Cinema, Censorship, and the State:
The Writings of Nagisa Oshima

Cinema, Censorship, and the State:
The Writings of Nagisa Oshima,
1956–1978

NAGISA OSHIMA

edited and with an introduction by Annette Michelson

translated by Dawn Lawson

An OCTOBER *Book*

The MIT Press
Cambridge, Massachusetts
London, England

MIT Press

0262150409

OSHIMA
CINEMA CENSOR STATE

© 1992 Massachusetts Institute of Technology
French edition (*Ecrits 1956–1978: Dissolution et jaillissement*) © 1980 Cahiers du Cinéma et
Editions Gallimard

This book was set in ITC Garamond by DEKR Corporation and printed and bound in the United
States of America.

Library of Congress Cataloging-in-Publication Data

Ōshima, Nagisa, 1932–
    [Selections. English]
    Cinema, censorship, and the state: the writings of Nagisa Oshima, 1956–1978 / edited and
with an introduction by Annette Michelson; translated by Dawn Lawson.
        p.   cm.
    "An October book."
    ISBN 978-0-262-15040-8 (hc : alk. paper)
      978-0-262-65039-7 (pb : alk. paper)
    1. Motion pictures—Japan.   I. Michelson, Annette.   II. Title.

PN1993.5.J30794   1991
791.43'0952—dc20   90-6259
                                                                          CIP

Contents

Acknowledgments

This selection of texts was established by their author for publication in 1980 by Editions Gallimard within the Cahiers du Cinéma series. To it has been added "Perspectives of Japanese Cinema."

It was immediately and incontrovertibly apparent, however, that theoretical and historical contextualization would be required for their fullest understanding in the West. For although the Japanese cinema has gained an audience and some scholarly attention,[1] the events and debates within Japanese film culture have remained largely undocumented and unexplored.

Our effort to remedy this situation, if only modestly, was facilitated by the collaboration of Hideo Suzuki, who brought his thorough knowledge of Japanese theory and practice to the preparation of a critical apparatus adumbrated in extensive footnotes. These are intended to clarify for the reader the origins, urgency, and resonance of the essays, manifestos, diaristic texts, and reportages produced within two critical decades of Japan's postwar resurgence. Hideo Suzuki's resourceful and scrupulous research have thus enriched this volume.

I have had, as well, the comradely assistance of Dominique Faccini, whose intelligent eye and keen ear have helped to clear a path through editorial problems that were, at the inception of this work, not wholly foreseen.

Melissa Vaughn of The MIT Press has given this manuscript much efficient and enthusiastic care. Roger Conover, Acquisitions Editor for the Arts, has been generous and unfaltering in his patient support of this project.

---

1.   Notably in the work of Joseph Anderson, Donald Richie, Noël Burch, David Bordwell, and David Dresser.

For the illustrative material, included in the hope of sharpening the reader's focus on films not yet in wide distribution in this country, we are indebted to Nagisa Oshima and to the Film Stills Department of the Museum of Modern Art, and to its director, Mary Corliss.

Annette Michelson

Perspectives on the Japanese Film

Introduction

Annette Michelson

"Banish Green!" is Oshima's categorical imperative, self-imposed at the very outset of his enterprise. He tells us that in making his first color film (the second of his career) he restricted himself to a color scheme from which green was excluded.[1] The foreseeable problems posed by that exclusion were, in some respects, easily solved. Objects, costumes, and city landscapes allowed for avoidance or removal of green elements. Camera angles could be determined so as to ensure exclusion.

It was rather the typical, sparsely furnished Japanese home, with its garden adjoining the living space, which epitomized the problem. It is that garden and adjoining rooms that often contained the tea cabinet—the mark of familial continuity and stability—that were the object of negation. "Characters, rooms, gardens were all utterly repellent, and I firmly believed that unless the dark sensibility that those things engendered were completely destroyed, nothing new could come into being in Japan."

We would, however, err in ascribing to Oshima the radical rejection of "the natural" familiar to us in the Baudelairean tradition of the Dandy. And indeed, Roger Caillois, in his review of *The Empire of Passion*,[2] was to invoke, with an eloquence impelled by his own characteristic sensitivity to the interest of natural phenomena, the manner in which, within that film, they are the privileged signifiers, the expressive agents of Oshima's practice. Thus, "the idea of passion is, as it were, distanced from thought, relocated so as to render it more mysterious, more inexplicable, dissolving the name of the empire into a realm congruent with that of nature, with that of roots asleep deep beneath the ear, and which spring forth as an immense tangle of trees. Nature is therefore constantly present and powerful: in the snow; in the pouring rain; in the trails of fog which rise from the field and path; in the yellow

1.   See page 208 of this volume.
2.   Roger Caillois, "Sur l'Empire de la passion," *Positif* 224, October 1978, pp. 2–4.

foliage of autumn; in the gust of wind which bends and straightens the branch of the needle-laden pine trees, the scratching of insects . . . in all this, there is, as well, a human order which is a kind of extension of nature."[3]

Oshima's stricture was, as it happens, formulated and published in reply to an inquiry from *Kyosensui,* a journal devoted to flower arrangement. One is thus amused to imagine a letter of request ("Dear Mr. Oshima, We should so much like to have your own personal view of our traditional art of flower arrangement."), and to imagine as well the reaction to his answer, which assumed the form of a manifesto.

The green excluded was that of a Nature long since tamed and integral to the order of Japanese domesticity. "Arranged," like flowers, it extends the space of the five- or eight-mat rooms of the traditional dwelling. It is within this extended space that a culture, its practices and traditions, now corrupt and defeated, is seen to have crystallized. To preserve that space meant to sustain and foster the festering growths generated by "the dark sensibility" of the culture.

One is led to recall the especial force of Adorno's critique of Kierkegaard, whose texts centered, in significant instances, upon descriptive accounts of rooms, corridors, houses. Adorno has analyzed, in a manner both subtle and trenchant, Kierkegaard's "interiority of thought," his "inwardness" as the direct articulation of the dwelling of the nineteenth-century bourgeoisie. "The ordering of things in the apartment is called arrangement. Historically illusory objects are arranged in it as the semblance of unchangeable nature."[4]

> The contents of the *intérieur* are mere decoration, alienated from the purposes they represent, deprived of their own use value, engendered solely by the isolated apartment that is created in the first place by the juxtaposition. The "lamp shaped like a flower," the dream orient, fit together out of a cut paper lampshade hung over its crown and a rug made of osier; the room an officer's cabin—full of precious decoration greedily collected across the seas . . . the complete fata morgana of decadent ornaments receives its meaning not from the material of which they are made, but from the *intérieur* that unifies the imposture of things in the form of a still life. But in the *intérieur* things do not remain alien. It draws meaning out of them. Foreignness transforms itself from alienated things into expression. Mute things speak as "symbols."[5]

3.   Ibid., p. 4.
4.   Theodor W. Adorno, *Kierkegaard: Construction of the Aesthetic,* trans. and ed. Robert Hullot-Kentor, Minneapolis, 1989, p. 44.
5.   Ibid.

In this passage Adorno postulates the congruence of "inwardness" and the landscape of bourgeois domesticity; the apartment as thesaurus is the site of retreat into the private, into melancholy.

For Oshima it was the "mute symbolism" of Japanese domestic architecture and its traditional reconciliation of interior and exterior that had to be destroyed, for it had survived to sustain the repressive ideology of "harmony" that prevailed in Japanese nationalism. To strike green from the palette of Japanese cinema was to attack "the root of many evils. . . . For it softens the hearts of Japanese . . . a certain intransigence was necessary . . . no opening for sentiment, for the past . . ." And the analysis, the prescriptions do not end here, for he speaks as well of the expectations surrounding the early stages of postwar reconstruction, of the hopes aroused by the sight of the high-rise housing built by the Japan Housing Corporation on a huge area of reclaimed land along the coast, of the sharp angles of concrete walls cutting across the sky, the "dream-like lines of mercury lamp," of the conviction that this architecture must produce a new "sensibility." Two and half years spent in the three-mat, concrete room of a studio apartment in such a development on the periphery of an industrial city produced the rage of scorn and anger that was subsequently to possess him. The films, then, were impelled by the conviction that here, too, was a proper object of attack so that, among other things, "I tried to eliminate completely all scenes with characters sitting and talking on tatami."

It is, then, in the space bounded by revulsion at the past and apprehension of the future that Oshima's cinema is constructed. The expectation is that it will prove vectorial in the formation of an order of equality, of democratic process, and of a greater range and freedom of discourse. This cinema was, in fact, to become the long chronicle of the difficulties attending the establishment of that order. Speaking of the production of the New Wave (to whose most seminal figure, Godard, he is frequently compared), he claims that a situation of greater gravity than in France directly determined the deployment of the camera—its framing, movement, rhythm—thereby inscribing within the shape and texture of the work the continual sense of crisis and contradiction. The study of this parameter might tell us whether indeed he can, together with Godard, claim for camera movement a moral and political dimension.

August 15, 1945, is the date of the unimaginable, impossible, unspeakable event: the acknowledgment by the emperor, speaking in an idiom removed from that of general currency, of the nation's defeat by the allied forces.

> The imperial broadcast was hard to hear and hard to understand. There
> was a great deal of static. Frequent air raids during the closing months of

the war had damaged transmission facilities, and the radios themselves were prewar models, old and worn. Since not every household had a set, radios were made available in public places where people could gather to hear the broadcast. A further difficulty was that the emperor had never before officially addressed the nation over the radio. He was not a trained public speaker; his voice was not easy to understand; nor was the imperial rescript, for it was couched in the traditionally formal, archaic, unfamiliar language of the court.

This broadcast—poorly transmitted, received and understood— was symbolic of the condition Japan found herself in that mid-August day.[6]

This acknowledgment of confusion became the hard ground of a generation's cinematic enterprise. Within two years of the defeat, however, there had developed the germ of an articulate and politically militant student movement. Originating in response to a sharp increase in university fees, the movement's first significant action was a general strike, called by twenty-nine universities within the Tokyo area, involving 200,000 students throughout the country. This current crystallized in the massive student organization recruited from 272 universities and known as the *Zengakuren.*

It was in this immediately postwar milieu of militant action, subject to internal debate, to factionalism, to the aporias inevitably generated by the vicissitudinous relation to the Communist Party, that Oshima was formed. It was in the struggle of 1959–60, against ratification and implementation of the U.S.-Japan Security Treaty, in both its original and revised versions, that the movement reached its culmination. Ending in defeat, the struggle, which left its mark upon the Japanese polity—and upon its artistic practices—must be seen as linked to the more general movement of opposition to the United States' Cold War policy. Oshima's texts on Korea and Vietnam solicit analysis in relation to his work in documentary television, within an historical framework which is also that of a period of alienation in exile from the mode of industrial cinematic production.

For despite the rapid advance of cinema studies within the past two decades, despite the broad range of historical and theoretical literature now available, the study of Japanese cinema still lacks adequate representation. Despite recent publications such as Kurosawa's memoirs, the Japanese cinema has been represented almost wholly by work originating in English; apart from interviews and journalistic texts, little or none of Japan's critical or theoretical production has found its way into

6.   Masataka Kosaka, *A History of Postwar Japan,* Tokyo, 1972, pp. 11–12.

our language. The issues and debates, the major discursive currents within Japanese film production have, unlike those of France, Germany, or the Soviet Union, remained undocumented for the English-language reader. Textual analysis and historical contextualization have remained largely uninflected by documentation of these debates and polemical exchanges, or by questions of reception.

It was, however, within a nexus of theoretical discourse that Oshima developed his demand for what he termed "a cinema of subjectivity." We are, of course, to understand by this a notion quite distinct from that of the American avant-garde of the same period, for although grounded in a similarly radical critique of industrial cinematic production, it nevertheless declares the necessity to come to terms with it as providing the inescapable conditions of production within the capitalist order. Rejecting an artisanal solution, he then went on to develop the notion of a cinema which we must understand as that of *the subject of history.*

Poised between the voiding of a national historical tradition and the "adventurism" of the left, confronted as well with a rising generation for whom the claims of victimization were becoming meaningless, one had to rethink the cinematic. An analysis of the dominant system produced the conviction that the cinema had to become one of an authorial subjectivity that confronts, rather than appeals to, its audience.

Questioning the system of production, rethinking spectatorship, meant for Oshima—as it did for others elsewhere in the postwar period—a certain flexibility with respect to established genres. It meant, as well, the rediscovery of the documentary form, the loosening of narrative codes. Thus, as Noël Burch has noted, *Death by Hanging,* Oshima's most seminal and internationally celebrated work, begins with the presentation of three successive coded modes in which editing and shot composition correspond to three distinct genres: that of the "objective" documentary, the militant film of propaganda, and that of fiction.

The cinema of "subjectivity" was, in the wake of the defeat of the movements of political opposition, to become increasingly directed against social *institutions.* The generative center of its narrative became, as Oshima has noted, crime, those acts of violence and transgression that mark the constraints and limits of an order sensed as oppressive. This cinema of "subjectivity" is now one of heterology which, in this era of Japan's economic hegemony, finds its resources, its material base, its audience, abroad.

Before asking whether the Japanese film has a future, I want first to ask whether the Japanese film exists.

The Japanese film definitely does exist. There are films made by Japanese in which there are Japanese on the screen speaking Japanese. Those are the Japanese films. Therefore, the Japanese film exists. Everyone thinks so without having to stop and consider it further.

I used the very vague "everyone" just now because not only do those who see Japanese films want to think the Japanese film exists, but almost all other Japanese think so as well, even if they have never seen a film.

Many think that the Japanese film is in decline. But that is probably not because they have seen the films and felt them to be in decline, nor because they have analyzed them and think they are in decline. It is merely that nearly all of them are convinced that the Japanese film is in decline. Or rather it is merely that they have been convinced of that.

So, who led them to think this?

Needless to say, it was journalism and the mass media.

But did the media spread that news on the basis of its own investigation or discovery of the decline of the Japanese film? That cannot be the case. The mass media and journalism aren't that diligent.

The news of decline undoubtedly came from among those involved with the Japanese film; this includes those who make their living directly from production, distribution and exhibition, for example, as well as those few who make their living through film-related activities such as criticism and journalism.

It is they who feel that the Japanese film is in decline. Or think that it is. Why do they feel and think that?

In a nutshell, although they feel that the Japanese film definitely exists, they feel its existence is weak at best.

I joined Shochiku Ofuna Studios as an assistant director in 1954. I wasn't a film lover; it was just that no other company would hire me, so I happened to end up at a film company. But I knew of the existence of the Japanese film based on the films I had seen up to that time.

However, the existence of the Japanese film as I perceived it after joining a studio was quite different from the way I had perceived it during my student days. Explaining this perception is extremely difficult, but in the context of asking whether the Japanese film exists, I would say that the Japanese film really existed then. In fact, my feelings about its existence were more effusive: "There really is a Japanese film! There is! There is!"

In other words, although as a student I had perceived the existence of the Japanese film as a concept I had actually been seeing individual films as separate entities. When I entered the studio, however, my first perception was of the Japanese film as a whole rather than as individual films.

There was that kind of heavy atmosphere in the studio, along with a feeling of unity. It could be called a happy atmosphere. Whenever anything is made in a group or a community, it is enjoyable, but it is an especially happy life when one can keep making dreamlike products like films without having significant doubts about making them. Shochiku films were being made there, but because there were only five kinds of Japanese film, it was natural to feel that the Shochiku film was the Japanese film. This was true at all of the studios.

Also, in those days this unity was felt by more than just the studio people. When the people in distribution and exhibition belonged to the same company, they had to market the films made at that studio, so it was natural that there was a widespread feeling of unity regarding the film.

Rather than asserting individual films' differences, those in the film world valued the homogeneity of the Japanese film; no matter what company's film they were marketing, they were intensely conscious of and felt joy at being part of the Japanese film organization. That consciousness and joy were enhanced by the fact that the Japanese film was then a very profitable industry in the vanguard of its time and society.

In other words, people perceive Japanese cinema to be in decline because those in the film world no longer share the feeling of unity that they once had.

Today, rather than feeling that they belong to the Japanese cinema as a whole, those in the Japanese film world feel more strongly that they belong to a certain film company. They attach even more importance to the department to which they belong within that company. Production always complains about distribution and exhibition and distribution and exhibition criticize production. And each fights to shift responsibility to the other department.

Of course, these things happened in former days as well. Even so, people's shared awareness of being in the same company and a part of the Japanese film kept events from reaching the point of catastrophe.

That the Japanese cinema is now generally thought to be in decline reflects the fact that people in the Japanese film world are no longer conscious of themselves as part of the Japanese cinema as a whole. In fact, more than feeling that the Japanese film is in decline, in actuality they feel that they have lost the Japanese film of old about which they felt unified.

Does this mean then that the Japanese cinema definitely exists in name, but not in substance? But how can those involved with film say that something exists when they don't feel it exists in substance? One would have to say that if one wants to continue to call what was previously called the Japanese cinema by that name, it no longer exists.

I express myself in such extreme fashion by way of response to opinion that scorns current Japanese films by comparing them with the old "Japanese cinema." Of course, some current films are merely inferior descendants of the "Japanese film" of old, but some artists are filling the void left by the extinct "Japanese film" with work using new themes and methods. The Japanese film's only future lies in the potential of these artists to continue the struggle as a source of inspiration and support for others.

However, let us refrain from proceeding directly to the future outlook of the Japanese film. I'd like to delve a bit deeper into nonexistence of the Japanese film and the reasons for it.

Superficially considered, the Japanese film ceased to exist because, as is evident the Big Three—Shochiku, Toho, and Toei—have practically stopped producing films. The number of films these companies produced entirely by themselves in 1986—not including productions by outside companies, subsidiaries, subcontractors, and collaborative works—was fourteen: four for Shochiku, nine for Toei, and only one, *Women in Love,*[1] for Toho. That same year, Fuji Television produced seven films, including *Milo and Otis,*[2] and New Century Producers produced nine.

1.   *Women in Love* (Koisuru Onnatachi, dir. Oomori Kazuki, 1986).
2.   *Milo and Otis* (dir. Hata Masanori, 1986), a film about animals.

During the days when those three companies, along with Nikkatsu, Daiei, and Shin Toho, monopolized the Japanese cinema in the three areas of production, distribution, and exhibition, that monopoly presented the biggest barrier to those desiring a revolution in the Japanese film. It was extremely difficult for films produced by independent production companies to find a distribution network and theaters for exhibition: independent distribution companies didn't last long, and independent theaters were forced to depend on the distribution network of the large companies.

On the other hand, by virtue of their monopoly the large film companies bore all responsibility for the Japanese film, and one can say that they fulfilled that responsibility. The reason the Japanese film was established as an entity that unified the Japanese film world was that it was supported by this monopolistic structure.

However, the production departments began splitting off in the 1960s, continued to do so in the 1970s, and broke away decisively in the 1980s. Japanese cinema was swept into a state of nonexistence; Shin Toho, Daiei, and Nikkatsu were destroyed.

From a business standpoint, this was a matter of rationalization on the part of management. It is natural to split off departments that are low profit and high risk. In the film business, production was thought of as a high-risk, low-profit department.

Certainly the production departments were very problematical. Some rationalization was necessary, since photography entails unforeseeable situations, difficulties in budgeting, and swelling numbers of studio personnel.

However, weren't the rationalization of the production department and its elimination two different things? Even so, the Japanese film industry didn't stop at the rationalization of production, but headed toward a complete discarding of production. The places that retain production departments today do so only because they have no alternative.

Why was production discarded? Isn't it because, from the outset, the film companies forced the production departments in their monopolies into a position of high risk and low profits, as compared to the distribution and exhibition departments?

Film companies are free to do this because they can divide their profits—admission fees paid by audiences—among departments as they like.

From the point of view of the film industry worldwide, production is definitely a high-risk department, but it is also one with a high earning potential. However, Japanese film companies used their monopoly to minimize the profits of production departments, by creating a system that forced them to assume all of the risks while holding down their earning potential.

That being the case, wasn't it easy for them to discard the production department?

By omitting production, the film companies probably managed to make their operations healthy. At the same time, however, they lost their ethics as film companies. As long as they were called film companies, the unifying factor of each company centered on filmmaking, and what they made was the "Japanese film." When they stopped production, the film companies lost their ethics, their unity, and identity, and the "Japanese film" ceased to exist.

Taken to extremes, what Japanese film companies most desire is that films like *Star Wars* and *ET*—or even *Rocky* and *Back to the Future*—come out every year, or that Kadokawa Haruki or Fuji Television sponsor some major work. An old Japanese expression refers to this as competing in sumo wrestling while wearing someone else's loincloth.

Today Japanese film companies think of nothing but competing in sumo wearing other people's loincloths. This is also the reason they make films with several other large companies from other industries as cosponsors. There is no logic beyond that, however, so when it comes to convincing the sponsors, either an animal ends up as the film's hero or it turns into a "tearjerker."

Consequently, *Twenty-Four Eyes*,[3] which was made by Kinoshita Keisuke in 1954, is clearly a "Japanese film," but the *Twenty-Four Eyes* made in 1987, when the "Japanese film" had already ceased to exist, was an exercise in futility.

In saying this, I may seem to be attributing all of the responsibility for the Japanese cinema's demise to the film companies. That is not my intention, however. I am merely pointing out that by discarding film production, the management of the film companies only confirmed the nonexistence of the Japanese film, or confirmed the fact of its not being able to exist. The fact came first.

If any fault is to be found with the management of the film companies, it is that they have acted as though the "Japanese film" still existed or that they are acting that way even now. Many film people, or people on the periphery of the film world, such as critics, reviewers, and journalists, are guilty of the same thing.

But why does the Japanese film no longer exist? Needless to say, it is because of the precipitous changes in Japanese society.

In the past, the Japanese maintained their homogeneity as one race and as a people who lived in one society. Today, too, the Japanese maintain considerable

---

3.   *The Twenty-Four Eyes* (*Nijushi no Hitomi,* dir. Asama Yoshitaka, 1987). A remake of the Kimoshita film (1954) of the same name.

homogeneity, but are clearly moving in the direction of placing more value on their differences as individuals.

A society or race can maintain its homogeneity only until it feels the winds of modernization. Modernization is, at the same time, internationalization.

Thus, the condition of a given society or race is most interesting when it is exposed to waves of modernization and internationalization. In Japan, beginning in the late 1860s, that happened from the time of the fall of the Tokugawa shogunate through the Meiji Restoration and into the Meiji period (1868–1912). Within the homogeneity of race and society are in an evident state of friction, producing the interesting condition of a race, a social structure and their individual subjects, in bitter struggle. The modern literature of every country comes into being under these circumstances; in the case of Japan, it was the literature of the Meiji period. The works of Meiji novelists Natsume Soseki, Mori Ogai, and Shimazaki Toson are expected to endure as Japanese literature because they were born in the midst of this struggle.

The film medium was born a little too late to be present at the modernization and internationalization of a race and a society. Nevertheless, it has had outstanding success depicting scenes of this struggle in various countries. Thus, moving scenes in many films depict the first operation of a train and the first time that a light goes on in a house.

The Japanese film, too, inevitably had to turn its attention to changes in the homogeneity of the traditional forms of the community, to the villages and towns, and to changes in the homogeneity of the family system that the modernization and internationalization of society brought about. (In the case of Japan, modernization and internationalization also meant militarization.)

In several articles I wrote around 1960, I pointed out that one characteristic of such Japanese films was that they were permeated with a victim's mentality toward war, the feudal system, and poverty.

This observation involved no sort of value judgment. It was based on a recognition of the fact that fifteen years after the war, Japanese society was changing and approaching the point of becoming completely modernized and internationalized, and it included the assertion that the Japanese cinema would have to change accordingly.

The "Japanese film" made no attempt to change, however. But for superficial fashions (the appearance of Ishihara Yujiro, for example), it is basically unchanged to this day.

One reason for this condition lies in the sensibility that should perhaps be called the "postwar renaissance."

Usually the modernization and internationalization of a people and a society are completed all at once, in whatever period of time is required, whether short or long. In the case of Japan, however, because Meiji society went the route of militarization, it encountered the frustration of defeat in World War II and thus was forced to modernize and internationalize a second time.

In one respect, this was fortunate. The Japanese people worked frantically and thought deeply. That work became the basis for the economic prosperity of today. And that thinking gave rise to a second modern literature, postwar literature. Japanese film produced masterpieces in this atmosphere. To think means wanting to look at your own face. The postwar Japanese film responded to this demand from the Japanese people: it reflected their faces. To my mind, however, what was reflected there looked just like the faces of prewar Japanese.

In any case, the period that might be called the "postwar renaissance" was all too short, because it was merely a review of the Meiji modernization and internationalization. While the Japanese were tiring of these concepts, a violent modernization and internationalization of economics and lifestyle began. The people were buffeted by these waves.

The largest total film audience in Japan was recorded in 1958; 85 percent of the total consisted of viewers of Japanese films, while only 15 percent saw foreign films. I saw both kinds of films in nearly equal proportions when I was a student and believed that to be the usual pattern, but through the latter half of the 1950s, Japanese who saw foreign films were actually a kind of elite.

When you consider this, the position of the "Japanese film" of that time becomes even clearer. Instead of saying "the Japanese film of that time," perhaps I should say the Japanese film as it had been since its inception. From its very beginning, the "Japanese film" existed completely separately from the foreign film.

First, films were imported. Then it was decided that films be made in Japan also, but with a very few exceptions they were produced, shown, and seen as something completely different from the foreign variety.

The "Japanese film" was able to exist precisely because it was so completely different from the foreign film. There was a homogeneity to the lives and feelings of the Japanese spectators, and that homogeneity was enough to make a sharp distinction between Japanese and foreigners, the "Japanese film" and the foreign film.

After about 1960, however, the conditions of Japanese society abolished this homogeneity. Generally, when the homogeneity of a society is eliminated, the first thing that happens is a generational war. The generational war lasted more than fifteen years, beginning in 1955 with the sun tribe and continuing through the anti-

United States-Japan Security Treaty demonstrations in 1960 and the All-Campus Joint Struggle of the late 1960s. It completely changed the face of the Japanese film, wrenching it from the hands of adults. Rather, you could say that the adults themselves let go of it.

The people in the "Japanese film" world were not so foolish as to not realize this. Because only children were going to the theaters. That's when the maneuvering of idols, such as Yamaguchi Momoe and Yakushimaru Hiroko, began to develop.

They didn't realize, however, that this war of the generations was taking place not only in Japan but all over the world. Young people in every country initiated an intergenerational war, and because they shared a single ideology, in almost no time they exchanged ideas, fashions, idols, and trends.

The international atmosphere that began in the late 1960s and continued into the 1970s cooled into the worldwide nationalism mood of the mid-1970s, but the cultural exchange that occurred as a reaction to nationalism was unstoppable.

Thus, the only audience for "Japanese film" consisted of young people who had never made any kind of distinction between Japanese and foreign films. Furthermore, it was an audience that recognized no particular difference between seeing a film in the theater and watching it at home as a rented video cassette.

In spite of this, those who believe, or want to believe, that the "Japanese film" exists are trying to attract the average Japanese to the theater by forcibly devising a "national film." If there is no feeling of unity about the "Japanese film" on the part of those making films, how can a popular "Japanese film" come about? Even if they are sometimes able to attract an audience, it will be deceptive, a fluke that won't recur. By deceptive, I mean that their films are imitations that rely on a homogeneity among the Japanese that existed only in the past. You would think that perpetuating this deception would be too depressing for those who make, sell, and see films.

The thing to do now is to get rid of the illusion that the Japanese film exists, as quickly as possible. There is no such thing as a popular Japanese film. Only individual films exist. If there is a Japanese film, it exists only in the worst common elements considered here.

When I first entered a studio, there were of course negative elements common to all Japanese films, but there were also positive ones. Needless to say, those elements were a response to the positive aspects of the homogeneity of the Japanese people at that time.

For me, however, the Japanese films that possessed such common elements were unbearable. I could not stand the heavy atmosphere in which a uniform entity called the "Japanese film," rather than the individual film, was made. At times I enjoyed my work as assistant director, but my aspirations eventually centered on making a new Japanese film unlike those made up to that point.

At the time, however, in talking about a new Japanese film, I was still caught up in thinking of the Japanese film as an entity. Rather than saying that I was "still" caught up in it, I should say that I was "sufficiently" caught up in it. In publishing studies of scripts, I had taken a critical stand, so I thought that as a director I would soon be able to effect some sort of a revolution in the Japanese film through my work and criticism. Other critics and directors of my generation thought and worked for essentially the same thing.

The new film that I was thinking of at that time consisted of overturning the notion of the "Japanese film" as having common elements that depended on homogeneity. I hoped also to bring forward artists who would make individual films that would in some sense be directed toward the liberation of mankind. Because all of us would be making films in Japan, we would be able to create a cutting edge of films directed toward the liberation of the Japanese people.

When I actually started making films, however, I soon discovered that revolutionizing the Japanese film as an entity along those lines was a hopelessly overwhelming task for one film director.

As I had hoped, people recognized that my films were essentially different from the Japanese films that had been made thus far, but for this reason they were also the target of many attacks, from both inside and outside the studio. Within a year of becoming a director, I had left the film company to become an independent filmmaker. After that, it was all I could do to continue making films. With the exception of ventures in which I cooperated with people on film production directly, I had no leeway to think about other productions, other artists, or the Japanese film as an entity.

Nevertheless, until the beginning of the 1970s I still had the vision of a cutting edge of new Japanese films. During the latter half of the 1960s, I had carved out a new method of film production that took the form of a collaboration between the director's production and A.T.G. In addition, a number of directors had emerged with independent production companies, and the activities of documentary filmmakers were brilliant. In some sense those activities were linked to and supported by the fight of the students in the All-Campus Joint Struggle and of the young people in the worldwide movement based on Chairman Mao's saying, "There is a reason for rebellion."

When I went to Europe for the first time, with *Death by Hanging,* Paris was blanketed by the smoky haze of the May Revolution, and Cannes was canceled because of the rebellion of French film people. However, students in Nice were passionately supportive of *Death by Hanging,* and that was the start of the acceptance of my films overseas.

Now, twenty years later, my strategy is extremely clear-cut. It isn't possible for me to make films like *Rambo* and *Top Gun,* which attract overwhelmingly large audiences in the United States and throughout the world. It is also impossible for me to make *Platoon.* For better or worse, these films are supported by the fact that they are made in a special country called the United States. Films conceived in the multiracial United States can become global films just as they are. Their expansive investments in production are possible because of a firm belief in this fact.

I·don't work under these conditions.

However, even if I can't attract large audiences everywhere in the world, I can make films that are sure to attract audiences everywhere, even if they are small. Although the numbers in each country will be small, they will add up to a certain total worldwide. That is probably what makes it possible for me to make my next film. This is how I would like to make international films.

This is not only my strategy; it is now shared by film directors who think that they would like to make films that they can call their own. I have confirmed this in conversations with Wim Wenders, Bernardo Bertolucci, Paolo Taviani, Theo Angelopoulos, Jim Jarmusch, Mrinal Sen, and others.

Young Asian directors such as Chen Kaige[4] and Lee Jang Ho[5] have shown such passionate interest in me because they have strong hopes and plans for the internationalization of their films as well.

Thus, the desire on the part of film directors for internationalization is a global trend. At first I wasn't always conscious of it; I merely sought to go abroad as one way of breaking out of my position in the Japanese film world. But I am pleased to think that I either inadvertently found myself in the midst of this trend or played some sort of a role in creating it.

However, this trend was not created merely through the hopes and abilities of a few film directors. It was expanded by the visions and efforts of people who worked in cooperation with the directors: independent producers such as Anatole Dauman, critics such as Gene Moskovitz, journalists, organizers such as Mr. and Mrs. Gregor

4.   A Chinese film director. His well-known films are *Yellow Earth* (1986) and *The King of Children* (1989).
5.   A Korean director. His films include *The Dance of a Widow* (1983), *Declaration of a Fool* (1983), and *No Rest for the Traveller* (1987).·

of the Berlin Film Festival, independent distributors such as France Film Company, and theater owners such as New Yorker Films.

But why is this trend global? It is because the film worlds of their own countries are ghettoes for these film people.

It is assumed that the Japanese film and its world have special conditions that differ from those of other countries. Of course, as I have pointed out, they are not lacking in special problems. Considered from a global perspective, however, there are no major differences between the state of the film in Japan and in other countries.

Not one country has been able to find a breakthrough point—which is to say that industrially the size of film audiences only decreases, while practically no films are made that broaden the artistic possibilities of the form.

In every country, the cinema appears to be breathing its last and film people are in fetters, groaning. If this is not a ghetto, what is it?

Those who recognize it as a ghetto naturally try to escape. This is the departure point for the noble effort to internationalize the film.

However, we must also point out that the desire to internationalize the cinema has also come from the side of the American film, or the pseudo-American film.

To put it metaphorically, the American film now rules the cinema globally. The fact that groans now issue from the ghettoes of other countries, pushes the American film into a reverse ghetto. The American cinema then becomes a violent torrent moving toward internationalization. Under these conditions, a movement within each country to make an "American film" will inevitably arise. This is what is referred to above as "the pseudo-American film."

When you look at it in this way, the state of world cinema is clear. The trend toward internationalization is already deep-rooted. Will it end in the one-dimensional violence of the American film (this is already half-accomplished) or will the tendency to place value on individual directors and their work be able to compete with it? There lies the problem.

In the case of Japan, the problem is equally clear-cut. It depends on how many internationally respected films it can produce and how many films that aspire to be international it will accept from outside.

It is not a struggle that can be viewed totally optimistically. It is fraught with difficulties. However, it cannot be thought that no film people in Japan are bravely volunteering for the cause. If there is a Japanese film, it shares a common future with these people. They may still be called Japanese films, but in actuality they are simply films.

I may have overemphasized the necessity of internationalizing film and its attendant difficulties. I would thus like to say one last thing to those shouldering the responsibility for the future of the Japanese film.

Placing yourselves in the center of the trend to internationalize the film may mean being hemmed in by the logic of necessity and the ethical problems of the difficulties as though they were your own to overcome. But before that, before all that, it is indescribably sweet. It is the kind of sweetness that allows you to say from your heart these words of Jean Renoir: "I am a citizen of the communist country Film."

The true essence of film is this sweetness; it has no national boundaries.

I Creation and Destruction of the Japanese Cinema
(1956–1963)

To Critics, Mainly—From Future Artists

There are critics who devote all their energy to reviewing the work of those ten or so filmmakers who create so-called artistic films. Others concentrate on denouncing the commercialism of film companies and polling the viewing public.

The important topic that is neglected and never subjected to criticism is the program picture—which forms 90 percent of all films screened in Japan—and the philosophy of its makers.[1]

This leaves future filmmakers (assistant directors) at a loss. Each longs to become an artist who will someday create an outstanding work. But even were one of them to become a Kinoshita Keisuke[2] or a Kurosawa Akira, that person would not

1.   This term covers mass-entertainment movies in general, as specifically contrasted with "idea pictures" or "theme pictures" during the U.S. occupation of Japan (1945–1952), when cinema was called upon to promote "democracy," "antifeudalism," and "antimilitarism," according to GHQ directives. Program pictures are later contrasted with "director's films," "filmmaker's films," or "author's films." Despite historical change—and especially after the introduction of nationwide television networks—all five major film-producing companies continued to see the program picture as the mainstay of the industry, until they realized that by the early 1970s program pictures had lost much of their audience. Daiei had by now gone out of business, and Nikkatsu started producing only film versions of the *roman pornographique*. The remaining three film companies—Shochiku, Toho, and Toei—drastically reduced their production. Because they owned many theaters throughout Japan, they concentrated on distribution. Program pictures were designed for association as brand names for each production company; genres, subject matters, and target audiences were divided up among social and generational strata and gender so as to share and secure the market. This strategy, although not unmarked by occasional intercompany squabbles, proved conducive to an insular consciousness of the Japanese cinema.

2.   Practically unknown to the Western public, Kinoshita Keisuke has been compared with Kurosawa Akira. Kinoshita joined the Shochiku Kamata Studio in 1933 as an assistant cameraman and transferred to the assistant director's department in 1936, working under Shimazu Yasujiro and later under Yoshimura Kimisaburo. He made his directorial debut with *The Blossoming Port (Hana Saku Minato,* 1943). In that same year Kurosawa began his directing career with *Sugata Sanshiro,* a judo movie. Kinoshita received the New Director's Award, Kurosawa the Yamanaka Sadao Award. Kinoshita's next film, *Army (Rikugun,* 1944), was another hit, but its excessive tracking shots of the lach-

contribute to the development of the Japanese film as long as dozens more were producing program pictures. If the future resembles the present, it will not be possible to call their work filmmaking, will it?

How did future filmmakers come to think in this way? By working in program pictures.

A printed script is passed out. It is ten days, a week, or only three days before shooting begins. The assistants meet with the director, whose own doubts about the quality of the film he will be making are subtly communicated. Naturally, the script they have read doesn't excite them at all.

Nevertheless, preparations must continue. The chief assistant director meets with the chief accountant to set the budget and decide on the schedule. Limits, limits, limits. The clothes aren't made to fit the body; the body is made to fit the clothes. The costumes are made to fit the women, not the roles. "I'd make a more realistic costume if the story were more realistic. But this will do." The assistant directors stand by silently.

The shooting continues—quickly, cheaply. The director's attitude pervades the crew.

Hurry! What poor actors! Test. Once, twice. It's no use. Okay, let's do it for real.

Hurry! It doesn't matter if the lighting in a corner like that isn't realistic. Brighter, brighter! Brightness is the number-one demand executives make of photographers.

---

rymose mother watching her son march off to war aroused the anger of the army. *The Osone Family* (*Osoneke no Asa,* 1946), made immediately after the war, is known to have been intended as an attack on the defeated army, despite his complaint that the censors of the CIE (Civilian Information and Education) section of the occupying allied forces were ordered to show no compassion whatever in their treatment of the army. Another "theme" film made by Kurosawa in the same year, *No Regrets for Our Youth* (*Waga Seshun ni Kui Nashi,* 1946), conveys a false impression. Its righteous professor is idealized and his students are presented as fighting for "democracy," "antifeudalism," and "antimilitarism" under the fascist regime as though this had actually occurred, as if he, Kurosawa, and the scriptwriter, Hisazaka Eijiro, had tried to transgress the directives of the allied forces. Although Oshima favorably compares Kinoshita's *A Japanese Tragedy* (*Nihon no Higeki,* 1953) and *The Garden of Women* (*Onna no Sono,* 1954) with other one-dimensional antiwar films of the postwar era that offered a view of the common people solely as victimized, he calls attention to Kinoshita's tendency to succumb to a common narrative device, the juxtaposition of beautiful scenery with the evocation of victimization within an impenetrable reality (*On the Experiential Post-War Film Image, Taikenteki Sengo Eizoron,* Tokyo: Asahi Shinbun Sha, 1975, pp. 152–167) . Oshima saw Kinoshita's next enormously popular film, *Twenty-Four Eyes* (*Nijushi no Hitomi,* 1954) as illustrative of this failing and as a monumental component in the restoration of the "Shochiku melodrama" genre of the prewar era. Of all the antiwar films, this film and another Shochiku megahit, *What Is Your Name?* (*Kimi no Na wa,* dir. Oba Hideo, 1953) had the strongest emotional impact on the Japanese public.

Hurry! I can't get the sound. They completely changed the position of the mike. Okay! We'll get the sound later and add it!

Hurry! It's okay if it's cloudy. It's the morning after the hero has been with a woman for the first time, and I was planning on bright sunlight—but going on location costs money. We've got to do it cheaply.

Cheaply. We are permitted to use only twice as much negative film as will be included in the completed work. Okay! It's okay if the actors are a little clumsy, if the camera movement is shaky. Film is expensive. Okay! Okay! It doesn't matter that the acting is much easier if we film a scene many times to give us our choice of the cut we will use. It doesn't matter if that would allow the editors to hone their skills. Film is expensive!

Everything must be cheap. Equipment, decor—absolutely everything. All right! No one understands anything.

Although everything has been done in a rush, there is a break in the shooting. The star is shooting another film and can't make it. Tears in the eyes of the scheduling coordinator and first assistant director. As a result, they have to work overtime the following day, and although the day after that is a legal holiday, they work nevertheless. The crew grows irritable. There is a dramatic drop in efficiency. The crew likes films. That's why they're here. The crew is making a film that they themselves wouldn't want to see!

The shooting is completed. It's organized and edited. They'd like to do retakes, but there's no time. The music is added. Having seen the film only once or twice, the composer has to create a soundtrack in a day or two. The director first hears the music that will accompany his work on the same day that it is recorded. That, too, is over in a rush.

Completion. Private screening. The directors and executives coming out of the screening seem to be trying not to think negatively about their own film. The same is true of the crew to some extent. No, the crew has forgotten all about it because they're already busy making their next program picture.

Program pictures are released. The public that is dear to certain film critics sees them. The critics, who may or may not see them, are silent.

But the future artists—the assistant directors—contemplate the road ahead. At some point, a few of them—no, all of them—will probably have to make a film that the critics will ignore.

While contemplating their future, they also look back at the road they have traveled.

For the crew, plans are a given. They experience them as something over which they have no control. But the crew's vague desire to make a good film never disappears.

The director tries to somehow shatter the stereotypes in a work that is assigned but unwanted. He tries to infuse the hackneyed characters with new life or rewrite the screenplay or bring something new to the shooting. Although the directors are rushed and forced to work under bad conditions, they focus all of their attention on screen composition—including technical elements such as the length of each shot, its size, and its composition—mise-en-scène, and the logic and drama of the work as a whole.

Can one really say that a program picture never has a scene to which the photography engineer[3] and his assistants have given special attention, even though they always have to shoot under pressure?

Although the recording engineer and his assistants may press the OK buzzer nonchalantly while on the set, who can say that their exhaustive efforts to collect additional sound effects and background sound after the filming will not come through on the screen?

And perhaps the hero's poor performance improved when the decorators—who always use simulated food and drink—gave him the real thing for once.

The artists of the future—the assistant directors—are there to increase speed and economy, but even as they point out script deficiencies and suffer through the rehearsals of inferior new faces, they are observing the actions of the crew.

Who can assert with confidence that among the program pictures ignored by critics—who probably assume that they are all alike—there are not parts in which the efforts and abilities of the crew, led by the director, shine through?

Criticism of Technique

Don't critics feel that criticism of technique is necessary? Or, if they feel it is necessary, do they understand film technique?

Don't they think that an important aspect of the critic's work is to locate outstanding new technical expressions in the uniform-looking program pictures and praise and foster them?

3.   Actually the "director of cinematography." The Japanese film industry tends to place a higher value on technical expertise than on artistry, simply because of the division of labor. Assignment to work in cinematography is preceded by years of apprenticeship and assistantship. The "recording engineer" is the "recording or sound director."

Ninety percent of Japanese films are program pictures, and the crews' techniques form their backbone. If film critics care about Japanese film and its development, why do they not review them?

Criticism of technique is needed not only for the production crew, but also for the executives who plan films and the audiences who see them.

Audiences see program pictures. Executives plan program pictures solely on the basis of this one fact: audiences see them. It is a vicious circle!

How are we to break out of it? There is but one solution: critics must become part of the audience. If they could apprehend the consciousness that sustains the reality of "seeing" and the lives that inform it, if they could locate and clarify the aspects of that consciousness and those lives that seek better films, then the executives would plan and the production crew would work accordingly. In addition, furnishing the audience with technical criticism of program pictures would foster a desire for better films.

As long as executives and production crews are influenced solely by the fact that audiences see program pictures, the only improvements in film we can anticipate will be spontaneous. Unless film critics sense their responsibility in this matter, we can't say that they are interested in the development of cinema.

While working on the production of program pictures, the artists of the future—the assistant directors—cultivate their artistic faculties by seeing films, writing scripts, and reading. In that respect, they are as diligent as their predecessors, today's directors.

While each hopes to become an outstanding director, each also gives serious thought to the development of the Japanese film. They will not be satisfied by a situation in which one outstanding director shoots masterpieces while all others listlessly make program pictures. Here tomorrow's artists appear as representatives of a generation upon whom, a decade after the war's end, the weight of history is still laid. They don't forget the belief in which they have been immersed: that films are made not by an individual but jointly by executives, production crew, and audience.

For this reason, the artists of the future believe in the immensity of the responsibility to be shouldered by the critics, who are the strong thread binding executives, production crew, and audience together in the context of film production. They pray for the healthy fulfillment of this responsibility.

(*Film Art,* December 1956)

Is It a Breakthrough? (The Modernists of Japanese Film)

In July 1956, Nakahira Ko[1] breezed onto the scene with *Crazed Fruit,* boasting, *"Season of the Sun* glorified the sun tribe and *Punishment Room* criticized it; I sneer at the sun tribe."[2] In the rip of a woman's skirt and the buzz of a motorboat, sensitive people heard the heralding of a new generation of Japanese film. Then in May of the following year, with *The Betrothed,* a wholesome, rational depiction of adolescence, Shirasaka Yoshio[3] proved that scripts of exceptional style can transcend the strengths of the director and determine the style of the entire film. At that time, even more people became aware that this new element could not be ignored when talking about the Japanese film. In September of that year, when Masumura Yasuzo[4] used a freely

1.   Nakahira Ko joined the Shochiku Ofuna Studio as an assistant director in 1949, working under Kawashima Yuzo, Shibuya Minoru, and Kurosawa Akira. He then moved to the Nikkatsu Studio, which had resumed film production after the war, where he worked under Tasaka Tomotaka and Shindo Kanato. His directorial debut was *The Pursued Man* (*Nerawareta Otoko,* 1956), but his next film, *Crazed Fruit* (*Kurutta Kajitsu,* 1956), was shown to the public first because of its timely "sun tribe" subject. He directed two other films, *Summer Storm* (*Natsu ni Arashi*) and *Milkman Frankie* (*Gyunyuya Frankie*) in the same year.
2.   *Season of Violence,* also known as *Season of the Sun* (*Taiyo no Kisetsu,* dir. Furukawa Takumi, 1956), launched a series of Nikkatsu Studio "sun tribe" films based on the novel of a young author, Ishihara Shintaro. The term referred to a generation of alienated youth in the 1950s. The Daiei Studio tried to compete with Nikkatsu by producing *Punishment Room* (*Shokei no Heya,* dir. Ichikawa Kon, 1956) based on another novel about the sun tribe by the same author. Its great success derived from the assured technique of Ichikawa Kon.
3.   Shirasaka Yoshio began his career in 1956, ascending immediately to stardom with his scripts for two Masumura Yasuzo films, *A Cheerful Girl* and *Warm Current.* Their collaboration was to endure. Shirasaka wrote the script for *The Betrothed* (*Nagasugita Haru,* dir. Tanaka Shigo, 1957), based on a Mishima Yukio novel.
4.   Soon after joining the Daiei Studio as an assistant director, Masumura Yasuzo went to Italy to study at the Centro Sperimentale di Cinematographia in Rome and visited Cinecitta (1949–1951). His first three iconoclastic films, *Kisses* (*Kuchizuke,* 1957), *A Cheerful Girl* (*Aozora Musume,* 1957), *Warm Current* (*Danryu,* 1957), or his fifth, *Giants and Toys* (*Kyojin to Gangu,* 1958), are char-

moving camera to depict a pair of young motorcycle-riding lovers in *Kisses,* this new generation had assumed a place in Japanese cinema as an intense, unstoppable force that could no longer be ignored.[5]

The camera does a 360-degree pan, following the youths at work in a car wash, who are running around the cars in order to wash them ever faster and more thoroughly. Characters looking down from the window of a building or walking on the street are also captured by the camera. A woman stares at a man, saying, "I have had an affair with that person," and another woman sees a man off to the station, screaming, "I'll be your mistress, your concubine. . . . I'll be waiting for you!" Quick speeches, dynamic action. Violent changes of scene, extreme ellipses. Active heroes, ultramodern settings, the establishment of events. Dispassionate depictions sustained by a richly modern spirit that unites all of these elements. In filming "things" in particular, Nakahira was at his best, using as his most powerful weapon the sharply critical spirit that views people as objects. Masumura has the force, the strength of thought to twist the subject of a script into a Masumuraesque subject, and he has the expressive courage to assert that subject by entrusting it to a character's human instinct. Shirasaka's genius lies in his ability to stylize the images of his rich, modern sensibility with a skillful critical technique. The formal innovations of these filmmakers' forms extended so brilliantly in so many directions that they created comic situations; people acknowledged that they definitely were onto something new, although they couldn't quite grasp the essence of it. Now, however, their newness must be analyzed, examined, strengthened, and publicized, because it probably represents the biggest breakthrough in the wall of the Japanese film.

---

acterized by dynamic direction and rapid editing. "Neorealism" seems to have had an adverse effect, as he judged realism of any sort, Italian or Japanese, to express an ideology of "resignation." Upon his return from Europe, he went to the Daiei Kyoto Studio to work under Mizoguchi, then embarking on production of his last three films. Upon the death of Mizoguchi, he returned to the Daiei Tokyo Studio to work under Ichikawa Kon.

5.   Oshima's critical assessment of the "modernists," written by an emerging filmmaker, is directed toward moderating the immediate impact of these men (Masumura, Nakahira, and the scenarist Shirasaka) who had rebelled against the Japanese cinema's inveterate tradition of naturalism and realism. Oshima came to see in their practice a formalist adoption of Western and American film strategies that did not engage questions of historical meaning. Unlike these modernists, he sought to engage with the problematic of history and its articulation within the Japanese cinema. This deepening of historical consciousness, seen by Oshima as a challenge to young Japanese filmmakers, reflected intense critical debates as to the responsibilities of those men of letters who had lived through the expansionism and militarism of Japanese capitalism as literary modernists and political leftists. At issue was the "conversion" of the writer in terms of his or her political stance. Readers are referred to Oshima's *On the Experiential Post-War Film Image* or *The Destruction and Creation of the Post-War Film* (*Sengo Eiga: Hakai to Sozo,* Tokyo: Sanichi Shobo, 1963).

The most fundamental characteristic of these new artists is their determination to create works that break with the traditions of the premodern Japanese film. The two established types of Japanese film were the period drama (*jidaigeki*), which drew on the Kabuki tradition, and the modern melodrama, which drew on the New Wave (*Shimpa*).[6] These forms and their requisite content were the most acceptable to Japanese film audiences; they were closely tied to the consciousness of the Japanese people, centered in the premodern Japanese social structure and in the premodern human relationships engendered by it. Of course, most filmmakers rebelled against these traditional forms. In the prewar period, the most effective form of rebellion was the naturalistic realism that reached its peak in the work of Ozu Yasujiro.[7] After the war, the tendency known as realism developed among left-wing independent production companies. However, because they were always conscious of the audience's receptiveness to the traditional forms—and because they could not resist their attraction—the realists were not able to generate a fundamentally new form. Kinoshita Keisuke and Imai Tadashi,[8] the most promising among them, main-

6.   The "Shimpa" theater, which emerged after the Meiji Restoration (1868), established a modern theater in opposition to the traditional and stylized Kabuki form. It eventually generated another stylized, but melodramatic, dramaturgy; its contemporary situations were presented in an acting style that broke with intended realism. *The Tower of Lilies* (*Himeyuri no Too,* dir. Imai Tadashi, 1953), *Twenty-Four Eyes* (*Nijyu-shi no Hitomi,* dir. Kinoshita Keisuke, 1954), *Rice* (*Kome,* dir. Imai Tadashi, 1957).

7.   Oshima sees Ozu as foremost in a "naturalistic realism," adopted in rebellion against Shimpa-derived melodrama and Kabuki-derived *jidaigeki,* or period drama. A closer analysis of his films reveals Ozu's treatment of his subjects as holding fissures of text and history at bay. The apparent "fatalism" of his narrative thereby differs greatly from the sort of agnosticism prevalent in "naturalism." This distance enabled his experimentation and development of formal strategies in the prewar period, as in *Only Son* (*Hitori Musuko,* 1936). However, *Brothers and Sisters of the Toda Family* (*Todake no Kyodai,* 1941) and *There Was a Father* (*Chichi Ariki,* 1942) mark a crisis in keeping text and history in balance.

8.   Imai Tadashi is representative of those "leftist" Japanese filmmakers who "converted" under the fascist repression during the war and cooperated with the regime, producing films in accordance with the war policy that justified the invasion of other Asian countries. There were only a few exceptions. Among these was Kamei Fumio (1908–1987), a documentary filmmaker whose passive antimilitarism in *Fighting Troops* (*Tatakau Heitai,* 1941) sufficed to bring him imprisonment. Imai had been a member of the Japan Communist Party, which was pronounced illegal during the war. Some members then went underground or were incarcerated, while others converted to the official ideology; Imai therefore had to rejoin the party after the war. He started to make antiwar films in accordance with the directives of the GHQ of the allied forces. When the Korean War began in 1950, the GHQ ordered the major film production companies to expel communists and communist sympathizers from their studios. Directors such as Imai, Kamei Fumio, Gosho Heinosuke, and Yamamoto Satsuo lost their jobs in this "red purge" and had to form independent production companies. This time Imai did not convert to the change of ideology of the allied forces. The issue of "conversion" was raised among filmmakers, although not as intensely as among men of letters. The founding editors of the magazine *Modern Literature* (among them Ara Masato, Honta Shugo, Hirano

tain a balance between innovation of form and content and audience receptiveness. The former does this by relying on his naturally sharp perceptions, while the latter sustains his persistent, desperate efforts with his tough, rational spirit. The results are *The Tower of Lilies, Twenty-Four Eyes, Rice,* and *Times of Joy and Sorrow.*[9] These works demonstrate a harmony both fortunate and unfortunate between the artists' content and form on the one hand, and the audience's receptiveness on the other. It is unfortunate because these films engendered not a single substantively new element. In this way, the existing relationship between the traditional form of the mainstream Japanese film and the Japanese consciousness and view of life is based on a strong conservatism.

New filmmakers like Nakahira, Shirasaka, and Masumura naturally rebelled against the traditional forms, injecting their films with the new forms that arose from their commitment to their own perceptions. Moreover, to make their work easier, they dared to ignore the old premodern side of their audience. This is their chief characteristic, and they are thus inevitably called modernists. These men therefore occupy positions as innovators in Japanese film today.

The modernists of the film world are conscious of method; this is what sets them most radically apart from earlier filmmakers, who were without consciousness or method. These men not only realize their method within their films, but they also take every opportunity to explicate and publicize their works and elucidate their methods. Earlier filmmakers did not use these strategies. Japanese cinema's confrontation with the social structure, its escape from a space of closure to one of openness, meant seizing the first opportunity to leave behind the premodern craftsman in his world of secrets; it also meant the renewal of artistic method.

The modernist Nakahira issues pronouncements against the solemnly serious faction. It is obvious, as he himself says, how disadvantageous this sort of stance is in the context of Japanese film today. Nevertheless he says, "I had to speak out." He talks frankly of his resentment that only the films he endowed with "the social as theme (plausibility), lyricism in the story (sentimentality), and composure and dignity (dullness)" were highly regarded by the critics. He thus expresses his resentment not only toward film journalism but also toward the Japanese social structure, which forms the basis for those films that win critical approval. This is clearly a losing

---

Ken, and Haniya Yutaka), which began publication immediately after the war, took part in these debates and proceeded to investigate the problem of the subject and subjectivity in ideological terms. These discussions were further pursued among philosophers such as Miura Tsutomu, Tanaka Kichiroku, and Umemoto Katsumi.

9.   *Times of Joy and Sorrow (Yorokobi mo Kanashimi mo Ikutoshitsuki,* Kinoshita, 1957).

battle, and it presents all the more reason for Nakahira to fight effectively, by limiting the problem to method. Using "a variety of things as weapons, such as narrative,[10] power of description, artistic sense, purity, refinement, and lightness," he must capture in his works the ultramodern customs that have broken off from the premodern elements of Japanese society; he must carve out one kind of modern world.

For the modernist Shirasaka, it is the "gonorrhea theory of the old film world": working in the film world is like sleeping with a woman who has gonorrhea. He boasts that, even so, his blood does not become infected. His weapon is his differentiation between his "sharp senses and strong spirit": he says that he has "always worked guided by his senses." He has aspired to "depict cultural confusion and social contradictions by borrowing the form of the lucid, full-bodied comedy of manners." Like Nakahira, he captured a transient social phenomenon and created a new style of comedy. This aspect of his work is definitely a product of his "senses." He knows, on the other hand, that "novelty is a problem of the spirit." And his spirit, which was "ignored" where works are created, pronounces *Times of Joy and Sorrow* "the worst film ever." He would have no recourse, however, if someone were to say, following up on his reaction to *Times,* that the efforts to formulate a prescription for the gonorrheic woman—who represents the vast Japanese society that supports this film— have been forsaken. His only response to date has been to continue to inject into his superbly stylish scenarios superficial social criticism based exclusively on his modernist sensibility

The modernist Masumura turns his back on the overriding lyricism, reality, and atmosphere of the Japanese film and the society that produces it: "My goal is to create an exaggerated depiction featuring only the ideas and passions of living human beings." Masumura, possessor of the sharpest sociological perceptions of the three, understood the inevitable: "In Japanese society, which is essentially regimented, freedom and the individual do not exist. The theme of the Japanese film is the emotions of the Japanese people, who have no choice but to live according to the norms of that society. The cinema has had no alternative but to continue to depict the attitudes and inner struggles of the people who are faced with and oppressed by complex social relationships and the defeat of human freedom." He made a decision:

---

10.   In Japanese parlance, "narrative" means a specific method of *storytelling* in which the narrator governs the voices of the characters. The modernist novel and the antinovel destroyed the identity of the character and the unity of the authorial voice. Oshima does not cherish the concept of narrative prevalent among film theorists in the West. The concept has no place within a Japanese theory of cinema: its place within Japanese theoretical tradition is confined to literary theory.

"After experiencing Europe for two years, I wanted to portray the type of beautifully vital, strong people I came to know there, even if, in Japan, this would be nothing more than an idea." Although reflecting that, "As for whether or not this is the right thing to do—in fact, the answer will probably be negative," he pelted the screen with a series of intense images: the young lovers of *Kisses,* the maid's daughter in *A Cheerful Girl,* and Ishiwatari Gin in *Warm Current.* The posture of the modernists is most discernible in the stance of Masumura.

All three despise and reject the premodern status of the Japanese film's traditional form. They recognize, however, that this form is inevitably sustained by the surviving premodernity of Japan. They also know that they must ultimately fight against the link between the two. At the same time, they are aware that many of their respected predecessors, who did understand their opponents' strength, fought and were defeated nevertheless. They thus rejected the idea of challenging the premodernity of Japanese society in favor of direct attack through the content of their films. They decided to shock their audiences, rather than persuade or move them, by filming images of people created on the basis of concepts that had no connection to that social reality and its forms.

And in this they succeeded. For the film people who had been nodding off and resting complacently within the traditional form of the Japanese film (and the stagnation of Japanese society that was its background), these were truly shocking events.

The emergence of these modernists within the Japanese film world was due not merely to their artistic temperaments or their social consciousness. Their sensitive reactions to Japanese society and the state of the film industry in the late 1950s made their emergence inevitable.

For some years after the war, the struggle against the premodern system and for human freedom and human rights was carried on passionately in the midst of a chaotic Japanese society. The film industry, too, retained works with the traditional premodern form and content on the one hand, while making films whose content struggled against the traditional on the other. At that time, artists like Kinoshita, Imai, and Kurosawa won the immeasurable support of the young film audience. Immediately after the war, however, the power of the government, in the form of a democracy-promoting institution, once again began to defend openly the premodern tendencies of Japanese society. A little later, such a defense occurred in the context of film as well. However, the quest for human freedom and human rights continued. Supported by that quest, artists like Kinoshita, Imai, and Kurosawa continued to fight a splendidly beautiful retreating battle from around 1950 onward. *Until the Day We*

Meet Again, Ikiru, A Japanese Tragedy, The Tower of Lilies, and *The Garden of Women* are brilliant monuments to this battle.[11] However, from the latter half of the 1950s, a decade after the end of the war, the chaos of that time initially receded and things basically stabilized materially. Politically, too, the balance of power between conservatives and revolutionaries became established, as did the opposition of the two major international power blocs, ushering in a period of a kind of mutual stabilization. In the film world, too, the young audiences, which had supported the violent struggles of Kinoshita, Imai, and others against the premodern, were now becoming entwined in the premodernistic structure of Japanese society and immersed in the conservative sensibility. Thus, these outstanding filmmakers, who were continuing their quest for human freedom and human rights in the context of a society that oppresses that quest, lost the base of support for their ideas. Kinoshita Keisuke, the possessor of sharp senses, promptly tried to retain the sympathy of his audience in the world of chronicles. Kurosawa Akira, true to his own philosophy, tried to nurture it genuinely in the context of the period drama. Imai Tadashi, whose eyes never strayed from reality, ultimately sought a new dramaturgy in the world of Chikamatsu.[12] The sufferings of these, the most talented artists in the Japanese film world, were evinced in their desperate efforts to rid themselves of the frightening stagnation of the innovative aspect of the Japanese film.

As innovation stagnated, there were fewer viewers of the melodrama, the traditional form of the Japanese film. Obviously while Japan's postwar democratization had only reached a certain point, it was also solidly successful up to a certain point. The way to find a new direction in the midst of this strange peace and harmony— the way to break through—had not yet been discovered.

During this miserable period, a strong rival to the film industry appeared: television. Film people were haunted by a vision of Hollywood's turning into a petroleum plant. The influence of television became apparent. The battles of Rikidozan[13] and the Sharp Brothers, boldly slapstick comedies, and the confrontation between Kaneda[14] and Nagashima[15] started to draw more viewers than foolish films.

---

11.   *Until the Day We Meet Again* (*Mata Au Hi Made,* dir. Imai Tadashi, 1950); *Ikiru* (*Ikiru,* dir. Kurosawa Akira, 1952); *A Japanese Tragedy* (*Nihon no Higeki,* dir. Kinoshita Keisuke, 1946); *The Garden of Women* (*Onna no Sono,* dir. Kinoshita Keisuke, 1954).
12.   Chikamatsu (1653–1724) is generally considered to be Japan's greatest dramatist.
13.   Professional wrestler who lived from 1924 to 1963, when he died of wounds suffered when he was attacked by a gang member.
14.   A great pitcher of the Kokutetsu Swallows, a Japanese professional baseball team.
15.   A slugger of the Tokyo Giants.

Exactly at this time, the modernists appeared. Nakahira, in his first release, *Crazed Fruit,*[16] created an incomparable depiction of the three S's—speed, thrills,[17] and sex. This was a well-rounded response to the demands of the film industry as it sought to oppose television. At the same time, his spirit as a modernist critic made possible that form of expression. He used the three S's to his advantage as material for his critical stance, and this made him a champion in the defensive battle against television. Nakahira carved out his artistic stance by always taking transient, superficial social phenomena and serving them up with his cynical, critical spirit.

Shirasaka's comedies started off having to be funnier than television comedies: if television had to be interesting at any given moment, so had Shirasaka's comedies. And so Shirasaka's scripts were completely stylized: every speech and every action was imbued with his modernist sense. Shirasaka could not take into consideration the fact that Japanese audiences, who lived in the climate of the first-person novel, were not comfortable with these stylized ideas.

The heroes created by Masumura also struggled with the heroes of television, whose conspicuous personalities and modes of behavior were needed to give the audience a sense of stability. Masumura put this necessity to use while struggling with it. He achieved shocking effects by creating characters with completely free hearts and bodies and heroes who behaved freely. And he continued to ignore the social realities of these human images as well as the composition of his audience.

The modernists thus raised the fiery hand of innovation against the stagnation of the art of the film. At the same time, they responded to the primary demands of the contemporary film industry.

In June 1958, the modernists began to throw themselves into a more difficult effort. The team of Masumura and Shirasaka released *Giants and Toys*[18] (shown abroad as *The Build-Up*), written by Kaiko Takeshi. This film grapples with a brave theme: humanism destroyed by a huge capitalist mechanism. In spite of the fact that the form of this film is an extension of their previous work, it clearly and solemnly introduced a new element of content—the social structure—that brings forth changes in form as well. How do they manage this? Is Masumura possibly trying to keep his faith in human beings by giving his characters a violent energy that is repeatedly regenerated, even as the characters are destroyed by the mechanism? How does

16.   *Crazed Fruit (Kurutta Kajitsu,* dir. Nakahira Ko, 1956).
17.   When the English word "thrill" is transliterated into Japanese, it begins with an "s" sound: *suriru.*
18.   *Giants and Toys (Kyojin to Gangu,* dir. Masumura Yasuzo, 1958).

this interact with Shirasaka's coolly sarcastic attitude? This work is a major experiment cast into the future by these two filmmakers.

Nakahira will release Niwa Fumio's *The Four Seasons of Love* after more than six months of silence following *The Wavering of Virtue*. For the first time, Nakahira's critical spirit attempts to progress from depicting frothy social phenomena to penetrating the psychology of human physiology, a realm in which Naruse Mikio[19] and Toyoda Shiro[20] excel. How will Nakahira express himself as he takes on this genre? And what kind of new world will he establish in Japanese film? This work, too, is an important crossroads at which we will ask whether Nakahira's critical spirit is indeed genuine.

While the modernists' foundation with respect to both content and form was becoming confused in the context of a relatively stabilized Japanese society, the Japanese film was exposed to the threat of television. The modernists were engineering a breakthrough by means of an innovation in form. Their next challenge is to progress further, to the level of content, innovating and modernizing as they confront the premodernity of Japanese film and society.

They will inevitably face that challenge because mere innovation in form will not earn them the overwhelming support of the audience, which is living in a partially premodern Japan and has premodern elements in its consciousness and view of life. At present, these filmmakers have only the support of a segment of stateless intellectuals and Japanese youths who are not yet completely integrated into the social structure. This doesn't compare with the national trust that Kinoshita, Imai, and others have attained as artists. But now even these trusted artists are confused, along

19.   Naruse Mikio joined the Shochiku Kamata Studio as a propman in 1920 and moved to the assistant director's department later. His directorial debut with *The Fighting Couple* (*Chanbara Fufu*, 1930) was made considerably later than that of younger colleagues such as Ozu Yasujiro, Gosho Heinosuke, and Shimizu Hiroshi. His next film, *Hold on, Lunch-Carrying Worker! (Koshiben Ganbare*, 1930), marked him as a promising director of the Shochiku "common people" or "little citizen" genre of film, but unfortunately Ozu had already established himself as the director of the same genre. It is reported that the studio director, Kido Shiro, said that they did not need two Ozu's. A successful third film, however, *The Ruined Spring* (*Mushibameru Haru*, 1930), showed Naruse to be a different kind of master director. Having made seven widely acknowledged films at Shochiku, he moved to the newly organized PCL Studio in 1933, which was to be incorporated into the Toho Company. His widely distributed film, *The Floating Clouds* (*Ukigumo*, 1955), was made at Toho.
20.   Toyoda Shiro joined the Shochiku Kamata Studio as an assistant director in 1923 and was promoted to director four years later with *The Painted Lips* (*Irodorareta Kuchibiru*, 1929). Critics praised his synecdochical use of a woman's feet pedaling a sewing machine in presenting her state of mind. After making a few unsuccessful films at Shochiku, he moved to a new independent production company and made the well-received *The Young One* (*Wakai Hito*, 1937), an adaptation of a popular novel by Ishizaka Yojiro. He came to excel in adaptations of successful, acclaimed novels. *Spring on Leper's Island* (*Kojima no Haru*, 1940) is generally considered to be his best film.

with the people. *Chushingura*[21] is breaking box-office records. This film features Ishihara Yujiro, who made his debut in Nakahira's *Crazed Fruit* as a symbol of rebellion, now transformed into a symbol of stability and good sense in his role as a devoted son and loyal younger brother.

The modernists are at a crossroads. One road would lead to gradual degeneration of their innovations in form into mere entertainment, bringing about their surrender to the premodern elements that are subconsciously included in the content of their films. In that case, they would simply live out their lives as mediocre technical artists. Another road requires them to exert all of their critical spirit and powers of expression in a persistent struggle that strongly and effectively pits the content of their works against the premodern elements of Japanese society.

We don't know what form that struggle will take; they probably don't know themselves. However, if they had been thinking of *Giants and Toys* and *The Four Seasons of Love*[22] as the first big steps along that road, then at least the germination of that method may be said to be in evidence. That they will select this, the road to innovation, rather than the former one, to degeneration, is highly probable. It is the only possible point at which the Japanese film can break through, and it is impossible to think of a breakthrough point as remaining closed. In some situation, at some time, the right innovator will certainly emerge to break through to a new situation, a new time. The form of the innovator will vary depending on the time and the situation. Compared to Kinoshita, Imai, and Kurosawa, who completed their preparations during the war and established themselves as innovators during the postwar age of emerging democracy, the modernists are unfortunate and their form may be inferior. However, as Jean-Paul Sartre said, "No matter what he does, there is no road on which the artist can escape; what we want is for artists to solidly embrace their own era. The artists' own age is his only opportunity. That age was made for that artist and that artist was made for that age." The burden of the glory and misery of today's Japanese film truly belongs on the shoulders of the modernists. Critics and viewers who desire the innovation of the Japanese film must shower their works with warm understanding and criticism. If the modernists don't maintain their innovative stance and continue to progress, it will be unfortunate not only for the Japanese film and Japanese society of today but also for the Japanese film and Japanese society of the future.

(Film Review, July 1958)

21.　　This film, based on a Kabuki play, dramatizes a well-known story of the Genroku era. The frequent remakes of this film would seem to point to a Japanese preoccupation with loyalty and vengeance.

22.　　*The Four Seasons of Love (Shiki no Aiyoku,* dir. Nakahira Ko, 1958).

A Review of "Sleeping Lion: Shochiku Ofuna"

I got angry when I read "Sleeping Lion: Shochiku Ofuna," the research on studios by Noguchi Yuichiro[1] and Sato Tadao[2] that was published in the June 1959 issue of *Film Review*. I hear that all of the directors and assistant directors who read it were also angry—but not because it was an attack on Shochiku Ofuna. We're saying, "You're cowardly, superficial! You're talking about a sleeping lion when you should be talking about a dead lion!"

A little later, though, the executive offices of the studio started to show a lot of interest in this piece. I heard that there was discussion about it in the planning department, particularly about the plan system. So this piece, which we considered worthless, actually served a purpose in a sense. Needless to say, bringing the problem into the public eye is a tremendous achievement. Our dissatisfaction, however, remains. Articulating that dissatisfaction will probably close the break between those who make films and those who review them and it may to some extent clarify the outlook for the future of the Japanese film.

The following is a summary of the main themes of Noguchi and Sato's piece:

1. Management! Wave your arms more powerfully! Make it clear that your ethic is "Work and you will be rewarded," and give your all to the fight against other companies!

---

1.   Literary and film critic.
2.   Film critic and social analyst. Although Sato is not a theorist in any strict sense of the word, his writings cover a wide range of cinema issues. He was associate member of *Film Review* (*Eiga Hihyo*) in the late 1950s and the editor-in-chief of *Film Criticism* (*Eiga Hyoron*) from the late 1950s to the early 1960s. His *Currents in Japanese Cinema* (trans. Gregory Barret, Tokyo, 1982) offers a characteristic historicization and theorization of Japanese filmmaking practice. His other publications include *The Art of Ozu Yasujiro* (Tokyo: Asahi Shinbun Sha, 1978), *The World of Mizoguchi Kenji* (Tokyo: Chikuma Shobo, 1981), *The World of Kurosawa Akira* (Tokyo: Asahi Bunko, Asahi Shinbun Sha, 1987), and *The World of Oshima Nagisa* (Tokyo: Asahi Bunko, Asahi Shinbun Sha, 1987). The book on Oshima contains a great deal of useful factual data.

2. Perfect the mass-production structure and establish a system of accountability.

3. Consider whether the Ofuna style, with its content and techniques centered on the emotions of the closed, introverted Japanese people, is really the right thing.

4. Improve your technique!

These are truly well-founded assertions, but I have to say that they all stop at a superficial articulation of the problems. The point is, why can't something that is this simple and clear be resolved? These two authors must take responsibility for failing to pursue this issue and thereby making the fatal mistake of leaving the responsibility for finding a solution entirely to management. Can the authors be thinking that one fine day management will arise and give a yell and the entire problem will be solved? That can't be the case. This problem will be solved only when the pursuit of innovation by those in the studio making films and the pursuit of reform by management come together in some form. The authors should have identified the two types of filmmakers: the type that is stagnant and conservative in both his feelings and actions, which reinforces the status quo, and the type that is innovative in both respects. The censuring of the former and strengthening and encouraging of the latter should have been their main point of emphasis, because the strength to defeat the stagnation of the Shochiku film—and, by extension, the Japanese film—lies only in the pursuit of innovation on the part of those who participate in the making of films in the studios.

However, the pursuit of that kind of innovation hasn't gathered sufficient strength. Why? That is the question at this point. I want to consider this problem in the context of Noguchi and Sato's third point: the Ofuna style as it relates to the content and technique of a work.

The authors are correct to seize on this phenomenon. They observe that the Ofuna works, which are based on a warm understanding of the circumstances behind the warping of the impoverished masses of seclusionist Japan, together with a splash of criticism—both the so-called artistic works, with their excellent critical sensitivity to society and people, and the romantic melodramas and merchant-district comedies, which are stripped of critical sensibility—all leave one with that same impression of seclusion. Such works quickly lost popularity once the wartime generation, with its visceral understanding of the Japanese tradition of emotional endurance, was no longer the center of the audience. They are also correct in saying that objective description centered on smooth segues had been the technique that was most appropriate for depicting this seclusionism. Given the fact that the content and method of this sort of work—which had peaked in 1954 with *Twenty-Four Eyes*—was already beginning to lose its ability to attract audiences and would soon lose it completely, why did works of the same type, in an even more degenerated form, keep appearing on the screens of Shochiku films?

Except for a very small group of specific individuals, most people at Ofuna today probably have doubts about the content and method of this kind of work. Surely many executives, directors, crew members, and actors believe that innovation is in some sense necessary. Even so, the sole reason that no innovation of any kind is taking place is that new content and method exist in only a few works; in a debilitated form they lack the strength to spread to all of the works.

What is the content and method of the new work? Noguchi and Sato seem to be saying that they must be able to capture the focus of the audience's active interest: they must take a stance exactly opposite to that of old Ofuna work, because by concentrating on the problem of warped feelings in human relationships, the old films were able to capture only the audience's passive interest. Films written now must be actively interesting, because the core of the audience consists of the postwar generation, which, unscarred by the war and brought up amid the collapse of Japan's feudalistic morality system, is able to believe only in a world of which they are the center—a belief that leads them to actively pursue their own individual desires.

The new work must center on the vivid desires and actions of people who grapple with the status quo. They must not depict feeble complexes, shabby emotions, or quiet virtue. The tendencies of individual works will vary with the artist. If the depiction is of someone who confronts his circumstances and triumphs, it will be a new melodrama singing the praises of human energy; if it poignantly exposes the meaning of a person's circumstances as he experiences them, it will be a new comedy. It will be possible for both to be applauded by the audience, who will feel liberated because they themselves are seeking the energy to break through their own circumstances. A modern tragedy that gives rise to a distortion of circumstances—that is, a work that depicts people who cannot break through their circumstances in spite of their fully mustering the energy and actions needed to combat them—can become a sharp thorn piercing the side of the viewers, who are searching for a way to triumph over their own circumstances.

To create works that are centered on the vivid desires and actions of people who are grappling with their circumstances, it is, of course, necessary to destroy the old naturalist methods. First of all, we must be liberated from the confines of storytelling for its own sake. We must destroy the illusion that films are characterized by the flat storytelling of the naturalist novel and affirm that what is cinematic is bold fiction and free structure. Next, we must do away with the naturalism present in each shot and in the way the shots are linked. Composition, lighting, camera movement, sound, and music must be used in accordance with the artist's bold subject and arranged solely for the purpose of expressing the theme. The method and technique of the Ofuna works were always the essence of constraint. Now we must brandish freedom of method and technique. And we must restore the appeal of the film itself.

I return to the initial question of why so simple a thing can't be accomplished. Is it, for example, because a conservative executive office steadfastly guarding the old Ofuna framework will not accept any attempt at reform? One often hears this offered as an excuse. But a far more serious problem is that the old Ofuna framework is solidly present in the attitudes of those who make films—those who must actively make innovations in them. The exterior condition called Shochiku Ofuna firmly binds the content and methods of works to something old because it has been internalized by every person who makes films. Is it possible for each individual to free himself of what is inside?

I said "every one who makes films," but what is the role of the director, who, among all who participate in production, must bear the brunt of the responsibility for making active innovations in film? Unfortunately, there are many directors who lead a peaceful existence having internalized the Ofuna framework and who never contemplate creating works with anything new in the way of content or method. In spite of this, these directors know that their works are losing their connection with the audience; moreover, because they are comfortable with that, nothing in their works is worthy of being called a theme. This does not stop merely with Shochiku Ofuna. The presence of this type of director in every studio is the chief cause of the crisis of the loss of theme in Japanese film in general. Noguchi and Sato should have pointed this out and censured it. However, some directors struggle against the old Ofuna framework within, and, because of this, they struggle with external conditions and try to accomplish innovations in content and method. Because it is an independent, lopsided battle, they end up compromising somewhat both inside and outside and aren't significantly successful, despite the massive energy they have invested. It isn't that their work lacks a theme but that their themes are only half-developed, and their connection with the audience is limited accordingly. Noguchi and Sato, however, should have discovered these directors and given strong support to their struggles. Why doesn't the number of such directors increase, given the desirability of such an increase? The problem is that over the past several years Ofuna has had no outstanding new directors. Why is that? Briefly put, it is because these people, who are called new directors and are in fact new as directors, have long been in the employ of Ofuna as assistant directors! How could the Ofuna framework not become completely internalized by someone who has worked for ten years in an Ofuna setting? Ofuna's new directors therefore must start their careers battling outside while also battling the Ofuna framework within. Most new directors have already abandoned that fight with their first work, while a small number of them manage a very feeble struggle at best. This is because the external framework imposed on new directors is too strong and they can fight against it only if they are completely independent. Noguchi and Sato should have been aware of the internal and external conditions faced by these new directors and offered them criticism and counsel.

It is obvious that the establishment of new content and method in film will come only with the appearance of a new class of directors whose inner consciousness is not yet completely dominated by the old Ofuna framework and who, moreover, have the strength to fight that framework and win. Those new directors will probably be of essentially the same age as the postwar generation that forms the mainstream film audience. The common goal of the postwar generation is to give spectacular cinematic expression to the vivid desires and actions of people grappling with their circumstances. That is precisely where new themes are to be found.

Here lies the only opportunity for remedy, not merely for Shochiku Ofuna but for the crisis loss of theme in the Japanese film as well. The Japanese film has become erotic and grotesque and endlessly degenerate because the desires and actions of the postwar generation are not given expression by the writers of their own generation and are portrayed instead in a mannerist style, with no thematic element.

That is precisely where the crisis of Shochiku Ofuna lies as well. Not only the directing department but every department involved in making films must give the postwar generation, which is capable of establishing the content and method of new works, the opportunity for self-expression. Moreover, we must precipitate the coming of this period before their consciousness is totally dominated by the old Ofuna framework. If Noguchi and Sato had made a concrete suggestion to Shochiku Ofuna, wouldn't this have been it? Shouldn't they have counseled them to censure the postwar generation members of every department in the studio for not trying to seize opportunities for self-expression? Shouldn't they have advised the executive to provide opportunities of this sort?

I began this article by saying that Naguchi and Sato should perhaps have titled their research "Dead Lion: Shochiku Ofuna." Our view of the future is darker than that of Noguchi and Sato, but it does have a bright side. That's because we have confidence in our ability to establish the content and method of new work, and because we can feel in our bones the desire for innovation throughout the studios. The only future possible for Shochiku Ofuna and the Japanese film depends on those two things.

Finally, those producing films and those who review them need to communicate more. For that reason, Noguchi and Sato's article is very effective. I have written this to enhance that effectiveness and encourage communication. I long for this communication to progress further based on the basis of the participation of more people.

(*Film Criticism,* August 1959)

I'm a new director. Once you've spent six years in the studio as an assistant director, though, you really begin to worry about whether a film will be successful. By successful, I mean that it will attract a large audience. And as an artist you naturally worry about the audience's reaction (though of course there are directors who worry only about attracting an audience, not about its reaction). At any rate, if a director is to do the kind of work he wants to do in the film industry, he absolutely must have the support of the audience. He cannot consider the film without considering the audience.

Recently I have been a bit irritated to see that films that don't play fair—such as *The Road to the Thirteen Steps*[1] and *A Man Blown by the Wind*[2]—have been successful. Audiences want to see "the real thing"—the real atrocities of the Nazis or Mishima Yukio as he really appears. I find it very irritating because what these films actually show is a fake dressed up to look like the real thing. And even more irritating is the fact that such works are rarely criticized openly.

The Road to the Thirteen Steps is nothing more than an entirely pictorial explanation of the fact that the Nazis perpetrated atrocities and were defeated in the war. The audience merely acknowledges that they have heard this for some time. Even if the atrocities portrayed surpass their expectations, they are merely surprised; the film doesn't appeal to them to consider the deeper meaning of the acts or how they relate to the present.

---

1.   This imported compilation film (*Der Nürnberger Prozess,* dir. Felix von Podomanizki, 1962) treats the Nazis' emergence, seizure of power, their final defeat, and the exposure of the death camps.

2.   *A Man Blown by the Wind* (*Karakkaze Yaro,* dir. Masumura Yasuzo, 1960).

This is because the artist's subjectivity plays has absolutely no role in the selection and organization of the scenes, the montage, the sound, or the use of music. It is merely a showpiece.

I don't know who made this film. He probably intended from the beginning to create a showpiece. The artist's subjectivity may not have much popular appeal. This probably occurred to the critics, and thus no severe criticism appeared. It is not a showpiece along the lines of a one-eyed boy-monster or a creature that is half girl and half bear. Clearly, it is difficult to forgive the type of attitude that treats this kind of material—material with important significance—as if unrelated to the artist's point of view. It thereby serves merely to reinforce stereotypes held by the audience.

Masumura Yasuzo's *A Man Blown by the Wind,* which starred Mishima Yukio, was not harshly criticized. That's not unreasonable. Everyone knew that Masumura was put in an impossible position. However, this is clearly Masumura's worst work.

First of all, why did Masumura set out to depict the gangster as a very stingy, miserable creature? I don't know. Masumura has consistently depicted modern heroes and heroines. He portrays and praises characters who expose their desires straightforwardly and act on them, ignoring the myths of their surroundings, eliminating atmosphere, and rejecting lyricism. Why, then, did Masumura attempt to portray the gangster as miserable?

I think it is probably because Masumura had to use Mishima Yukio as his leading man. Wouldn't Masumura have had some hesitation about using Mishima as a hero? The play (by Kikushima Ryuzo and Ando Hideo), of course, was the old story of a gangster who reforms. If this were the Masumura we have seen so far, he would have had to change the story dramatically, because no concept is further from his mind than that of "reform." However, Masumura merely changed the hero of the play, portrayed as a shining example of a gangster, into a feeble coward. Of course, this change demonstrates Masumura's extraordinary originality, which a journalist friend of mine praised highly. However, although this shows the solidity of Masumura's social consciousness, the role of his subjectivity is another question. I should have preferred him to portray Mishima as a modern hero, as usual. If he had to be an unfeeling man, he should have been portrayed as a consistently unfeeling one, not as one who reforms; as a shining example of a gangster. That would necessarily have been a Masumuraesque character. By creating that type of character with a completely subjective use of the camera, Masumura makes his works independent worlds in themselves, generating—for the first time in Japanese film—a tension with society that serves as a critical mechanism. What you see there is not film incorporating reality; rather, it is Masumura's subjective world. That is Masumura's greatest achievement; all artists coming after him must be indebted to him for it. But making the hero of *A Man Blown by the Wind* a miserable gangster precipitated an error in the construction of the Masumura world. How did such an error—the casting of Mishima as a miserable gangster—come about?

What most perplexed Masumura about starring Mishima Yukio in *A Man Blown by the Wind* was probably the question of how to bring Mishima, a hero in the real world, into his own artistic world as a hero. Masumura's solution was to give the Mishima character in his work an image that was the exact opposite of Mishima's image in the real world. Masumura probably thought that by doing so he could maintain the purity of his creative world by preventing Mishima's real-world image from creeping in. However, from this point his thought process can be construed in two ways. One is that he thought that the audience would disregard Mishima's image in the real world—or at least think of it in the same way as that of the actress Wakao Ayako or the actor Funakoshi Eiji—and so become absorbed in his portrayal of a miserable gangster. The other is that he intended to constantly remind the audience that Mishima Yukio was portraying a miserable gangster. Had he opted for the former, the audience couldn't really have completely disregarded Mishima's real-life image, and, needless to say, it would have been a mistake because there was a wider gap between Mishima and his role than in the case of Wakao or Funakoshi. It is interesting to consider Masumura's position had he opted for the latter. Whenever it is made clear that a person is playing the role of another person, the audience doesn't assimilate this and is alienated; this alienation becomes a critique of the actor playing the role and of the situation in which he finds himself. Mishima, however, did not try to flaunt the role; he tried to become the character. In that case, even if Masumura had intended it, Mishima's performance could not have become that kind of critique. Therefore a work that was not a Masumura's world came into being.

Here I would like to raise a crucial question: Was Masumura trying to create the same kind of world in this work as in his other films; did he want to depict a miserable gangster? I don't think so. What must have interested Masumura was not the miserable gangster; it was Mishima Yukio himself—just as it was Mishima himself who interested the audience! The object of Masumura's criticism must have been not the miserable gangster but Mishima Yukio. Had he been aware of the effect of this on his own point of view, he probably would have been able to create a Masumuraesque world using his criticism of Mishima, even with Mishima cast as a miserable gangster. Masumura would probably have been able to imagine a different type of hero as well.

Because Masumura made this film without an awareness of this inversion, he produced something that cannot be called a Masumura work. Masumura should not be censured for having more interest in Mishima Yukio himself than in the character. Given the circumstances, that was only natural. What should be censured, however, is Masumura's lack or incompleteness of self-awareness, which caused him to make a film that ran counter to his desires as well as to those of his audience; he probably felt dissatisfied al the while without knowing why.

Masumura has swerved from his own philosophy. A close comparison of *A Man Blown by the Wind* and his previous work reveals the extent to which his subjectivity is absent from the film. *A Man Blown by the Wind* has a one-cut, one-cut,[3] terribly crude look. Although he employs the same type of direction as in his previous films, the weight given to each shot is completely different. Even when the shots in *A Man Blown by the Wind* are from the same angle and have the same size and arrangement of characters as shots in his other films, they are so light as to seem in danger of blowing away.

This is what being a filmmaker is all about. A filmmaker does not invent an infinity of different types of shots and scenes. Rather, he invests each individual shot and scene with his philosophy.

I once had the opportunity to see two works by the American documentary filmmaker Robert Flaherty in one day: *Nanook of the North* and *Louisiana Story*. *Nanook of the North,* the 1922 depiction of the icebound lives of Eskimos that was his first film, contains the following scene. The Eskimos are catching seals. They trick one seal and pull it up onto the beach. To them, the seal represents precious spoils that provide food and fulfill many of their other survival needs. The seal struggles. They engage in a desperate tug-of-war with it. At that point, there is a cut to the seal's companions in the open sea; they are floating in the deep black sea as if grieving for the seal that is being pulled away. It is a cruel, harsh image, revealing the filmmaker's intensely active attitude toward the tenuous conditions of existence.

On the other hand, the subject of Flaherty's 1948 film *Louisiana Story* is a primitive youth living in the marshlands when machines and oil wells penetrate the area. There is also a tug-of-war scene here, a struggle between the youth and an alligator. In the midst of it there is a cut to the youth's anxious father. Ultimately the youth escapes serious harm. The scene has a playful mood, as if the filmmaker is watching all of this at a safe distance, with half-closed eyes.

---

3.   Japanese directors say "shot" or "cut" irrespective of the difference in concepts.

The depth of Flaherty's active involvement in these two scenes, both of which feature a cut to a third party watching a struggle, varies tremendously. Rather than attributing this to Standard Oil's having sponsored *Louisiana Story* as a commercial film, I believe it is due to Flaherty's having aged and become debilitated—an unbearable thought.

I call it unbearable because the problem haunts me. I find *A Man Blown by the Wind* unbearable for the same reason. I lament the fact that the signs of decline have appeared so soon in Masumura. Of course, it is not as though he has completely declined all at once. However, all artists stand perpetually on the edge of that abyss. Once they lose their active involvement, the decline is all too swift. Afterward, the filmmaker is but a cog in the automatic manufacture of films. In fact, the position of a director in a modern mass-production studio is normally that of a cog. To preserve his active involvement, a filmmaker must begin by resisting becoming a cog. This resistance is all that supports the continuous renewal of the artist's active involvement.

Jean-Luc Godard's *Breathless* is a truly wonderful film in that it reminds us that the appeal of the film lies in the continuity of discontinuity. The beauty of the work is that the artist is not trying to earn his living as a film director. And perhaps that is why the filmmaker's active involvement penetrates the work so splendidly.

This is not true of Japan's impoverished directors and those other film people, who must consider their work an occupation. Naturally, pitfalls exist. In a sense, an easier fate awaits one who has lost his active involvement. The only way to avoid that is for the artist to check constantly for his active involvement in every film, every shot. Only by doing so can he achieve a genuine bond with the audience.

It may seem strange that I, who have completed only one film and am at long last about to begin shooting my second, should be talking about the debilitation of filmmakers. However, under present conditions such is the threat to his active involvement that it is not strange at all. I have no choice but to be acutely conscious of this while continuing to preserve and renew my active involvement in my films.

My second film, *Cruel Story of Youth,* will focus on the cruelty of our situation and most particularly on youth as victims of the contradictions arising from it.

(*Documentary Films,* June 1960)

Beyond Endless Self-Negation: The Attitude
of the New Filmmakers

The audience, which consists merely of people who go to the theater out of habit—no matter what film is showing—is tired of today's Japanese film. The new films need to give this indolent audience a shock and at the same time create a new audience.

To generate a new audience, new films must, first and foremost, express the filmmaker's active involvement as an individual. Until this is realized, a dialogue between filmmaker and audience cannot be established and the film cannot function, in tension with reality as critical commentary. Cinema can develop in no other way.

In spite of this, films that actively express the involvement of new filmmakers have not appeared. People say that this is because the walls of film companies are thick barriers.

The walls of companies are indeed thick barriers. The works of new scriptwriters aren't readily made into films, and new directors have tremendous difficulty in getting projects accepted in the plans of a new director. That is because there is no sense of stability from the business point of view—the companies don't have a clear idea of the nature of the work being produced by new scriptwriters and directors. The inherent conservatism of business has an inevitability that transcends the talent and good intentions of those involved. But filmmakers who use the thick walls of film companies as an excuse for failure to become actively involved deserve condemnation.

Furthermore, when the film industry is in this kind of unstable period, the companies themselves seek new films that can attract a new audience. One must understand that the biggest opportunities for innovation in film lie exclusively with the filmmakers.

In spite of this, new films don't readily appear. When they do, they seem to bear the marks of old film methods.

This is not simply because the companies constrain the filmmakers but because established methods of self-restraint have deeply penetrated the filmmakers as well.

The work of new filmmakers must begin with the systematic crushing of these hidden methods of self-restraint. Next, filmmakers must have active control over every aspect of the film.

Suppose that new films were to be made in this way. Suppose that a new audience for them were to emerge. That filmmaker and that work would give a kind of security to the company. The company would probably demand that the same artist produce the same sort of work using the same method every time.

However, if the second work were made by exactly the same method as the first, that method would no longer be one of active involvement on the part of that filmmaker; he would merely be repeating an established method. Naturally, the work would lose any real relationship to the filmmaker himself, and there would no longer be any dialogue with the audience. The decline of the filmmaker would have begun.

This is what is meant by the walls of the companies. Those walls are far more frightening when they take away the filmmaker's active involvement than when they reject it.

How is this possible?

It is possible only by means of endless self-negation.

Once a filmmaker has created a work, the method expressive of his active involvement must be thought of as part of his external reality. To reuse a method that has become part of his reality signifies the loss of an involved attitude and a surrender to reality.

Instead, only the maintenance of a state of tension with reality and the discovery of a new method of perpetual active involvement will enable him to make works that are a true expression of himself.

Thus the filmmaker must always seek a new tension with reality and constantly negate himself in order to continue to create a new artistic involvement.

This is an immensely difficult task.

But there is no other way to accomplishment as an artist than to endure this difficulty.

And the renewal of the Japanese cinema will come only through the appearance of many filmmakers able to endure it.

(*Scenario,* July 1960)

What Is a Shot?

I call a "shot" what in drama film studios is ordinarily called a "cut." Broadly speaking, it is "one fragment of a film that is shot continuously." (This definition is not complete. The short section entitled "The Meaning of a Cut" in Itami Mansaku's *Notes in Repose* contains a more detailed discussion of this.[1])

I have been asked to write about various issues related to the shot. At present, I haven't the necessary means (particularly the time) to produce a thorough analysis of the definition of a shot and related issues. Thus, what I have written below is merely my own personal hypothesis drawn from limited experience.

To me, a filmmaker's method is the way his temperament (which probably includes his aesthetic consciousness) and his perception of reality are synthesized (some filmmakers merely have temperament and lack a perception of reality—and the really awful ones have no temperament at all!). A filmmaker's method is present in even a single shot; from a single shot we must be able to get a sense of his temperament and his perception of reality.

My most recent work, *Night and Fog in Japan*,[2] has only forty-three shots. As a rule, this means one scene, one cut.

1.   Director and scriptwriter Itami Mansaku (1900–1946) was also a noted essayist. *Notes in Repose* (*Seiga Zakki*, 1943), and another collection of essays, *Notes on Cinema* (*Eiga Zakki*, 1937) are included in *The Complete Works of Itami Mansaku*, 3 vols. (*Itami Mansaku Zenshu*, Tokyo: Chikuma Shobo, 1960). His intellectual treatment of character is best seen in *Akanishi Kakita* (*Akanishi Kakita*, 1936).

2.   Alain Resnais's *Night and Fog* (1956) had been distributed in Japan. Resnais's other films, including earlier documentaries—*Van Gogh* (1948), *Guernica* (1950), *Toute la Memoire du Monde* (1956)—and a feature film, *Hiroshima, Mon Amour* (1959), were also introduced to Japan. These films and their camerawork were the subject of intensive discussion among Japanese documentary

This method attaches importance to and respects real time. It is designed to avoid interrupting the filmmaker's stream of consciousness. One of my basic rules is to make a shot last as long as possible with the camera moving freely. (This is also related to the complete construction of one scene. Long ago, stopping in the middle of a scene was held to be the proper method. Now it is necessary to finish constructing a scene once you have begun it.)

The next rule after the continuity of shots is that of instability of shots. For that reason, I use a telephoto-type lens. With it, the characters you are shooting are enlarged so that the screen soon becomes unstable with even the slightest move by a character. This is remedied by the camera's movement, and the character moves again—with the repetition of that process, the filmmaker's unsettled stream of consciousness becomes settled in the stream of the scenes.

The filmmaker's stream of consciousness and subjectivity flow through these two rules. Their role is critical.

Every shot must be critical. The field of each shot must incorporate the filmmaker's critique of the subject and the situation and at the same time serve as a critique of the filmmaker (this is also a rule of the work as a whole).

The problem is that existing films and the stereotypical images held by filmmakers keep them from taking any shots that incorporate critique. It is as if artificial people were manipulating the camera. (In that respect the camera is completely undependable. There is no way that the camera can take shots that incorporate critique by accident. That is simply the filmmaker's conscious attempt to use accident to destroy his own inevitable tendency to take routine shots.)

Thus, the only way to change the film is to crush the established stereotyped images contained in each shot. (Film logic that gives priority to the story is being turned on its head—it has been negated considerably, but not enough as yet. Lurking

---

filmmakers and theorists, among them Hani Susumu, Okada Susumu, and Matsumoto Toshio, in their journal, *Documentary Films (Kiroku Eiga)*. Although Oshima may have not seen all of these films, the theorists apparently discerned a certain affinity between the style of Resnais's films and that of Oshima in *Night and Fog in Japan*, especially with regard to the use of the very long, sustained take. Oshima was invited to contribute an article concerning his methodology. Hani Susumu must have been one of the first documentarist/theorists to argue for the use of the sustained take in relation to Alexandre Astruc's "camera-pen" theory via Mizoguchi Kenji. Beginning in 1957, Oshima was associated with the journal *Film Review (Eiga Hihyo)*. His text, "Is It a Breakthrough?" was published in July 1958. Other associates of *Film Review* included Hani Susumu, Matsumoto Toshio, Noda Shinkichi, Nagano Chiaki, Sato Tadao, Sato Shigeomi, Kuroda Kio, and Yoshida Yoshishige. The journal's last issue was published in January 1959.

within the works of filmmakers who are called avant-garde are also shots whose only purpose is to explain the story.)

The first films worthy of the name will be those in which every shot incorporates the same level of critique that informs the work as a whole.

Don't make even one haphazard shot!

(*Documentary Films,* November 1960)

How tasteless is the liquor drunk in the evening after you've done a production entirely by the book, making absolutely no changes to the stage directions or speeches. In contrast, how incredibly delicious is the liquor drunk on a day in which you've shot things that aren't in the script.

What does this mean? A production must not be an explanation of the script; it must be a reality-based negation of the images expressed in the script and a discovery of new images using that negation as an opportunity.

Here, a reality-based negation of the images expressed in the script does not in any way mean a negation of the importance of the script. Rather, the script has a definite importance. The script is the basic plan for the filmmaker's interaction with reality. It must be a total and dynamic vision of the inner person and the outer circumstances, superimposed on the filmmaker's consciousness of reality. At the production stage, the filmmaker's job is to relate his vision to reality once more and to use the camera to discover new images. When scripts with outstanding vision are related to reality, they make possible the discovery of new images.

This accumulation of new images becomes a work and thereby gives the filmmaker a new consciousness of reality. When he is preparing for the next work, it shapes his total and dynamic vision of the inner person and outer circumstances. The filmmaker goes on to discover new images as he works on each production, testing and negating his vision.

The filmmaker is headed toward decline if he doesn't place himself squarely in the midst of such endless exercises. By deifying and making absolute his ego's images, he renders himself unable to grasp all reality except in the context of those images.

Reality, however, is always changing. Thus, the filmmaker who is unable to grasp it immediately ceases being a filmmaker and degenerates into a mere crafter of images.

Constant self-negation and transformation are necessary if one is to avoid that debilitation and continue to confront circumstances as a filmmaker. Naturally, that means preparing a new methodology. Moreover, those transformations and that methodology must not themselves be made into goals of the ego, but, as weapons used to change reality, must always follow through with their objective of revolutionizing consciousness. With this in place, the law of self-negating movement is not merely a law of production or of the filmmaker, but a law of human growth and of the development of the human race—a law of the movement of all things.

The filmmaker must uphold that law.

(*Cinema Biweekly*, April 1961)

In Protest against the Massacre of *Night and Fog in Japan*

With unrelenting anger, I write in protest against the massacre of *Night and Fog in Japan*.

On behalf of all of us—myself, Ishido Toshiro,[1] Kawamata Ko[2]—and the entire crew, who unraveled a difficult subject and treated the project as if it were their own work; all of the actors, starting with Watanabe Fumio, who called himself a nonacting participant; and everyone on the outside who made endless efforts to improve it as if it were their own work, begrudging neither criticism nor counsel throughout the production process—representing all of them, all of their sadness and anger, I write in protest of the massacre of *Night and Fog in Japan*.

This massacre is clearly political oppression. This is demonstrated by the film's having been withdrawn in spite of the fact that its box-office figures were only slightly lower than usual, and by the sudden way it was withdrawn.

If this isn't political oppression, let even one theater, one independent screening group, give it one opportunity to be shown! Lend it out!

I understand that all such requests are being refused. If this isn't political oppression, what is it?

1.   Ishido Toshiro joined the Shochiku Ofuna Studio in 1955 as an assistant director and collaborated with Oshima during the first ten years of Oshima's directorial career. He coscripted *The Tomb of the Sun* (*Taiyo no Hakaba,* 1960), *Night and Fog in Japan* (*Nihon no Yoru to Kiri,* 1960), *The Catch* (*Shiiku,* 1961), and *Amakusa Shiro Tokisada* (*Amakusa Shiro Tokisada,* 1962). Ishido quit Shochiku with Oshima in 1961 and joined Oshima's independent production company, Sozosha, which he left in the early 1960s to work as a freelancer and eventually as a novelist.
2.   Kawamata Ko entered the Shochiku Ofuna Studio in 1945 as an assistant cameraman and became a director of cinematography with *Let's Go* (*Donto Ikooze,* dir. Nomura Yoshitaro, 1959). His second job as cameraman for Oshima's *The Tomb of the Sun* (*Taiyo no Hakaba,* 1960) launched his career in the Shochiku Studio as a director of cinematography much in demand, for his striking photography was immediately noticed. His collaboration with Oshima lasted until Oshima left Shochiku on the other two films, *Cruel Story of Youth* (*Seishun Zankoku Monogatari,* 1960) and *Night and Fog in Japan* (*Nihon no Yoru to Kiri,* 1960).

Night and Fog in Japan. 1960.

I direct my protest to Shochiku's executive offices.

You have succumbed to political oppression, massacring *Night and Fog in Japan* using excuses like "No one comes to see it. No one understands it."

You must have known from the beginning that this film wasn't going to be a big hit and would be difficult for the audiences of *The Manager and the Apprentice* to understand.[3]

This work was an appeal to the audience that usually turns its back on movie theaters, the audience that takes life seriously. You are forgetting to appeal to them and using the low box-office figures as an excuse for massacring *Night and Fog in Japan.*

With unrelenting anger, I write in protest.

It's not too late. Even one theater would be enough. Even one independent showing would be enough. Give it the opportunity to be shown! Lend it out!

I also direct my protest to one segment of art journalists.

You didn't seek the true meaning of the facts. You didn't use your pens to explore the question of political oppression.

You took Shochiku's announcement at face value, making an issue of the low box-office figures and a fuss about the collapse of the "New Wave." What do you mean, "New Wave"?[4] Have you ever used the term "New Wave" as anything other than a synonym for sex and violence? Where is the sex and violence in *Night and Fog in Japan*? What relationship does that film have to your so-called New Wave? By taking a concept that has already been smeared with your dirty hands and forcing it on *Night and Fog in Japan,* by sweeping the revolutionary aspects of that work into the realm of public morals, you are giving support to the political and artistic reactionaries.

With unrelenting anger, I protest.

3.   This film, a program picture, replaced Oshima's *Night and Fog in Japan,* which was withdrawn from circulation on its fourth day of public distribution. Oshima's fury at this treatment of his work by the Shochiku management is evident.

4.   The name, "Shochiku New Wave," modeled on the "French New Wave," was proposed by an editor of the *Weekly Yomiuri,* which published feature articles on *Cruel Story of Youth* (1960). In an effort to counter a series of box-office failures, Kido Shiro, director of Shochiku's production department, promoted some young assistant directors and enabled them to make their first films from their own original scripts. They are *Town of Love and Hope* (*Ai to Kibo no Machi,* dir. Oshima, 1959), *Only She Knows* (*Kanojo dakega Shitteiru,* dir. Takahashi Osamu, 1960), *Cruel Story of Youth* (dir. Oshima, 1960), *One-Way Ticket of Love* (*Koi no Katamichi Kippu,* dir. Shinoda Masahiro, 1960), *Tomb of the Sun* (*Taiyo no Hakaba,* dir. Oshima, 1960), *Volunteering for the Villain* (*Akunin Shigan,* dir. Tamura Takeshi, 1960), *A Good-for-nothing* (*Rokudenashi,* dir. Yoshida Yoshishige, 1960), *Night and Fog in Japan* (dir. Oshima, 1960), and *The Blood is Dry* (*Chi wa Kawaite Iru,* dir. Yoshida Yoshishige, 1960). This policy lasted only one year. The majority of these filmmakers were more radical politically than their French counterparts.

Stop using the term "New Wave" once and for all! Evaluate each film on its own merits!

And put your energy into getting *Night and Fog in Japan* shown again! That is journalistic work in its true sense.

I really think that what killed *Night and Fog in Japan* is the same thing that killed Kamba Michiko[5] and Asanuma Inejiro,[6] and I protest with unrelenting anger.

What is it? It is everyone and everything that is displeased when the people try to effect reform from their side, to carve out new conditions for themselves. The enormous strength shown by the people in the fight against the security treaties terrifies and intimidates them, ultimately sending them into a frenzy.

I swear before the three skeletons of those who were massacred by the power of that frenzy that my film is the weapon of the people's struggle.[7]

I don't have high hopes for that struggle.

I know that in any case *Night and Fog in Japan* was unable to mobilize the majority of its audience and cannot gain the acceptance of the audience that enjoys *The Manager and the Apprentice.*

But I am not giving up.

I believe in the potential of the audience—that is to say, of the people. I believe they can change.

The audience has been given too many foolish films for too long. *Night and Fog in Japan* is the first memorable Japanese film to reach those in the audience who take life seriously. And as *Cinema Report*'s Minami Hiroshi and *Weekly Opinion*'s Mr. T. have noted, the future of the Japanese film depends on whether works like this continue to be made.

I will continue to make work like this.

Voices protesting the massacre of *Night and Fog in Japan* will continue to spread quietly.

5.   A student in Chinese history at Tokyo University who was killed in a clash between student demonstrators and the police in front of the parliament building. Her death produced an emotional ripple among the participants that developed, on the following morning, into uproar among the wider public.

6.   Asanuma Inejiro, the chairman of the Japan Socialist Party, was assassinated by youth of the extreme right when about to deliver a speech at the party congress.

7.   There were, in fact, four skeletons in 1960. One is that of Kamba Michiko; another is that of Asanuma. The third would be that of the wife of the president of the publishing house Chuo koron Sha. The fourth would be that of a coalminer murdered by a right-wing thug in a clash between strikers and nonstrikers, assisted by gangs of strikebreakers, which took place in front of the hopper of the Mitsui Miike coal mine. This site was to become a symbol of the defeat of the postwar labor movements in their struggle against a change of state energy policy that had been shifting from coal to petroleum.

Give the film another opportunity to be shown! Lend it out!

That is the voice of the people demanding that the future of the Japanese film be directly tied to their own future.

Along with my colleagues in production and criticism, I will continue to respond to these voices. The future of the Japanese film depends on us.

(*Film Criticism,* December 1960)

First Interlude: In Korea and Vietnam (1963–1965)

I returned from my two-month stay in Korea a little thinner and with a stronger sense of personal resolve. The Koreans are fighting a tough battle, trying to weather a difficult situation and triumph over it. I spent each day there feeling as though my eyes and my heart were being purified.

As I traveled along a road lined with blooming cosmos on my way into Seoul from Kimpo Airport, my first impression was, "Ah, this is just a big Kamagasaki."[1] The confused structure of the town, the squalid scenery, the large number of people camped along the roadside, and, especially, the dirty children—the people's energy that flowed from the midst of all of this had a violent effect upon me. Just as in the past I had fallen in love with the Kamagasaki district of Osaka and made *The Tomb of the Sun* there, I now fell in love with this city at first sight.

In Japan twenty years already passed since the end of the last war, but in Korea it has only been ten years. Korea, moreover, is in the same state of military preparedness and is as politically oppressed as it would be if a war were actually in progress. It is understandable that the reconstruction of Korean cities is progressing slowly, if at all. They are in the same state that Japan's cities were in three or four years after World War II.

It pains me to think that my saying these things will displease my Korean friends. In that respect, the Korean national consciousness is tremendous. When I told the Korean people with whom I became acquainted that I was there to gather material for television, most of them—from government officials to filmmakers, from journalists to bar hostesses—asked me not to photograph or mention poor or dirty areas. Only a handful of filmmakers and journalists asked me to show things as

1.   Former name of the very poor part of the city of Osaka that is now referred to as the Airin district.

they were. The reason for this was, of course, that most Koreans didn't want their national embarrassments exposed to a foreign country. I was impressed, first and foremost, by the ferocity of that national consciousness.

However, if mankind is ever to achieve peace, it will be necessary to dismantle the framework of that national consciousness. To this end, people in my line of work must always seek the truth and communicate it. Even though I sensed the ache behind the words spoken by my new friends, I still felt that I could not report about Korea without mentioning the poverty.

Considered in the context of their national consciousness, I can see that it is only natural for Koreans to have extremely strong feelings about Japan. My stay in Korea coincided with the nation's excitement about the Tokyo Olympics, and there was controversy about Son Kichong, the marathon winner at the 1936 Berlin Games, which were held during Japan's occupation of Korea. Son's comment during an interview in Japan that he hoped the Japanese would win the marathon in Tokyo had angered Koreans and was being hotly debated in the Korean press. It was said that Son was losing his sense of national pride.

At first I thought this was a clear case of narrow-mindedness. Son probably had some nostalgia for Japan, and his remark was obviously meant to be diplomatic. But to the Koreans it went far beyond that. In 1936, when Son won as a representative of Japan, a major Korean newspaper, the *Dong-A Ilbo,* ran a front-page photograph of him with the rising sun on his shirt inked out. This was because he was Korean, not Japanese, they said. When news of the picture spread, publication of the newspaper was suspended and its editors imprisoned [by the Japanese occupation authorities]. This incident illustrates the tragic history of the Korean people's racial and national consciousness. To injure their national pride, no matter how minimally, is unforgivable.

This is not to say, however, that the Koreans have only negative feelings toward the Japanese. There are many young Koreans now studying Japanese. Seoul's Japanese bookstores even carry copies of a collection of my essays (of which only two thousand copies were printed). Furthermore, many people I met expressed a sincere desire for their nation to develop a harmonious relationship with Japan. They emphasized, however, that the relationship must always be that of two equals. They said that when they considered the disparity in the economic strength of the two nations, they felt oppressed by Japan's economic power. When I traveled through a small fishing village in South Korea, I met a man who wept when he saw me, saying that I was the first Japanese he had seen in twenty years. When I asked him if he didn't feel hatred for the Japanese, he responded that he did feel hatred and bitterness, but also nostalgia. Hatred and bitterness alone are not enough to close the door on a future relationship.

I am not worried about people like him, but how will it be for the children? I was thinking about this on the train from Masan to Pusan. I was looking at the youth sitting next to me, who had fallen asleep leaning against me, breathing softly and peacefully. He had no way of knowing I was Japanese. Feeling his warm breath, I thought: When will the day come that two peoples as close as this can develop a truly friendly relationship? When this boy and my son grow up, will they help each other rather than try to kill each other? We all must work to make that day possible.

(Asahi News, 1964)

It is with a heavy heart that I speak of Korea.

I knew this would be true before I went to Korea. The belief was confirmed during my two-month stay there and has been like a thorn in my side since I returned to Japan. Perhaps one of the reasons that speaking about Korea is painful for me is that while I was there I observed Japanese journalists at work in Seoul. It may also be because I am a provincial person whose trip to Korea was his first to a foreign country (in some ways I am rather proud of this fact). It left me feeling that I could swear that, among all of the Japanese journalists stationed around the world, the ones in Korea were pursuing their calling with the most passion and dedication.

These Japanese journalists are trying desperately to communicate the actual conditions in Korea to the Japanese people, because they believe that telling the truth is absolutely essential to any future relationship between the two countries. Of course, it is probably just as difficult to communicate to the outside the truth about any particular place in Japan. However, these journalists must also fight not only the kind of barriers to journalistic truth that are present in Japan but also those in Korea and those inherent in the Japan-Korea relationship.

One small example of these difficulties occurred last June around the time martial law was declared. A violent censorship campaign was mounted in Korea against a Japanese newspaper that had reported that the poverty of rural areas was one reason for the student demonstrations. The reporter in question is, in my opinion, one of the most heroic of the extraordinary Japanese correspondents in Korea. Compared to the standard of living of most Koreans, a foreign correspondent's salary is enough to place him in the aristocracy, but this correspondent dresses as shabbily as the average Korean and eats in Korean restaurants where other grains are mixed in with the rice. He pays no attention to the Korean geisha houses frequented by Japanese traders and high Korean government officials; he goes to open-air stands where he drinks a raw Korean liquor called *makkoli*. Whenever the battle over freedom of speech breaks out between the Korean newspaper companies and the government, he visits the camp of each newspaper company, bringing moral support in the form of bottles of the imported whiskey that is sold only to foreigners. How could a journalist like this bear ill will toward Korea? How could he write an article with malicious intent? He is not the only one of this type. Most Japanese correspondents there live this kind of life and have this type of attitude toward Korea.

Nevertheless, the articles that reported on Korea's poverty had to be subjected to censorship. These are the conditions under which the Japanese correspondents in Korea struggle to write their articles and send them to Japan. Just read carefully the articles in any Japanese newspaper that are signed "XX, Seoul correspondent." If you continue reading them, a sense of the real Korea will inevitably emerge. Even though my two months is a longer stay than the average traveler, I still did not become a resident, so there is no way that I can give as good a report as these correspondents can. If they have a hundred things they would like to say and are allowed to say only twenty, would it really be better for me, in a freer position, to say thirty?

If a Japanese feels heavy-hearted in speaking of Korea, if he feels constraint, a Korean feels all the sadder, all the more constrained.

I had met a university professor who had shown deep confidence in students and a broad, sustained understanding of them. Everyone thought it would be good to meet him and have him talk on Japanese television, to express his ideas on Japan. He was far more circumspect than we had anticipated. We were disappointed, but what he did say during a conversation that followed pierced me to the heart: "Aside from politicians and businessmen, there is not a single Korean who has ever, at any time in his life, said what he really thinks of Japan."

In this country where, for everyone, to speak of a neighboring country represents a painful task hedged around by constraint, I was above all aware of practicing a profession whose object is the most complex and impenetrable one possible: the human heart. The weight that I felt derived, no doubt, from the fact that despite the distance and alienation between men, their emotions are always and everywhere the same.

I then had an idea. The Koreans I saw in Japan were either rich and disagreeable or poor but potentially friends. In Korea I had seen that between these two extremes there existed countless ordinary people. They are the ones who wear white shirts and ties, punch time clocks, return home early or, sometimes, when they have a bit of cash on hand, go drinking, speak ill of their superiors and, on arriving home drunk, receive the jeers of their wives. Among these ordinary folk you also find fans of Japanese professional baseball, and those who express themselves more enthusiastically than we do on the Sino-Russian dispute. In these respects, Koreans are no different from us Japanese.

Once I had met these people, the existence of Koreans I saw in Japan seemed strange. Similarly, isn't the life of Japanese as seen in Korea odd in relation to that of other Japanese? Unless you see people living in their own country, their true identity escapes you. The tragedy thus grows clear; the Japanese and Koreans have superficial and uncertain views of each other, and cannot see things in their true light.

This surely explains why Koreans are extremely sensitive to criticism of their country's poverty. For thirty-six years Korea lived in subjugation to Japan, reduced to a colony and maintained in poverty. Those Koreans who crossed the sea into Japan were treated in the same way. For the Japanese, Korea became synonymous with poverty. That idea is almost inextinguishable in our country; to the Koreans that idea is intolerable. We Japanese ought to ponder this question.

If poverty is incontestably real in Korea, the signs of poverty are not universal. The splendor of their schools, for example, and of the universities is an eye-opener. Since I, as a student, often made my way through poor and dirty school buildings as a participant in student demonstrations, I had imagined school buildings in Korea, where events of this sort are very frequent, to be dirty. But this was not at all the case. The several universities that I visited were dazzling. The campuses were vast, planted with sage; students sat on benches, quietly reading. There was not the slightest trace of those sudden eruptions of student demonstrations. On the contrary, one saw concrete proof of the Korean's love of knowledge and desire for self-improvement. Nevertheless, I see in that splendor an element of Korea's reality: the enormous gap existing between the ideals of its people and the reality of their lives. Koreans are not lazy. They are studious and show a will to learn, an intensely questing nature. However, given the heavy consequences of a foreign policy for which they are not responsible, the distance between their ideals and the reality of their lives is far too great. The poverty of certain countries may derive from apathy. Such is not the case for Korea. And saddened, depressed by the perceived gap between desire and existence, they ask "Why are we so unlucky, so unhappy?"

One answer lies, of course, in the splitting of the country. And at the same time, Koreans cannot feel other than ambivalently toward Japan, the neighbor who, after thirty-six years of domination, is now rich.

This is confirmed in their attitude toward the problem of the maritime line established by Syngman Rhee. I traveled in the villages of the fishing region. Almost all those who live by fishing feel that from the point of view of international law there is a problem; they add, however, that for Korean maritime fishing, this line is a vital necessity. If the Japanese fishing boats cross that line, it will destroy Korean fishing which, in equipment and technique, is far inferior to Japanese fishing. Impelled by deeply rooted national feeling, the students of Rika Women's College—the most eminent of its kind in Korea—organized a fund-raising campaign for the construction of coastal barriers. This is merely one small example of the strength of national feeling.

The Rhee line is, from the viewpoint of international law, illegal. But it is my own view that the rich should tolerate the support of illegalities committed by the poor. Otherwise, relations of true friendship between Koreans and ourselves will never be established. One might assume that Koreans as a whole commit illegal acts, but such is not at all the case. The individual Korean possesses that energy which enables him to tolerate the personal difficulties, to transcend them and to carve out a path for himself. If the Japanese do not show a similar energy, Korea and Japan will never maintain relations of equalilty and reciprocity. For the Japanese, nobility would consist in being prepared to shed one's blood for maintaining and developing those relations of equality and reciprocity. Tolerance of illegalities committed by the poor forms part of the resolution. With our own blood, we as Japanese hope to restore the blood shed by our ancestors.

The hard struggle of the special correspondents for Japanese newspapers forms part of that compensation. It is their example that has led me, with heavy heart, to write this text.

(*Japan Reader's News*, 1964)

Are the Stars and Stripes a Guardian Deity?

Many of Korea's young people go to study in the United States. You see them practically every day receiving a splendid send-off at the entrance to the Bando Hotel, Seoul's version of our Imperial Hotel. One of the returning students told me that the most most painful experience he had had in the United States was when he spoke with American mothers who had lost their sons in the Korean War.

Almost 100,000 American sons shed blood in the Korean War. And what did the United States gain from this? The American Embassy faces the entrance to the Bando Hotel. The American flag blows in the breeze out front as though it were this country's guardian deity of freedom. And yet, the building used to belong to Japan's Mitsui Trading Company. What a way to do things! Are they incapable of comprehending the depth of the wounds left here by Japan's thirty-six-year occupation of Korea? Don't they know that they should avoid any overlapping of their image with that of Japan, a past ruler? This kind of insensitivity is bound to damage the friendly relations of the United States and Korea. In spite of the fact that the United States is still expending blood and wealth on behalf of Korea, is it impossible for Americans to understand the feelings of the people of this country? It must be made possible—so that soldiers spending their youth in a foreign land eating unappetizing steaks in the Walker Building don't have to die. So that the mixed-blood orphans you see on the streets will have a chance at future happiness.

The World's Fourth Leading Army

On Sundays, the streets of Korea's capital turn yellow. No, not yellow, for that is the color that signified the old imperial Japanese army. This is actually green. It is that same dark green worn by the American army and then by the occupation forces that we Japanese became accustomed to seeing. Off-duty soldiers fill the streets.

Every face is young and tanned. Some are with friends and some are with lovers. A few slightly older ones go shopping or picnicking, babies in tow.

The Korean armed forces number 630,000, with the 570,000-member Korean army ranking fourth in the world in size. Some stupid Japanese wanted to attack Korea over the problem of the Rhee line, but if there were a war today, Japan might end up the loser.[1]

No matter how you look at it, however, 630,000 soldiers for an entire population of 26 million is too many. The Korean defense budget is over 30 percent of the nation's gross national product.

This is too heavy and too tragic a burden for one country to have to bear. Can it be that the United States and the Soviet Union feel no responsibility to share this heavy burden? And what about Korea's neighbors, Japan and China?

Now, however, there is no one sharing it, and Korea bears the burden alone. There are those who try to rid themselves of this excessive weight—in other words, the draft evaders. Recently, though, government enforcement of the draft law has become stricter, and evaders are prosecuted and drafted into the Land Development Army in lieu of regular military service. In this respect, the national army is the mainstay of the lives of the Korean people.

At the time of the May 16 military revolution in 1961, one of the military leaders behind the revolution said, "The only organization in the country that is trusted by the Korean people right now is the army." There is some truth to this. But what a sad truth—just like Japan before World War II.

The People on Street Corners

The most beautiful buildings in Korean cities and towns are Christian churches. There are a great many of them. This is partly because the country was under the influence of the United States for twenty years after the Japanese occupation, and partly because many patriots of independent activity, beginning with Syngman Rhee, were Christians. But the strong beliefs of the Korean heart are also partly responsible. Koreans are very strong believers and have a profound respect for their ancestors. During their Festival of the Dead, all Koreans leave their houses to go to the ancestral graves located on the outskirts of the towns. They offer flowers and wine and spend an entire day there. They wail as loudly as they can to mourn

1.   Artificial line established in international waters by Korean president Syngman Rhee in 1952 to ensure major fishing rights for the Koreans. The Japanese protested, and the disagreement was not settled until 1965.

the dead. The Korean moaning sound, *Aigo,* fills the mountains, sounding like a lament for the destiny of the land of their ancestors—a destiny of occupation and division. One large communal graveyard in the suburbs of Seoul has been exquisitely named the "Land of Forgotten Sadness." Graveyards, made to comfort the dead, also give solace to the living. It is only in the presence of the dead that the people can forget about the logic of this world. The logic of this world is the logic of "selling things." In the cities of Korea, an infinite number of little stands offer things for sale. In the huge markets of the Namdaemun and Tongdaemun districts of Seoul there is probably no commodity that can't be bought, but even there, on both sides of the street outside the regular stores, stands are set up to sell things. These lines of stands extend as far as the eye can see. The merchandise for sale may be a basket of persimmons or dried fish. What I call baskets range from small bamboo containers that fit in the palm of the hand to metal basins. Most of the sellers are women, over half of whom are accompanied by children. The children sell too, of course.

The children walk around selling newspapers, plastic umbrellas for 30 won (one won is about 1.40 yen),[2] and handfuls of chewing gum. The children who shine shoes contract with an office to shine the shoes of twenty of its employees every day for a month and earn about 500 won. Koreans' shoes are very shiny. It is a sad sight, just as the sight of things being sold is truly sad.

(*Sun,* 1964)

2.   In 1964, the U.S. dollar was worth 360 yen.

The People of "The Forgotten Imperial Army"

"The Forgotten Imperial Army," the documentary I wrote and produced for Nihon Television[1] (August 16, 1963), has turned out to be the most meaningful project I have done this year. In search of material for "Nonfiction Playhouse," Noguchi Hideo and I were looking for Koreans currently in Japan who had fought as part of the Japanese army during the Pacific War and as part of the Korean army during the Korean War. It is difficult to describe in words our shock when we discovered that all of the white-robed disabled veterans begging in the streets of Japan are Korean. We decided to produce "The Forgotten Imperial Army" immediately.

There are now only seventeen living members of the "forgotten imperial army," formally called "The Organization of Disabled Korean Veterans Living in Japan Who Had Been in the Japanese Army." All of them were wounded as Japanese citizens serving in the Japanese army or in the civilian component during the war. Because their Korean citizenship was restored after the war, they were not able to gain complete acceptance into the Japanese social security system, and they were excluded from the army pension program.

These people, who met in army hospitals and naturally formed a group, have petitioned the Japanese government many times for reparations. As recently as last June they sent a letter to the entire cabinet and received not one reply. On May 31 of this year they also submitted a formal petition to the prime minister through Dietman Ando Kaku (about half of these people live in Kanagawa Prefecture, which is Ando's district), but that also had no effect. I quote the main points of their petition:

> Because it exists in perpetuity, a polity can build relationships with no temporal restrictions, but a human life is short. We who have already

1. One of the major privately owned, mass-media corporations that operates national networks of radio and TV broadcasting.

lived over two-thirds of our lives idly in pain cannot suppress our impatience. . . . For us, reparations, because they would represent one of the body parts we have lost, taking its place and enabling us to find suitable jobs, are something we cannot live without. We earnestly hope that you will implement reparations as soon as possible and stop forcing weak individuals to make this unjust sacrifice in the interests and convenience of the polity. . . . In Korean there is a saying, "If you abuse it too much, even the dullest cow will jump the fence." This saying applies to our situation as well. . . . If it seems that the reparations issue will stretch out for another year or two, although it is unprecedented we believe that we will have no choice but to make a direct appeal to His Majesty the Emperor and rely on his benevolence. We urge you to introduce new legislation during the next special session of the Diet at the latest and apply the pension law and the relief law to us within the year. At the same time, we ask the government for a clear answer to the question of when and how it intends to implement reparations.

The response of the Japanese Foreign Ministry and others was that if the Korea-Japan talks were resolved, Japan would make a lump-sum reparations payment to Korea, so the veterans should petition their own government.

The Korean mission said that these people's wounds were received on behalf of Japan, so the Korean government had no responsibility for them; the people should make their demands to the Japanese government.

Consequently, these people have no place to go. They have no desire to go home to Korea; they know that if they returned, veterans wounded in the Korean War would not give them a warm reception because they had fought on behalf of Japan. As an illustration of these people's tendency to grasp at straws, it is worth noting that two people in this group were born in North Korea and were of that nationality, but changed to South Korean nationality amid the compromising mood of the Korea-Japan talks because it seemed that doing so would make it easier for them to receive reparations.

In reality, though, not even a straw for them to grasp has surfaced as yet, and with two or three exceptions all of them are eking out a living doing piecework or begging in the streets, as they are likely to continue to do.

It is clear from the words of their petition that there is something a little perverse about the appeal of these people and their way of going about it. Ushiyama, the producer, and I had been against the idea of an army pension. But if there is something perverse about their assertions and their method, that in itself becomes part of their appeal because it is evidence of their condition. We made "The Forgotten Imperial Army" because, above all, we wanted the Japanese people to experience the condition of these people as their own personal wound.

I put this on film because I wanted all Japanese to see these people's cruel wounds and pitiful lives. But even more than that, I wanted to capture on film and engrave on the heart of every Japanese something more cruel and pitiful than their physical wounds and their lives—their psychological wounds. I think that those who saw the show on television understood that I was expressing this by depicting the family quarrels at the banquet after the demonstration parade and the bitter tears that flowed on that occasion. However, there was something even darker in what I saw and heard during the shooting. I can't say what it was here. But I did frequently hear these words from the lips of those people: "If I get reparations, do you think I'd ever hang around with these people again?" Ah! Forgive me for repeating the last words of the televised narration. I ask the Japanese people: Is this acceptable?

(Japan Readers' Newspaper, 1963)

Vietnam: Land of the Interminable Decisive Battle

"It would have been better if there had been a decisive battle on Japan's mainland, too, after all." I began to have curious feelings like that as I rode along in a shaky bus going full speed down National Highway 19, which runs from the town of Plei Ku, a base on a plateau in the middle of South Vietnam's front line, to the seaside city of Qui Nhom. "A decisive battle on one's own territory" is a phrase from the Japan of twenty years ago. Hemmed in by the U.S. army from Saipan to Okinawa, the people started having drills in preparation for fighting the enemy with bamboo spears. However, when the announcement of the end of the war suddenly came dancing down on that hot summer day, the Japanese people had managed not to have to fight a "decisive battle on their own territory."

Twenty years after the war, is it really better that it ended without such a battle?

If Japan Had Become a Battlefield

What would have happened if there had been a "decisive battle" on the Japanese mainland? The conditions along the road traveled by the bus offer an answer. Every two or three hundred meters, the beautiful paved road laid down by the Americans has been dug up and destroyed, exposing red clay. The concrete bridges, having been blown up, are falling down, and iron bridges take their place as a stopgap measure.

Large and small earthworks have been constructed at the foot of each of the endless number of bridges; some are guarded by the regular army or the militia.

Here and there along the roadside lie charred jeeps and trucks and, occasionally, the carcass of a bus. Armored government cars always stand ready in the shade of the small trees dotting the fields that extend from either side of the road. In the woods a vertical column of patroling soldiers extends endlessly, like ants. There is a pregnant woman on the bus, and an old man who isn't feeling well. That is the everyday world. These people get up early every morning and go to the bus depot in the center of town, where they board their buses, hurried along by the drivers, who shout, "Ride my bus!" Meanwhile, the bus doesn't leave until it is completely full.

Finally the bus sets off along a road that has just been reopened after having been blockaded by the Viet Cong for a time this February; it can't be characterized as completely safe. In each of the villages in which it stops along the way, the bus is surrounded by large crowds of people selling things. Sugar cane, coconut, bread—the people on the bus purchase their wares and, delighting in them, give themselves up to the vibrations of the bus. They don't seem to notice the scenes outside the window, each of which strikes me, as a foreigner, so forcefully.

Having "a decisive battle on one's own territory" means living in a world like this, in which the everyday and the extraordinary mingle strangely. This would probably have been true in Japan as well had such a battle taken place there. In some towns, for some people, it might have been as if everyday life were going on as usual. But that everydayness would have been tenuous, because at any moment it could have become embroiled in extraordinariness.

If the enemy army had come ashore, Japan definitely would have been split into a pacifist faction and a faction wanting to wage all-out war. The two factions would have coexisted and intermingled. A guerrilla war would have been fought, and Japanese blood would have been shed at the hands of other Japanese. In spite of that, do I still say that it would have been better if Japan had had a mainland war? Why?

"The Dogs of a House in Mourning" and the Naked Girl

One village, along National Highway 1, was completely burned out. The highway, which once ran along the coast from Saigon to Hanoi, has been destroyed in various places by the Viet Cong and, under their sway, it doesn't go very far beyond the larger villages. I rented a small three-wheeler called a Lambretta to go from Qui Nhom north to the front line just this side of Bonson.

April is the hottest month in Vietnam. It is the kind of heat that is scorching in the middle of the day. In Saigon, it is the time when people take a siesta. The village was situated along both sides of a red clay road that had dried to white. It was dead.

It looked as though everything that would burn had been burned and then had been washed by a violent squall. Only the crumbling whitish walls remained, lined up like a large grave. A strong fragrance emanated from the green grass coiled around the wire fence. I entered the village through a hole in the wire fence and held my camera at the ready. Suddenly, a dog jumped out of a dead house and started barking. There were two, a gray one and another spotted like a tiger. They were small and emaciated. Their barks were sharp; their teeth were like fangs.

I suddenly thought of the expression "skinny as a dog in a house of mourning." But these dogs already had the look of wolves. Images of a yellow dog and a green dog ran through my head—a nightmare I always had when I was running a high fever. At that moment, beyond the barking dogs, I saw the shadow of something that was not a dog. It was a person, a girl about five years old. Behind her came a slightly older girl. And then a smaller boy. The children had hardly any clothes on. I took a step toward them. When my eyes followed a girl trying to hide in the house, I saw another, larger silhouette in the gloomy darkness.

It was two people, apparently female. The girls, an older one and a younger one, were squirming faintly. With my eyes unaccustomed to the darkness, I couldn't make out their poses or their expressions with certainty.

I pressed the shutter continuously to see if my camera, being a passionless machine, would be able to make them out for me. The barking dogs had disappeared and, with the exception of the sound of the mine- throwers reverberating like distant thunder, only the sound of the shutter could be heard echoing over the burned earth.

I didn't have the courage to move closer. I returned to the road and grabbed the nearest passerby, asking why the village had been burned and by which side. The first people who passed, militiamen, carelessly answered that the Viet Cong had done it. When I asked them why, I didn't receive an answer. Next I stopped a small bus that came barreling along and asked the driver. He acted annoyed but replied that it was destroyed in a bombardment by the government army. He didn't offer a reason. I wasn't satisfied.

However, no cars or people came by. The sun was gradually beginning to set. The night belongs to the Viet Cong. Our safety wasn't necessarily guaranteed. I thought about going back. My brain was clouded by nonsensical thoughts like, "A village has been destroyed; nobody knows by which side. That's all right too, isn't it?" Just then, two dark shadows appeared beyond the road. It was a farming couple wearing black clothes and trailing long shadows. Incredibly, they lived in this completely dead village. The old woman answered my question.

The village was created by the government army for the farmers who had fled territories occupied by the Viet Cong. It had been burned by the Viet Cong. Before burning it, the Viet Cong apparently issued warning after warning, saying, "Abandon this place and go back to your own villages."

The people who evacuate territories occupied by the Viet Cong are of two types: the first are those who fear the wrongdoings they had accumulated by being the former rulers of the villages, and the second are those who fear being shot and bombed by the government because they are in Viet-Cong-occupied territories.

Naturally, the majority belong to the latter group. The people in this village had fled for that reason as well; however, they seemed to be at a loss in the face of this advice from the Viet Cong. In the end, though, they didn't follow it. The Viet Cong are said to have replied, "We are going to burn down this village two hours from now, so carry out your valuables and your furniture." I imagine the moving of valuables and furniture that probably took place during the night, soundlessly, and the lighting of the flames that burned down the village, also soundlessly. What sort of facial expressions did the people have as they watched their homes burning? And what kind of flame was burning in the hearts of the Viet Cong soldiers?

A Vietnamese Marine Dangling a Head

I recall another burned-out village. The fires were seen by a cameraman for Nihon Television's "Nonfiction Playhouse." He followed the Eagle Flight of the marines, who prided themselves on being the strongest branch of Vietnam's government army. The operation was successful, and the marines chased the Viet Cong out of that village. When they entered the village, however, there wasn't a single farmer left. That's when they burned the village.

In the midst of that action, a man was discovered hiding in a house. The marines, angered that their triumph had been so insubstantial, panicked. They took their explosive feelings out on the prisoner. They walked along, dangling the man's head from a sword, ultimately casting it aside. I understand that the cameraman captured it all. But inside that severed head, what did the prisoner make of the burning of his village—seen with his dead eyes, which must have been shining brilliantly?

The government army and the U.S. army are winning the large battles fought by battalions. The more they win, though, the more alienated the farmers become. Even farmers who fled the Viet Cong territories to go into houses built by the government do not communicate to the government the Viet Cong's warning that if they don't evacuate, their villages will be burned.

Furthermore, even in villages from which the Viet Cong and the farmers have been driven by the Eagle Flight, the evacuees will always return when the marines move to another theater of war. Even if the government army and the U.S. army are winning battles, they are losing the war.

There is no question that in terms of fighting spirit and fighting capability, the government army and the U.S. army—particularly the latter—are superior. The Viet Cong probably won't be able to drive them into the sea. But the government army and the U.S. army definitely won't be able to annihilate the Viet Cong completely, either. This war will go on for a long time.

In Korea I was mistaken for a Korean; in Hong Kong I was asked if I were from Shanghai. I was expecting to be mistaken for a Vietnamese in Vietnam. Instead I was, unbelievably, mistaken for an American.

It happened far to the southwest of Saigon in a village on the banks of a tributary of the Mekong River heading toward the Cambodian border from a village called Long Xuyen. I was taking pictures in a peaceful primitive village not 300 meters from the national highway. Yet it was not a village, but rather a small hamlet with a few houses scattered in a grove of palm trees. Before I knew it, I was surrounded by villagers.

Where did all these people come from? Moreover, those in the front were all sharp-eyed young people—whom you'd normally expect to have been taken by the draft. Now what? I felt a chill go down my spine. Furthermore, they are calling me an American. I have never regretted my potbelly more than I did then. "I am Japanese," I protested earnestly.

Once they seemed convinced of that, one of them cried out shrilly, "Aren't they saying that the Japanese are sending soldiers over to Vietnam to help the government?" I turned pale. I hadn't heard that until I arrived in Saigon, but it had been reported prominently in the Vietnamese newspapers. In actuality, this had been said by only one Japanese person, but much was being made of it, and one couldn't blame the Vietnamese for taking this to be the sentiment of all Japanese.

But any young people who were aware of this type of political issue in an area like this had to be Viet Cong. I protested more strongly. I even said that the Japanese were making every effort to ensure that peace would be restored in Vietnam as soon as possible. One reason for my earnest protests was that I wanted to avoid any physical danger; the other was that I was frightened when I realized the position in which Japan was being put in Vietnam.

Their expressions didn't change, and, though I was reluctant, evening was approaching and I had to leave. Finally, I asked one question. "How do you think this war will end?" One of the young men smiled for the first time. "Without a doubt, we will drive the U.S. army out of Vietnam."

I said earlier that that would not be an easy thing. However, if an ethnic pride was going to emerge among the Vietnamese, it would have to come from the Viet Cong, who fought the world's strongest army, that of the United States. That is to say, it would have to come from the struggle at the front lines to liberate the South Vietnamese people. This is why a "decisive battle on their own territory" is necessary for a people.

If the Japanese are to attempt to do anything regarding the Vietnamese, they must begin by correcting their posture as a polity. If not, no one will bother to listen to what any Japanese has to say.

Visions of a Hundred Years' War between the United States and China

"Ultimately, it's a war between the United States and China." I heard these shocking words without much surprise. "The Vietnam War is merely a prelude to a hundred years' war between the United States and China." These were the words of a Japanese newspaper correspondent at a Chinese restaurant in the middle of Cholon, a Chinatown that occupies a completely independent location in what should either be called the outskirts of Saigon or, perhaps, an independent town next door. It actually seemed that half of the newspaper correspondents in Saigon shared this view. Even among those who disagreed, it seemed that much of what they felt when watching the Vietnam War could be summed up by this kind of observation. However, those feelings did not necessarily show up in the articles they sent home.

It won't be easy to resolve the conflict between the army with absolute rights to the land and allied with the people of that land (but lacking airplanes) and the army that possessed airplanes and all manner of overwhelming material strength, but completely ignorant of the land and thus powerless over it. This is because neither can completely overpower the other. Under these conditions, it is entirely natural that the United States chose to bomb North Vietnam as a way to use its strength to gain the maximum advantage.

Rather than negotiating directly with the Viet Cong, they bring out the North Vietnamese as a negotiator. That is because doing so makes it a confrontation between North and South and legitimizes the present government in South Vietnam and U.S. support for it.

North Vietnam, however, would not accept this. It is obvious that the next goal of the United States is China. The United States would probably like to involve China as an even bigger negotiator. Not only that, it is easy to guess that the global strategy of the United States is probably to defeat China at this level and delay China's development, including its development of nuclear weapons, for five or ten years. If so, it would be strange to think that the current Vietnam War won't develop into a war between the United States and China. One can just say that it has been avoided so far merely by chance.

What is chance? Perhaps it can be said to be the rare endurance of the likes of Ho Chi Minh, president of North Vietnam, who didn't explicitly seek help from China even when bombings by the U.S. army had destroyed so much of the country he had labored to build up.

According to one theory, Vietnam's traditional wariness of China explains why it does not seek its neighbor's help. Except for the eighty years during which it was occupied by France, Vietnam has been occupied by China or been at war with China during almost all of its modern history.

That theorist said that were Ho Chi Minh completely destroyed by the bombings, he would again turn to guerrillas rather than seek aid from China.

If that is true, what superb politicians Ho Chi Minh and his party are! At any rate, it must at least be acknowledged that for whatever reason, the crisis of a war between the United States and China has been avoided because of the sacrifice of North Vietnam.

Even so, China's historical influence over Vietnam defies imagination. The clothes of Vietnamese women—even the *aodai* that people admire—are all ultimately merely imitations of Chinese clothing.

The top half of the garment is Chinese, with pants worn underneath only because of the split that goes from the waist down. There is no question that the cloth that reaches the feet of Vietnamese women is beautiful when it flutters in the wind, but it is not something originated by their people.

This case serves to symbolize all the rest. The so-called folk art, too—the ivoryware, for example—is all an imitation of the Chinese. The food, too. You might as well think of Vietnamese food as a bad-tasting, spicier version of Chinese food.

Possessing a cosmopolitan stomach, I have never found a food disagreeable, and, in the case of Vietnamese food, I enjoyed eating the hard-boiled eggs. (They are boiled just before they become chickens. Thus, the inside already has the shape of a chicken, and the beak and feathers are right there with the yolk.) I didn't get particularly attached to Vietnamese food, however.

Thus our newspaper correspondents fight off starvation in a Chinese restaurant in Cholon.

However, the reason that particular correspondent considers that restaurant to be particularly good is that his taste buds have become Vietnamese. In actuality, this restaurant does have a good reputation, and it seems that many American soldiers come here. Wire netting was even put out as protection against Viet Cong hand grenades. I felt, though, that the food served by this Chinese restaurant was just a shade better than Vietnamese food.

But whether or not it is becoming slightly Vietnamese, the sight of a whole city in the middle of Vietnam consisting of just such Chinese people's shops—flourishing as if it were a Hong Kong, in spite of the war—is indeed spectacular. Omitting the hundred years of modern history and taking this sight together with the historical strength of China as the perpetual occupier of Asia, you can't help sensing a war between the United States and China.

The New Master of Asia's Champs-Elysees

Would it be going too far to say that Cholon and Saigon aren't Vietnam? On the contrary, I'd even venture to say that none of the large and medium-sized cities above the splendidly paved national highway are Vietnam. If I say that, the implication would be that none of the places the government army and the U.S. army are securing are Vietnam, but I'd still venture to say that. The cities and the farm villages are entirely too different.

Saigon is dirty. That's not surprising. The twenty years of our postwar period have been twenty years of war for the people of this town. Thus, the large buildings all date back more than twenty years. They are fancy white or French-style buildings of egg-yolk yellow. They have balconies and venetian blinds; the restaurants have chairs lined up outside as well.

However, they are all old and dingy. In the past it was the French who gathered around this small Asian Paris and Champs-Elysees; nowadays it is the Americans. Serious, tense American soldiers. Among them a very few Vietnamese, dressed in suits, go in and out of those buildings. The rest are the masses of Saigon. Except for a few shirts of black and deep red, nearly all wear white shirts, and most of those are dingy. It is also rare to see women wearing colorful clothing: the finery of the women students consists of a white *aodai* with black pants underneath. And a hat resembling a farmer's straw hat. By wearing these farmer's hats, are the students trying to show that they, at least, are Vietnamese?

However, I wasn't able to feel the strength it would take to set in motion the Vietnam of tomorrow in the figures of the Saigon masses, including these women students.

They definitely aren't poor. No, they may be poor, but it is not the type of poverty that drives one into a corner. I ate my morning meal at the town cafeteria every day. Japanese-style noodles for the equivalent of 15 to 25 Japanese yen, or Chinese-style noodles. And a meat bun. Sometimes rice gruel. That may seem like a poor breakfast, but with the noodles there was always as much meat as is in the Japanese-style noodle dish containing roast pork fillet. It was never *raamen*. The number of calories appeared to be more than sufficient, perhaps because the amount required by the body is greater in this hot weather. I thought it was far superior to the food I saw the masses eating last year in Seoul.

But the people who ate these noodles with meat and the meat buns and on top of that the duck eggs can't get up out of their chairs very easily. They drink tea and sit and talk endlessly. Children who aren't even old enough to start elementary school hang around them, smoking cigarettes. I found this in all of the cities. Moreover, the bigger the city—Saigon or Hue, for example—the longer they stay at the cafeteria. I thought this was not a good thing.

Seoul also used to be a colonial capital, but it isn't any longer. The people may be poor, but their appetite for increased independence and their efforts and energy are tremendous. Compared to that, Saigon is still a colonial capital. Even people's spirits have been violated and ooze laziness. Can this be because it's so hot?

However, that customary afternoon nap, the siesta, bothers me. For all of the activities of the town to come to a stop between noon and about three is quite unbearable—no matter how hot it may be. This will delay progress. The concerned parties may be able to dismiss it by saying that it's hot, but does that mean that they'd have no will to win in a competition against a place with a cold climate?

If so, then hasn't the victor in the conflict with the North already been decided? In other words, is that how it will turn out?

Witnessing a Nun's Attempted Suicide by Fire

Perhaps I have bad-mouthed Saigon and other Vietnamese cities too much. However, my hypothesis is that the French occupation, and the administration by the Vietnamese government that followed it, extended only as far as the cities and the roads that connect them.

The brave, sincere missionaries may have been the only ones to pay a visit to the farm villages and mountain regions; the administration must not have spread that far. If that were not the case, there wouldn't be such a big difference between the cities and the farm villages.

So, the farm villages that are now said to have been taken by the Viet Cong were not really taken; they were not possessed to begin with. Coming into being in those regions where the administration left a vacuum, as it were, the Viet Cong penetrated and created a unified administration. It is natural that, like the old Eighth Army, it is a phantom army.

I should have looked in Saigon and the other cities for the strength to form a grassroots organization—something like the Viet Cong in the farm villages, or something to resist the Viet Cong. However, as a free traveler I opted to walk through many farm villages. That's because there were so many newspaper correspondents in Saigon. Nevertheless, on the day before I was to leave Vietnam, I came to Bien Hua Dai (Vietnam's national temple), the Buddhist regimentation area.

From the outside it looked like a quickly built circus tent. Worshippers came to a main hall that could easily be called a wooden fence, and they came continuously. More than half of them were old women. With the exception of their poor clothing, the people—with their dark skin, wrinkled faces, and piercing voices—looked like people at a Japanese temple on a holiday. Buddhism really is something, I thought. But if it is merely a matter of assembling people, plenty of that goes on in Japan, so I didn't think much about it and left. Then, I stopped in my tracks because I sensed that the people were suddenly standing still.

It occurred to me that the number of people had been steadily increasing over the last few minutes. To one side there was the structure that looked like a main hall, and to the other side—was it the place where the priests gather?—there was a long building like a cafeteria. The area in between was packed with people, about to overflow with them. This can't be normal. It occurred to me that the people's voices sounded out of the ordinary.

Finally I gleaned the reason. Two days earlier a sixteen-year-old priest had set himself on fire in the garden of this temple. I had been walking around the farm villages and hadn't heard about it.

When you are in Vietnam's remote areas, you don't hear anything about Saigon or the bombings in the North. You hear more when you're in Japan. The people who live in remote places know only about the struggles taking place where they are. To them, that is the war. Even in the middle of Saigon, there is no newspaper delivery. How did these people get wind of this and gather here? People had assembled because of the rumor that today would be his funeral. They were wearing small pieces of yellow cloth on their chests, a sign of mourning.

For whatever reason, however, there wasn't a funeral on this day. The highest-ranking priest didn't seem to be present. Even so, the people made no sign of leaving. They went to the outbuilding that held the casket containing the remains of the young priest and prayed. Then they went to see the place where the young priest had burned himself to death—pebbles had been placed in a line in the middle of the garden to mark the spot. Then they returned to the side of the main hall and continued their loud conversations. Suddenly sounds rang out from a microphone in the main hall. I thought it was saying, "Today there will be no funeral. Please disperse." I remembered the security treaties.

The sounds from the microphone stopped, and the people's voices were louder than ever. The sun was finally starting to set, but it was still burning hot. At that moment, I smelled the strong odor of gasoline. There was a commotion. Following the heads of the people, I peered in that direction. A priestlike form was being carried by the people. The match hadn't caught. An attempted suicide by burning! I stumbled to the front.

In an instant, however, the "thing" was being carried into the priests' quarters. It was a young girl.

"I'd really like to go to Vietnam."

"Indeed."

I had had that conversation with the producer of "Nonfiction Playhouse," Ushiyama,[1] the summer before last. Now I was seeing this. I trembled.

Is Suicide by Fire Part of the Strategy?

According to what I heard later, she was a twenty-two-year-old priestess. What was the purpose? I don't know. This priestess tried to take her decisive action in front of a large gathering of people, but the young priest had been alone when he poured the gasoline on himself in the sweltering heat of the garden during siesta time; not a soul was around.

---

1.   Television producer of the "Nonfiction Playhouse" program of NTV, Ushiyama Junichi later founded his own independent TV documentary production company. Most of Oshima's documentaries were produced by Ushiyama. He persistently opposed the "nonpartisan neutralism" and the alleged objectivism of TV documentaries perennially produced by the hegemonic NHK (Nihon Hoso Kyokai or Japan Broadcasting Society, a state-owned institution), insisting that documentaries articulate the documentarist's or director's point of view while at the same time offering a dramatic structure.

I understand that Buddhist leaders are excellent strategists, never revealing their true motives. It is also said that each suicide by burning is part of a grand strategy that, even if not ordered explicitly, is carried out as part of a silent understanding.

But I can't understand this. I'd even dare to say that it seemed to me to be one result of an awareness of powerlessness—the powerlessness of not being able to organize to stop the war. However, because they are aware of that powerlessness, the Buddhists can perhaps be called the faint hope of Vietnam.

We Japanese are powerless as well. However, not one of us has burned himself to death. Because we aren't aware of our powerlessness. Because we feel we have accomplished something merely by having displayed an inoffensive slogan like "Peace in Vietnam!" We will be sitting down as we watch the opening of the war between the United States and China and, as an American base, we will suffer China's atomic attacks.

Is that good enough? Are we truly powerless? As far as Vietnam is concerned, the time for reportage has passed. It is time for political action.

(*Heibon Punch,* 1966)

Defending the Cruelty Depicted in "War Chronicle of a Marine Troop in Vietnam"

It seems that there was a very strong reaction to "War Chronicle of a Marine Troop in Vietnam—Part I" broadcast by Nihon Television on its "Nonfiction Playhouse" on the evening of May 9 [1965].

Apparently people were violently shocked by scenes of actions they felt were overly cruel: a government army soldier taking a farmer prisoner, torturing him, and cutting off two of his fingers; a battalion chief, stripped to his shorts, seizing what appears to be a fourteen-year-old Viet Cong youth, bellowing at him and whipping him until he is covered with blood; and a youth being murdered and his head cut off and thrown along the roadside by a soldier.

I myself wasn't assigned to gather material for this specific episode. I had traveled to Vietnam as a member of the reporting team for "Nonfiction Playhouse" and had seen and heard of a great many such scenes. Seeing them on television, however, I felt a deep shock all over again. And so it is only natural that people seeing these things for the first time, with no background knowledge, would want to cover their eyes. As expected, a maelstrom of arguments for and against the piece has ensued.

Since the night of the broadcast, the staff of "Nonfiction Playhouse" has had to answer constant telephone calls, and the newspapers have published all kinds of opinions.

Here is one type of argument: "When I finished watching, I had a really terrible aftertaste. . . . I began to wonder if it is really necessary to expose the ugliness of war to this extent. These are facts, and it may be necessary to make people aware of them. But is it actually right to deliberately emphasize such hate-provoking cruelty? Of course, in the standards for television programming there must be some provision prohibiting this. Those responsible for the broadcast say that they did it in the name of disavowing war. But does the exposure of such inhumanity really accomplish the goal of disavowing war?" (Mr. Shirai, of *Japan Sports*).

"This is neither whitewashing nor light reportage. Its objective is to communicate the reality of war exactly as it is. . . . In another situation, one might feel reluctant from the point of view of the television code to show a freshly severed head. But when the cruel, inhumane, criminal reality of war is perversely covered up, the result is whitewashing, which gives rise to the danger of easy affirmation of war." This was the defending argument by the author of the *Yomiuri Newspaper*'s "Editor's Notebook."

In addition, the Tokyo Customs House protested that Nihon Television had violated the policy that "Things that are contrary to the public peace and laudable practices must be previewed by the customs house." That is because material filmed outside of Japan is considered imported. In a related development, it came to light that since last year the importation of a number of photographs taken by AP correspondents and Okamura Akihiko[1] have been prohibited. Nihon Television's films could perhaps have suffered the same fate.

After this much commotion, an even larger number of people were expected to watch the rebroadcast on the morning of May 13, but a different film was shown at that time. Furthermore, the broadcasts scheduled for the16th and the 23rd were canceled altogether. It is too bad.

Of course, Nihon Television must have made the cancellations of their own free will. However, you'd probably have to say that in doing so, they yielded to so-called good sense.

I feel great anger at that "good sense." It is definitely not good sense in the true sense of the word. "There is only one way to save those who suffer oppression and those who oppress others, not knowing what they do: by making it public."

These are truly words of good sense. Whose words? They are from a letter sent to the *Times* by Tolstoy on behalf of the Dukhobors, who were persecuted in Russia when they unconditionally renounced war beginning in the early nineteenth century (Kimura Takeshi, *The Story of the Dukhobors*).

Sharing Tolstoy's beliefs, as it were, the staff of "Nonfiction Playhouse" chronicled the Vietnam War and made it known to the public. Hey, you people of "good sense," do you have anything to say in response to these words?

There is something else I want to say to you people of "good sense." Have you ever put yourself in the place of the youth who was decapitated. The position of a youth whose life of ten-odd years was tragically cut short? In spite of that, will you

---

1. Still photographer known for his reportage of the Vietnam War, during which he demonstrated that the sturdy Nikon F camera was a real tool for war reportage.

still cover your eyes? What I am trying to say is that closing your eyes to cruelty is itself cruel.

There have been many films shot in Vietnam before this. But there had never been a film that depicted the battlefield so graphically.

Why is that? It is because the method of coverage was different. What method did "Nonfiction Playhouse" use?

Within the city of Saigon, there is no place where it is dangerous to brandish a camera. There is, rarely, a bombing of the American embassy or the fatal shooting of a youth, but to cover these occurrences you have to wait for them.

Of course, waiting is important. The work of journalists sent to Saigon consists almost entirely of waiting. Newspaper correspondents in other foreign countries usually set up a special agreement with the leading newspapers and wire services of the country to be contacted by them as soon as a major incident occurs. In Vietnam, however, there are neither newspapers nor wire services substantial enough to make agreements with, and no consistent statements are made by the police or the government agencies. The correspondents have no choice but to go to the USIS building every evening—apprehensively, because the building has been bombed repeatedly by the Viet Cong—and listen to the reports of the U.S. army, or to independently seek out their own questionable sources in an effort to obtain some accurate news.

In spite of this, Japanese newspaper correspondents were able to exchange news because nearly all of them were staying at the same hotel, the Majestic. Recently, however, seemingly reliable reports that the hotel might be bombed circulated (initially it had been thought that the Majestic would not be bombed because a large number of Japanese stayed there, but, possibly because of that, many members of the U.S. military had since moved in). And so, concerned about their safety, the Japanese correspondents moved to a number of different lodgings, and the exchange of news became more difficult.

Thus, whenever they heard a big bang, they ran off toward the sound, thinking that a story might be unfolding. Being out chasing possible stories sometimes even led to their missing events such as the bombing of the U.S. embassy. Among the Japanese in Vietnam, then, those most to be pitied are the newspaper correspondents on regular assignment who are envious of all the groups sent over temporarily. One of the regular correspondents compared his feelings upon seeing them to those of a Korean fisher whose game is taken away by speedy Japanese fishing boats.

The easygoing pleasures of the correspondents seem to consist of heaving a sigh of relief each day that the U.S. bombing of the North had continued but not reached Hanoi. They sometimes go to a middle-class nightclub, where they drink beer while worrying about the number of cocktails their female Vietnamese companions are putting away in rapid succession. Even so, they say that when they happen upon the occasional clever woman who speaks English fairly well, they have to worry that she may be a Viet Cong spy, so it is a comedy that you just can't laugh at.

In fact, that is why, when a certain American minister was attacked and killed in the suburbs of Saigon en route to the home of a woman—it isn't known whether the woman accidentally made it known that he was coming or whether she was actually a spy—the gentlemen correspondents straightened their collars and began to behave more prudently.

First of all, we should probably be sincerely grateful to the press in Vietnam for all of their waiting. The fact that the reporter in this case, Kaiko Takeshi, was able to encounter a youth being shot is precisely because his stay lasted for over one hundred days.

What happens to those in the press corps who can't stay that long? Generally they use U.S. military planes to fly from base to base. If they do that, they can get the news of the bases. And there is always a battle going on near a base. When they hear that there has been one, they rush over. Then they can get pictures of the scene after the battle. They can get pictures of dead bodies lying all around.

But that alone is boring. The producer of "Nonfiction Playhouse" thought, "I really want to shoot a battle in progress. How can I do that?"

Some of the crew of "Nonfiction Playhouse," including the cameramen, followed the ground troops. Rather than flying from base to base in military planes, they followed the army on foot from battle to battle.

They bought military clothes at Saigon's black market. They put rising sun emblems on the clothes. One reason given for this is that, once dirty, the outfits would definitely be mistaken for Korean uniforms. For whatever reason, in spite of their having gone to this trouble, the Viet Cong, shooting from a distance, didn't make that distinction. In life and in death, they were the same as the soldiers.

They followed the Vietnamese marines, who pride themselves on being the strongest of the Vietnamese military. Looking like leopards in their horizontally striped green and black clothes, they do appear strong. They walk between forty and fifty kilometers a day. They walk steadily. The cameramen carry heavy cameras, with a bag of film on their backs. They are among enemies. If they fall behind, death awaits.

Whenever they camp at night, there is an enemy attack. There are even eight-hour-long night raids that last from around ten o'clock until sunrise. The gunfire comes from straight ahead, so they are safe if they lie down. The trench mortars are scary, though. They come down in an arc. For eight hours, they can't lift up their heads for even an instant. Setting up their cameras is out of the question.

Gradually, the sky brightens. The chickens crow—the ones they are carrying around for food. They are completely disgusted with being fed those chickens every day, but they are as grateful to hear their voices as if they were the voice of God.

It's an operation. The marines get into one-hundred-odd helicopters and fly to the villages held by the Viet Cong. A few meters above the ground, following the soldiers, the cameramen jump out, carrying their loaded cameras. It is strange that they don't bend their knees. They plunge into the village. There is no one there. They search the houses. The youth is discovered. He is tortured severely.

The soldiers have come here after spending every day in terror along the way. Every day in the course of merely walking and camping at night, there are three to five deaths per troop. They think to themselves, "I have one chance in thirty or fifty of dying." And they don't encounter the enemy. Terror invites terror; cruelty inspires cruelty. If they take this youth back to the base he will still be tortured, although more mildly—rationally. But this is the scene. The battle scene. The soldiers are crazy. The youth's head is cut off.

It is truly a cruel scene. But it is war.

At that moment, the cameraman forgot his fears for his own life, lost his everyday sensibility, and just kept pushing the button. He was a person who had become film, and on the film was a human figure with the war printed on him.

"Nonfiction Playhouse" had a producer determined to risk acting like a member of a land army and cameramen willing to follow along.

Okamura Akihiko did that, and continues to do it. Mr. Kaiko[2] and the cameraman, Mr. Akimoto, did it also. Hey, you people with good sense! Are you going to say that what they did was bad?

Two of "Nonfiction Playhouse"'s three cameramen wanted to take pictures of the war badly enough to come to Vietnam at their own expense, and they were added to the crew at the scene. Happily for them, their passion for their work meshed well with their producer's Tolstoyan intentions. One of them was so young that it still seemed appropriate to call him a youth. He had left Japan four years earlier to live on his own in Southeast Asia. He had been Okamura's assistant at one time.

"Aren't you afraid?" I asked him.

---

2.   The writer Kaiko Takeshi, whose *The Radiant Darkness* (*Kagayakeru Yami*) was based on his stay in Vietnam during the war. His *Giants and Toys* was made into a film of the same title by Masumura Yasuzo in 1958.

"Yes, I'm afraid. But as a cameraman I am specializing in war; I'm a war specialist," he replied, with a sweet smile that showed his white teeth.

"Don't die," I said as I left Vietnam. He gave me his marine cap. I gave him a white baseball cap in return. Ah, where is he now, wearing that white cap? It is already the rainy season in Mekong. I don't want that youth to die.

(*Yomiuri Weekly, Heibon Punch,* 1965)

Strange things certainly do happen. An appeal directed at the makers of films about Vietnam is published by the Committee of Filmmakers for Peace in Vietnam. The names of about one hundred scriptwriters and directors are listed as the founders of the group, mine among them. The strange thing is, I have no memory of agreeing to be a founder of the group and no memory of having approved the use of my name in connection with it.

Of course, before this document was published I did receive a postcard asking me to be one of the founders of the Committee of Filmmakers for Peace in Vietnam. About fifteen people were listed as founders on the postcard, some of whom are trusted friends of mine. However, the words written on the postcard were so childish and crude that I felt like showing it to someone and ridiculing the fact that they were saying those things at that point in time. At the very least, the language was vastly inferior to that normally used by these friends of mine. Other than thinking it ridiculous, I wasn't moved by it at all. I didn't respond.

In spite of that, my name is linked with the Committee of Filmmakers for Peace in Vietnam. What is this? Should I call it laziness or nonsense? As a matter of fact, at an August 15 meeting the Committee of Filmmakers for Peace in Vietnam acted only as an adjunct of a number of other groups, and I have never heard of their carrying out further activities of any kind.

I've been to Vietnam. I have no intention of bragging about that. I went merely because I was one member of an outstanding team called "Nonfiction Playhouse." We were already talking about going to Vietnam as early as the summer of 1963, when the first Buddhist monk committed suicide by fire. Last year when I went to Korea, I resolved that I would go to Vietnam as well. This year, as team members flew to Saigon one after another, I belatedly followed them.

A Town of Love and Hope. 1960.

The Catch. 1961.

The "Nonfiction Playhouse" team intended to go to Vietnam three times this year. The plan was to make one big work that covered all aspects of the Vietnam War. If possible, the work was to be sent to the United States and all over the world to communicate the reality of the war. When I flew to Vietnam, I was supposed to formulate a plan to unify the entire project. "War Chronicle of a Marine Troop in Vietnam" was the prelude to that. It was, however, a prelude of foreboding, which wouldn't end with the prelude. The foreboding hit the mark and shocked people violently, but we lost our chance to continue a project that would communicate all aspects of the Vietnam War in detail.

Why would I have any reason not to desire peace in Vietnam? However, the call of the Committee of Filmmakers for Peace in Vietnam did not move me. Not only that—none of the calls regarding Vietnam moved me. Not those of the established political parties, not those of the small factions that call themselves revolutionary, not that of the Alliance for Urban Culture, and, finally, not that of the Volunteer Corps to Support the Viet Cong.

My personal feeling is that none of those groups had a specific slogan that called for action. I had been to Korea and seen the student demonstrations there. To them, the significance of whatever slogan they were displaying at the time was that they would die for it on the spot. Their slogans, the result of a careful consideration of the strengths of their allies and their enemies, were displayed right at the border separating them from their enemies as their most effective combat weapons. By displaying those slogans, they expanded the power of their allies to its maximum strength, and they exposed the weakest points of their enemies. They organized the ultimate battle based on those slogans. Conversely, they displayed slogans that consistently made the ultimate battle possible. Sometimes they were against the government, sometimes they were against Japan, sometimes they were against the United States, sometimes they were for unification; sometimes their slogans were a combination of all of these views. The troops at the front moved forward thinking that they could die for that slogan at any time, and, moved by this, the general public proceeded with the same feeling. Who among the Japanese, calling himself a leader or a member of a leading party, had ever reached that kind of conclusion based on the slogan "Peace in Vietnam"?

So saying, I probably cannot escape responsibility. If political leaders or leading parties can't come up with an effective plan, why don't I come up with one myself? But I can't come up with one right now. This self-condemnation, this pain, grips my heart. Thus, I am not effective and do not add my voice to that of the Committee of Filmmakers for Peace in Vietnam or to the calls of other groups. I think it is, to some extent, more appropriate for me to mull over the reasons that I am unable to do anything now.

The above is one thought, an extension of an idea I had previously heard somewhere. I have another thought—one that is relatively new to me.

I saw Vietnam. If you merely say you've been to Vietnam, that doesn't necessarily mean that you can say you've seen it. This is what all of the proponents of avantgarde art have been saying since *Hiroshima Mon Amour.* Can I definitely say that I've seen Vietnam? I think I definitely can. When I went to Vietnam, something was born inside of me. No, to be precise, I would have to say that something broke inside of me.

It occurred to me that to look at human beings and think that you ought to do something is always futile. An emaciated dog and some children living in an abandoned house in a burned-out village. Women who come running out to the bus under the blazing sun to sell one pineapple. With the sound of artillery nearby, soldiers who will fight for 40 yen a day, bragging that they kill people just because they're there. I got caught up in the thought that it was probably futile to believe that one ought to do something for these people, or that they can do something for themselves. I saw those people in Korea last year as well. A prostitute with short bobbed hair and wearing only a sweaty shirt, lying in a room not even one mat wide, in which two people wouldn't be able to lie down comfortably. The youths who crowd around when the taxi stops, selling gum, newspapers, and umbrellas and polishing shoes. Men who are probably disabled veterans begging for money in the marketplace, holding a different baby every day, probably borrowed.

Do the people have political responsibility? Can they attain happiness on the basis of politics? I was assailed by the impulse to say no to both questions. The people don't have a political responsibility. Who can ask them to take responsibility? If so, the people are nothing more than the perpetual victims of politics. If they are victims, wouldn't it be better for the people not to embrace the illusion that politics can bring them happiness? These ideas blew through me like gales. These are the two ideas. This is the second idea. Embracing this idea, which was new to me, at least, I went home.

According to this idea, as one of the people I have no responsibility to Vietnam. There is no need to make excuses about not being effective or not being moved: from the beginning there is not one responsibility that I must fulfill regarding Vietnam. This is the second reason that I didn't respond to the Committee of Filmmakers for Peace in Vietnam or any of the other appeals.

Just now I said "the second idea." A new idea did come into being inside me, but that did not mean that the previous idea disappeared. They coexist. It is a coexistence, but not a peaceful one.

That I was able to make my first film in three years, however, was probably because of that second idea. I said I was "able" to make a film—as if I had been "unable" to—but although there were, of course, other objective conditions that prevented me from making a film, it was perhaps chiefly because my subjective conditions were not fulfilled. At any rate, it may be more correct to say that I had several opportunities, but didn't make the artistic preparations to take advantage of any of them.

What I mean by that is that I was completely stuck on the dead-end street of the first idea mentioned above: "I have to tell the people that we have to do something. I don't know what that something is, but we have to do it."

This is not to say that I made my start as an artist thinking that way. As an artist, the only concept I had in mind was that if we, the oppressed, are to take action, our action would inevitably be antisocial in nature, and it would probably be punished and frustrated by our oppressors. The problem that naturally came next was that of active responsibility for our actions. This was the period from *A Town of Love and Hope*[1] to *Cruel Story of Youth*[2] and *The Tomb of the Sun*.[3] When the problem of active responsibility arose, some of those who had previously supported *A Town of Love and Hope* could no longer see my films. Rather than a search for the subjective will of a given victim of oppression, this was an investigation of the real responsibility of the oppressed in general and of that on the part of militant movements. I call this a "direct" confrontation because, before this, symbolic ones had already appeared in my work. But to confront it directly in this fashion invited support from many beyond the film world and opposition from even more. That the screening of *Night and Fog in Japan* was suspended, and that there was a group within the antisystem movement that applauded that suspension, serve conversely as proof that this pursuit was important. As a result of this incident, whether I liked it or not, I had to take the position of someone in the movement or someone critical of the movement. Or so I was forced to think, at least. Rather than a search for active responsibility by the oppressed themselves, it was a search for active responsibility on the part of the oppressed from the point of view of an oppressed activist (who, in a sense, had

1.   *A Town of Love and Hope* (*Ai to Kibo no Machi,* dir. Oshima Nagisa, 1959).
2.   *Cruel Story of Youth* (*Seishun Zankoku Monogatari,* dir. Oshima Nagisa, 1960).
3.   *The Tomb of the Sun* (*Taiyo no Hakaba,* dir. Oshima Nagisa, 1960).

achieved independence from the oppressed) and on the part of the movement of the oppressed. The emphasis was on the former in *The Catch*[4] and on the latter in *Amakusa Shiro Tokisada.*[5] Compared to *Night and Fog in Japan,*[6] which, fortunately, was able to be a search for responsibility that skewered the oppressed and the oppressed activist from the point of view of someone who was both simultaneously, those films were both one-sided and unable to portray a colossal vision. Of course, the responsibility for this lies with the filmmaker, but it might also be said that it was a reflection of myself as filmmaker at the time, of my having been put in the difficult position of being both realistic and artistic. In *Amakusa Shiro Tokisada* in particular, I—an oppressed activist forced to become independent and to attempt to criticize the oppressed themselves and the movement itself—project my shadow all too pitifully. Frankly, I had no sense of where to go from there. Believing only in the correctness of what I had done up to that point, and taking strength only from the fact it that would be communicated again to later generations, I had no alternative but to ensconce myself in my castle and make pronouncements from there. At that time, a certain critic said that one possibility would be to send provisions to Oshima Nagisa in his castle. Was that really true? Perhaps it was. Perhaps it wasn't. In any case, the fact of the matter is that from that time onward, I became invisible to the eyes of people who look at things solely through the narrow framework called the film.

When I finished shooting *Amakusa Shiro Tokisada,* I was still planning to continue making films, but, thinking about it now, there was no reason that I should have been able to continue making films after writing an ending like that. Of course, I'm not referring to external conditions. I mean subjective conditions. Curiously, the destiny that would subsequently envelop me was even foreshadowed in *Amakusa Shiro Tokisada.* I didn't kill Shiro. I wasn't able to write to the point of his death. Was his being alive the only proof of my existence? Or was I hoping that Shiro would reappear somewhere else, totally transformed?

Earlier I said that I had been to Korea and Vietnam, and new ideas had come into being for me in those places. To be precise, though, should I say that they had come into being hazily beforehand and were merely confirmed when I saw Korea and Vietnam? If that is the case, perhaps I should say that with the television documentary "The Forgotten Imperial Army"[7] in the summer of 1963 and the television

4.   *The Catch* (*Shiiku,* dir. Oshima Nagisa, 1961).
5.   *Amakusa Shiro Tokisada* (*Amakusa Shiro Tokisada,* dir. Oshima Nagisa, 1962) As he was born, raised, rebelled, and killed in Amakusa, Amakusa became his surname.
6.   *Night and Fog in Japan* (*Nihon no Yoru to Kiri,* dir. Oshima Nagisa, 1960).
7.   "The Forgotten Imperial Army" ("Wasurerareta Kogun": TV documentary, dir. Oshima Nagisa, 1963).

Amakusa Shiro Takisada. 1962.

drama "The Scream"[8] in the fall of that year, I again began to make films from the point of view of the oppressed. And perhaps I should say that the radio drama "The Golden Age Passes"[9] in the spring of 1964 marked the end of my self-examination. Then I went to Korea during the summer and fall of 1964 and to Vietnam in the spring of 1965.

Even so, why was 1965 the year in which I had to begin making films again? It is undoubtedly because 1965 was a year of ordeals, certainly a year of ordeals for film. Beginning with *Tokyo Olympiad*,[10] continuing through *Black Snow*[11] and *The Secret in the Wall*[12] and on to *Pleasure of the Flesh*,[13] there had never been a year in which film had received so many attacks from outside. That is probably precisely why Japanese film needed me. *Pleasure of the Flesh* was my response to that.

To write further would result in an interpretation of *Pleasure of the Flesh*, which I would like to avoid. I have never annotated any of my films. I may be thought of as a talker and a lover of debate, but my intention has been to remain annoyingly silent on the subject of the works themselves.

Regarding movements and circumstances, I may have made all kinds of comments out of a feeling of obligation. But I would be annoyed if those comments were perceived to be directly related to the works. Of course, I wouldn't say that they have no relationship to the works; rather, the works should always be independent.

I have never responded to criticism. All criticism, no matter how bad—even censure—touches me deeply. At any rate, it moves me much more than something like the appeal by the Committee of Filmmakers for Peace in Vietnam. I consider myself someone who understands the critics.

Accordingly, I also think of myself as understanding the feelings of people who try to judge my present or my present films based on my past or my past films. I think of myself as understanding them painfully well. Therefore, for the benefit of those people, I have merely tried to explain the changes that have taken place inside me since I dropped out of sight. I don't mean to brag about them or rationalize them. I have tried to do it in the same way that I might explain one aspect of my current state of mind to an old friend at a bar.

8.   "The Scream" ("Sakebi": TV documentary, script by Oshima Nagisa, dir. Eto Jun, 1963).
9.   "The Golden Age Passes" ("Oogon no Toki was Sugiyuku": radio drama, script by Oshima Nagisa, dir. Miyagawa Shiro, 1964).
10.   *Tokyo Olympiad* (*Tokyo Orinppikku,* dir. Ichikawa Kon, 1965).
11.   *Black Snow* (*Kuroi Yuki,* dir. Takechi Tetsuji, 1965).
12.   *The Secret in the Wall* (*Kabe no Naka no Himegoto,* dir. Wakamatsu Koji, 1965).
13.   *Pleasure of the Flesh* (*Etsuraku,* dir. Oshima Nagisa, 1965).

Going a step further and drunkenly asking your leave to say one thing through my hat, I would like to say that my present life and works should be judged from the point of view of my future, not my past. Looked at from the point of view of the future, the meaning of my modest works, at least, ought to be as plain as the nose on your face—as long as your vision is not that of an elderly person, to whom distant things are clear but close things are completely obscure.

If I were asked, "Whither have you been going?", I would probably respond, "Along the road to freedom." As film experienced its season of ordeals, and conditions became more constricting, I gradually felt myself becoming freer, oddly enough. That I was able to make *Pleasure of the Flesh* is an indication of this, while at the same time I can also say that making it allowed me to become freer. That freedom, however, is still a small freedom. Just as *Pleasure of the Flesh* was a destitute pleasure. I think that our only route to freedom and our only route to pleasure can come after we have first recognized that freedom and pleasure are not possible in this world.

We are free because freedom is not possible. Ending with that statement, I am left with a very heavy burden. Is it something I can cast off a bit at a time with each film I make? No, I don't think so. Rather, I feel that the burden increases a little with each film I make: at first I was saying something about the second idea, but just because a second comes into being, the first idea definitely doesn't go away. If that is the case, can we become free as we increase our baggage, piece by piece? And, if so, does that mean that we can't become completely free unless we take on all of the baggage in the whole world? My road to freedom extends far into the distance.

Right now I am making a kind of documentary, entitled *The Diary of Yunbogi,*[14] consisting of a montage of the diary of a Korean youth made with pictures I took of children when I went to Korea last year. This is my third treatment of Korea, after the two television documentaries "The Forgotten Imperial Army" and "Monument to Youth."[15] It is also my humble message to the Korea-Japan Treaty. At present, there are no plans for it to be shown in the theater or on television. There will be one private showing, and then it will be available for borrowing on request. I am glad, however, that I am now able to make this type of film. By saying that I am able to make it, I mean that I both want to make it and have the foundation that allows me to make it.

14.   *The Diary of Yunbogi* (*Yun Bogi no Nikki,* dir. Oshima Nagisa, 1965).
15.   "Monument to Youth" ("Seishun no Ishibumi": TV documentary, dir. Oshima Nagisa, 1964).

Pleasure of the Flesh. 1965.

The Diary of Yunbogi. 1965.

When this is finished, I will probably begin to write the script for my next dramatic film. Right now, I think I would like to continue making films without interruption. I think I will be able to, which is good. This is my road to freedom.

Finally, if I might be allowed to inject a hopeful observation, as I am wont to do, it seems as though a number of my friends have definitely begun to walk along the road to freedom. If that is the case, then the Japanese film also has begun to walk along the road to freedom. I am starting to think that there is freedom and hope in the future of the Japanese film.

(Film Art, 1965)

II The Demon of Expression and the Logic
    of Organized Struggle (1965–1970)

The Concept of Demons and the Concept of a Movement

*In the first place, to make films is a
criminal act in this world.*

As I have written elsewhere, when you begin making a film, you don't know everything about it. There are even times when you don't really know what you're trying to do when you're writing the script, and you finally grasp it only when you're shooting. That can happen even fairly late in the shooting process. One of the reasons I set out to make *Violence at Noon* was that I was attracted to the concept of a "demon."[1] By demon, I mean the "demon" in the teenage rifle-shooting demon and the "demon" in the typhoid-poisoning demon, for example. The story of Ri Chin'u, which I had previously wanted to do and for which I had written a script, was also the story of a demon. Because I was attracted to demons, it is only natural that I latched onto *Violence at Noon,* although I myself didn't understand the reason why.

The filming of the rural part of *Violence at Noon* was done in the village of Kawashima in the town of Tatsuno in Kami Ina district, Nagano prefecture, where I stayed in a country house with my assistant director, art department, and others. This was the first time I had art director Toda Shigemasa[2] on my crew, but, as he had

1.   A precise translation of this title would be *The Passing Demon by Daylight.* It adds a delicate difference of connotative nuance to the acts of the rapist and the victims. The word "demon" here is a translation of the Chinese character that is pronounced "ma" in Japanese and signifies an evil spirit with a strange power to make a person do evil things. The character "ma" is often used to create compound words referring to the perpetrators of particularly heinous crimes in Japan; the teenage rifle-shooting demon was an eighteen-year-old who shot one policeman and seriously injured another in 1965. The typhoid-poisoning demon put typhoid germs in food. The film was adapted from a novel by Takeda Taijun.
2.   Toda Shigemasa began as an assistant to Mizutani Hiroshi for Mizoguchi's last works. He became art director for Kobayashi Masaki's *The Entanglement* (*Karamiai,* 1962), going on to work with him for *Harakiri* (*Seppuku,* 1962) and *Kwaidan* (*Kwaidan,* 1964). He then collaborated with

already demonstrated in his marvelously talented work with the directors Kobayashi Masaki[3] and Shinoda Masahiro,[4] he is truly a great artist. If *Violence at Noon* is a good work at all, I believe it is so principally because I had the good fortune of meeting up with this man. He is also quite a drinker, and we drank together night after night. One of those nights—I forget what we were talking about that triggered it—a thought glimmered in my mind like a divine revelation.

I too have aged and become forgetful. Most of the time when I have a good idea while drinking, I forget it by the next day. Not embarrassed or concerned in the least about my reputation, I have taken to making notes on whatever paper is available. This may be considered disagreeable, but I am no longer of an age to feel embarrassment or shame. Actually, Toda Shigemasa is also a practitioner of that system, fortunately. Thanks to that, I was able to make a note of this thought without embarrassment.

The thought that glimmered in my brain had to do with the concept of "a crime of conviction" (*uberzeugungsverbrechen*). Of course, the concept of a crime of conviction did not originate here in my brain. I have thought that I would like to make

---

Shinoda Masahiro on *The Dry Flower* (*Kawaita Hana*, 1964) and *The Island of Execution* (*Shokei no Shima*, 1966). Beginning with *The Passing Demon by Daylight* (*Hakuchu no Tori Ma*, 1966), he began to work extensively with Oshima, as in *A Study of Japanese Bawdy Songs* (*Nihon Shunka Ko*, 1967), *Japanese Summer: Double Suicide* (*Murishinju Nigon no Natsu*, 1967), *Death by Hanging* (*Koshikei*, 1968), *Three Resurrected Drunkards* (*Kaettekita Yopparai*, 1968), *Diary of a Shinjuku Thief* (*Shinjuku Dorobo Nikki*, 1968), *Boy* (*Shonen*, 1969), *A Secret Post-Toyko-War Story* (*Tokyo Senso Sengo Hiwa*, 1970), *The Ceremony* (*Gishiki*, 1971), *Dear Summer Sister* (*Natsu no Imoto*, 1972), *The Empire of the Senses* (*Ai no Korrida*, 1976), *The Empire of Passion* (*Ai no Borei*, 1978), and *Merry Christmas, Mr. Lawrence!* (*Senjo no merri Kurismasu*, 1983). Oshima acknowledges that Toda's contribution to these films went beyond that of art director as traditionally understood, for one can hardly imagine them without Toda's freewheeling imagery and strong political metaphors. He was an indispensable co-worker.

3.   Kobayashi Masaki joined the Shochiku Ofuna Studio in 1941 as an assistant director, but was immediately drafted into the army and became a prisoner of war. Repatriated in 1946, he returned to the same studio and was promoted to a directorship with *Son's Adolescence* (*Musuko no Seishun*, 1952). His third film, *The Room with Thick Walls* (*Kabe Atsuki Heya*, 1953), which dealt with an innocent war criminal, aroused anxiety among Shochiku executives as to the American reaction. They withdrew it from immediate distribution, not releasing it until three years later. He is known in the West for *The Human Condition* (*Ningen no Joken*, Parts 1–6, 1959–1961), *Harakiri* (*Seppuku*, 1961), and *Kwaidan* (*Kwaidan*, 1963).

4.   Shinoda Masahiro joined the Shochiku Ofuna Studio as an assistant director in 1954. His first film as director was *One-Way Ticket of Love* (*Koi no Katamichi Kippu*, 1960), which dealt with the idolatry of a star of a rockabilly group. His second film, *The Dry Lake* (*Kawaita Mizuumi*, 1960), launched him as a talented new director. He stayed with Ofuna much longer than did Oshima, Ishido Toshiro, Tamura Takeshi, or Yoshida Yoshishige, and he produced some memorable films: *The Dry Flower* (*Kawaita Hana*, 1964), *The Assassination* (*Ansatsu*, 1964), *With Beauty and Sorrow* (*Utsukushisa to Kanashimi to*, 1965). Shinoda left Shochiku in 1967 to found his own production company, Hyogensha. His *Double Suicide* (*Shinju Ten no Amijima*, 1969) is well known in the West.

a film with a crime of conviction as its theme a number of times. However, the idea would just pop into my head from time to time and not come to fruition as an image of a concrete work. This time, the instant that the idea of a crime of conviction came into my head, I clearly understood the meaning of it for the first time.

I somehow seem to be on a path whose purpose is to make a model of a crime of conviction. I started out making films about people who appeared to the world to be morally upright but who commit crimes unknowingly because of poverty. That continued for a time, but recently I have been thinking that I would like to portray demonic criminals—people who recognize an inner impulse to commit crimes, but don't understand it. And when I graduate from that, I want to make a film about a crime of conviction. This seems to be the path I am on.

Even while thinking this, however, it also occurs to me that although crimes of conviction are interesting in literature, they may be overly logical and thus dull on film. But this may also be because I don't yet have sufficient ability to make a film about a crime of conviction. At any rate, it is demons that are of interest to me now. Naturally, I think this is because I have some demon in me. At the press conference announcing the production, I said I made the film because I am the Daylight Demon, and Sato Kei, who plays the demon, said the same thing, but this was by no means in jest. In the first place, to make films is a criminal act in this world.

Doesn't this also explain why it is difficult to establish a movement in the film world? It is easy for one person to commit a crime, but it is really difficult to commit a crime in a group. People who try to commit a crime in a group are inevitably shot down. Thus, even if we were to establish the "phantom" studio and the "phantom" journal in the Japanese film world today, it would not be possible for a distinct movement to come into existence.

For a movement to exist, two or more people must openly join together and share the same clear aspirations. When I had to leave Shochiku and said that I was sorry it had come to this, Ishido Toshiro replied that to be in a movement was to lose together. That is certainly the truth. Today, however, losing together is too serious a loss. This is a difficult era—an era in which we can't lose together. Since we formed Sozosha, no movement in the Japanese film world has openly declared that its members would lose together. (In Wakamatsu Koji's group,[5] that implication is not lacking

5.   Revered as a pioneer independent maker of pornographic/political films, Wakamatsu Koji's first film was *The Sweet Trap* (*Amai Wana*, 1963). The intense political activity (1959–60) of groups opposed to the Japan-United States Security Treaty was followed by a burgeoning of eroticism and pornography. A small number of "ero-duction" (erotic film production) companies were formed. Their products, although marginal and limited, were in general distribution throughout Japan. Nat-

entirely. I won't go into that here, however.) This tells the tale of how difficult an environment the world of the Japanese film is for activism. I have no intention of boasting about myself or censuring others. I do think, however, that people who consider themselves activists should understand the situation properly.

In this situation, pseudomovements like the "phantom" studio and the "phantom" journal have no choice but to play the role of movements. Parties may even play a role of sorts. Our Sozosha should also be playing some role. The only people able to ignore all that and say that there is no activism here are the new people who are coming onto the scene with new movements (naturally, all of those first manifested themselves as pseudomovements). Those who merely pride themselves on being activists in other fields and judge that there are no movements in the Japanese film world today have to be called spectators.

In addition, another, completely different problem comes up in the case of activism in film, but is not an issue when activism is present in literature: literature and its criticism are presented in the same medium. In other words, it is possible for the two to coexist on the pages of the same journal. In the film world, to be appreciated as a film, the work must be shown at a theater or at least at a place with screening facilities, whereas film criticism must always take place in journals. I sometimes think that the journal *New Japanese Literature* is meaningless, but when I read, for example, the literary criticism by Takei Akio that the journal has been serializing

---

urally the major film companies and some noted directors, including Oshima, showed interest in them. Although obsessively "soft-core" because of the obscenity code, these films were distinct in their treatments of sexuality from those made in the 1950s. At that time, the major studios made *seiten mono* (films on sexuality) that dealt with teenagers' sexual awakening or "sun tribe" films dealing with sexual/social rebellion among upper-middle-class youth. Wakamatsu sent his *The Secret in the Wall* (*Kabe no Naka no Himegoto,* 1965) to the Berlin Film Festival, which produced a storm of protest over what some termed a "national disgrace." In this film participants in a series of sex scenes in an apartment of a high-rise public housing unit (of the kind that sprawl out over Tokyo's suburbs) are "watched" by a huge poster of Stalin, as if to indicate the limitations of the working-class struggle for political/economic empowerment. They are seen as confined within the small cube of anonymous space of their hard-won public housing quarters. Soon after this "incident," the filmmaker founded his own independent production company, Wakamatsu Productions. He made *When the Embryo Hunts in Secret* (*Taiji ga Mitsuryo Suru Toki,* 1966); *Violated Women in White* (*Okasareta Byakui,* 1967); *Jin Pang Mei* (*Kin Pei Bai,* 1968), which was distributed by Shochiku; and *Go, Go! You Are a Virgin for the Second Time* (*Yuke, Yuke, Nidome no Shojo,* 1969). All were distributed in the West. It should be noted that these productions were influenced by the participation of an ultra-left avant-garde filmmaker, Adachi Masao. This collaboration culminated in the production of *Red Army-PFLP: Declaration of the World War* (*Sekigun-PFLP: Sekai Senso Sengen,* 1971). This filmmaker made two films with A.T.G., *Ecstasy of the Angel* (*Tenshi no Kokotsu,* 1972) and *The Holy Mother Avalokitesvara* (*Seibo Kannon Daibosastu,* 1977). Wakamatsu was a Japan-side producer for Oshima's *In the Realm of the Senses* (*Ai no Korrida,* 1976). He has made well over forty films.

since the January issue, I am glad that this journal and this movement exist. I think this literary criticism is a challenge to the artist; while issuing that challenge to the artist, however, I think that Takei is screaming to the writer, "If you have something to say, write. Write your next work." And I think he is screaming, "If you write your work and there is no place to publish it [actually, even if there is another place to publish it], publish it in *New Japanese Literature*." Because of the guarantee that they can be published in the same forum, criticism can be so harsh on the work. Although I have some disagreements with the critical essays on an individual basis, I think that Takei is here at the height of his powers as a critic and activist.

By comparison, I think that the fact that the media for films and for film criticism are different is fatal to those whose only image of a movement in film is that of the movements already in existence. It seems as though there can be no mutual guarantee of a medium. A filmmaker who cannot produce a work has no recourse, no matter how much he is criticized or how much he tries to write criticism himself. These are the decisive factors in what has recently been called the impoverishment and decline of film criticism. For example, Matsumoto Toshio[6] has lately been unleashing frequent critical assaults on me, but there is no need for me to reply, because his impatience at his own lack of productivity is leading him astray.

Thus it is tragic to read his writings, which are transformed by feelings of inferiority and its opposite, superiority, toward the drama; by excessive praise and exces-

---

6.   Unlike the majority of noted Japanese filmmakers, Matsumoto Toshio first joined New Scientific Research Film Company (Shin Riken Eiga Sha) and made experimental documentary films and formally experimental public relations films for various institutions and corporations. After winning the *grand prix* at the Venice Film Festival for his documentary, *Nishijin* (*Nishijin,* 1961), which dealt with a traditional textile manufacturing process, he founded Matsumoto Productions. He is also a founding member and theorist of the Society for Film Image Art (Eizo Geijyutsu no Kai). His surrealist-inflected theory of documentary filmmaking conflicted with Oshima's theatrical cinematurgy. As Oshima later confessed, he learned a great deal from debates with Matsumoto. However, their arguments were apparently confined to the practical level of image making and compositional method. (One is reminded of the debates between Eisenstein and Vertov in the 1920s and the polemical arguments of Godard and Gorin of the Dziga-Vertov group against "bourgeois film practice" in the late 1960s.) None of these debates probed basic problems of image and of language in relation to issues of cognition and expression. Matsumoto did not initiate these debates in the early 1960s out of a void. A few years before, in the 1950s, critics, theorists, novelists, and poets including Okada Susumu, Masaki Kyosuke, Abe Kobo, Nakahara Yusuke, and Sasaki Kiichi had started questioning the basic issues of cinema. And they turned out, finally, to be not so basic. Should cinema emphasize image making instead of storytelling? Is expression through image possible without linguistic mediation? Should cinema strive to be literary or antiliterary? Yoshimoto Takaaki, poet and stringent polemicist, raised the debates to a level upon which fundamental issues of image and language could be raised. Two of Matsumoto's well-known films, coproduced with the A.T.G., are *Funeral of Roses* (*Bara no Soretsu,* 1969) and *Pandemonium* (*Shura,* 1971); both have been distributed in the West.

sive disparagement of the documentary films made by his colleagues; and by an unusual introduction of emotionalism toward Buñuel, who (he thinks) filmed masterpieces after decades of obscurity. I can prove each of these charges, but I will stop here. Although I don't shy away from a hard fight, I do want to avoid mudslinging. Also, I know the difficulties of our movement; I am sadly aware that our movement doesn't guarantee us a place to present our works.

When will there be a movement in film that will guarantee us a place to present each other's works? In the past, Takei Akio, in a Sozosha leaflet entitled "Proposal of a Fantasist," shared with us the following dream of the regeneration of the film: the 400 million yen that Sohyo (General Council of Trade Unions of Japan) had completely wasted on *New Weekly* would be given to the film movement, with each of twenty units making a film with a budget of 20 million yen. This was in early 1962, but in the intervening four years, has the dream become closer or more distant?

As fantasist and optimist and at the same time a businessman, I would like to say clearly that the dream has become more attainable. Sozosha became independent in 1962, even though I was about to embark on a period of three years in which I was unable to make a film. Now, four years have passed, and both Shinoda Masahiro and Yoshida Yoshishige[7] are making films independently, with Ishido writing Yoshida's screenplays and Tamura Takeshi[8] writing mine: both are going strong. It has also become clear that one can make a film for 3 million yen.

7.   Yoshida Yoshishige joined the Shochiku Ofuna Studio as an assistant director in 1955. His made his directorial debut with *A Good-for-nothing* (*Rokudenashi,* 1961) rendered somewhat in the manner of the French New Wave. He made his mark as a director with his fourth film, *Akitsu Spa* (*Akitsu Onsen,* 1962), an elegy for the generation that had come of age at the end of World War II. A clash with Shochiku erupted when the company put his sixth film, *Getting Away from Japan* (*Nippon Dasshutsu,* 1964), into circulation after cutting the entire final sequence of the protagonist's insanity. He immediately left Shochiku and founded a production company, Gendai Eiga Sha, in the same year. His major effort was *Eros Plus Massacre* (*Erosu purasu Gyakusatsu,* 1969), in which the historical present is constantly drawn into the enunciative present, with the historical past floating between them. This film deals with the life of a well-known anarchist of the 1920s, Osugi Sakae, and the three women with whom he had sexual relationships. In *Martial Law* (*Kaigenrei,* 1973), he tackled the most charismatic political philosopher of modern Japan, Kita Ikki. Despite his decentered handling of the subject, Yoshida had difficulty situating his protagonist, for this enigmatic national socialist, a prototype of Japanese fascist ideology, allegedly advocated a coup d'etat to abolish capitalism in the name of the emperor in order to redress the worsening conditions of the peasantry and the working class in the mid-1930s. Ishido Toshiro wrote scripts for his lyrical films of the middle period, including *A Story Written by Water* (*Mizu de Kakareta Monogatari,* 1965); *The Woman's Lake* (*Onna no Mizuumi,* 1966), and *The Trembling of the Ice-Covered Trees* (*Juhyo no Yoromeki,* 1968).
8.   Tamura Takeshi joined the Shochiku Ofuna Studio in 1955 and worked as chief assistant director for Oshima's first feature, *A Town of Love and Hope* (1959). He directed only one film, *Volunteering for the Villain* (*Akunin Shigan,* 1960), which was based on his own script. He left Sho-

In the Japanese film world today, movements appear to be both dissolving and forming. *Violence at Noon* can perhaps be said to portray these conditions of dissolution and formation as well.

(*Film Art*, 1965)

---

chiku with Oshima and joined his new production company, Sozosha, where he served as Oshima's main scriptwriter until the company was dissolved in 1973. His scripts include *The Catch* (*Shiiku,* 1961), *Violence at Noon* (*Hakuchu no Torima,* 1966), and *Boy* (*Shonen,* 1969). He coscripted *A Study of Japanese Bawdy Songs* (*Nihon Shunka Ko,* 1967), *Japanese Summer: Double Suicide* (*Muri Shinjyu: Nihon no Natsu,* 1967), *Death by Hanging* (*Koshikei,* 1968), *Three Resurrected Drunkards* (*Kaettekita Yopparai,* 1968), *Diary of a Shinjuku Thief* (*Shinjuku Dorobo Nikki,* 1969), *The Ceremony* (*Gishiki,* 1971), and *Dear Summer Sister* (*Natsu no Imoto,* 1972). His formative participation in these films is strongly evident. After writing the script for *Young Murderer* (*Seishun no Satsujinsha,* dir. Hasegawa Kazuhiko, 1976), he turned to writing novels.

Shame is an intrinsic emotion of those who bear the burden of being destined to take the initiative.

Japanese women are always saying, "Oh, I'm ashamed," and the language contains an adjective, *hanahazukashii,* that applies to virgins. It seems that shame is thought to be more characteristic of women than of men.

I don't think so, however. I think that shame is a particular characteristic of men. Furthermore, I think that it is an exclusive characteristic of men and that women have it only in exceptional cases; in the extreme, I think that women probably don't even understand shame.

The protagonist of *Violence at Noon* is a brutal criminal who goes to the doors of unfamiliar houses in broad daylight, putting the girl who answers the door off guard by pretending to ask directions or inquire if the head of the household is in. Once he ascertains that there is no one else around, he suddenly turns on her, threatening her and committing any violent act he chooses. Common sense says that his is an existence that doesn't merit a shred of sympathy. To me, however, this appears to be a pitiful expression of man's sense of shame.

From the first, *Violence at Noon* had one model: the real-life criminal who went on a crime spree as far west as Kyushu and as far east as the Kanto region, causing an uproar, mostly from the spring of 1957 until the following spring, that was called the second Kodaira case or the Daylight Demon case. The film was based on Takeda Taijun's novel, *The Daylight Demon,* which used the court decision on the case as background. The case underwent a transformation first in the novel and then further in the film as the age, occupation, birthplace, and other facts about the pro-

Violence at Noon. 1966.

tagonist, the Daylight Demon, were changed; however, his basic personality does not differ from that of the real-life model.

With the number of crimes for which he was formally prosecuted totaling thirty-five, all of which were attacks on girls who were home alone, the real Daylight Demon terrorized Japanese society. The hallmark of his crimes was that he always choked his victims unconscious before violating them. Thus, it can be said that the Daylight Demon may have been capable of feeling desire for a woman only when she was unconscious.

I see in this an extreme manifestation of man's sense of shame. I don't know whether there were secrets of some sort in his past. In any case, at some point in his life he may have experienced an unconscious realization along these lines: "My sense of shame is too strong. I can't engage in sexual activity under normal conditions. If I make the woman an unconscious object, I can be free sexually without being obstructed by my sense of shame."

We can also glean the degree of this man's sense of shame from the fact that he always drank before committing a crime. He started in the morning, drinking one or two pints of cheap Japanese distilled liquor, and then committed his daylight violence under the influence. Needless to say, sexual intimacy while under the influence is extremely foolish, but these are things that, unpleasant though they are, we have to see or otherwise come into contact with in our daily lives. Couldn't *Violence at Noon* be termed an extreme exaggeration of the physiology and psychology of men who are that foolish and that pitiful?

Takeda Taijun, added a brilliant invention regarding how the Daylight Demon of Violence at Noon came to be. The Daylight Demon found the woman with whom he had been in love unconscious; the persimmon tree branch, from which she was hanging while attempting double suicide with her lover, had broken. While caring for her, he raped her. In other words, he raped a woman who had become essentially a dead body. Raping a woman who was unconscious and for all intents and purposes dead, with the dead body of a man hanging from a tree branch overhead, the Daylight Demon originated in this scene from a daytime nightmare in a hushed thicket. Was it only in such a dream that the Daylight Demon could cast aside his sense of shame reveal himself as unique?

Thus the Daylight Demon could surmount his sense of shame and confront a woman only after she had been transformed into a dead body, but if, for example, that woman-turned-dead-body had begun to show signs of life, his sense of shame would have returned immediately and he would have suspended sexual activity and run away. The decision reads: "He tried to force himself on the woman, but upon learning that she was pregnant, he showed signs of pity and stopped thinking of intercourse and didn't go through with his original intention. . . . When he tried to force himself on her, he saw that the woman was defecating as a result of being choked into unconsciousness, and his lust suddenly disappeared, so that he was unable to succeed in his goal of intercourse . . ." This must be an extremely delicate sensibility. This is the inner reality of the sex criminal feared as the Daylight Demon and famed as the second Kodaira.

It goes without saying that in the film *Violence at Noon,* I wasn't trying merely to depict or justify the tragedy of the protagonist's sense of shame. However, if in real life I had had to appear in court on behalf of the Daylight Demon, I believe I would be able to make a sufficient defense for his criminal acts by reducing my argument to this one point: the sense of shame.

When one talks like this, the Daylight Demon's sense of shame is surely understandable, but one must naturally anticipate the question of whether it is abnormal. It is an example of an unusually strong sense of shame. But I, of course, believe that all men have this sense of shame inside them.

At the announcement of the film's production I said, "I myself am the Daylight Demon." Sato Kei, who plays the role of the demon, said, "I, too, am the demon." I see the archetype for all male-female relationships in the world in the relationship between the demon and the two women in his life, particularly in the relationship between the demon and his wife. As long as that is the case, I am unmistakably depicted in *Violence at Noon,* through the real-life Daylight Demon and that of Takeda Taijun. Furthermore, my own sense of shame will undoubtedly be heaving a sigh within the film. To top it off, my wife, Koyama Akiko, plays the demon's wife. Under those circumstances, there is no way that signs of my own feelings about love and sex—and delicate nuances of all kinds of related emotions—would not be hidden therein. There is no way that my own excessive sense of shame would not be revealed. However, trying to express something, one wants to say that one is the whole world—that the whole world is the same as one's self. For that reason, I will provide one more example to make my point.

It is the example of that boisterous debate about the restoration of prostitution. At first, I didn't really understand what that debate was about. I understand well that even if there were a law prohibiting prostitution, it would undeniably exist. It was confirmed that prostitution had gradually become more widespread and was flourishing; so be it. However, I didn't understand at all this concept of reviving prostitution. No, they say that they weren't suggesting that it should be revived, they were suggesting that it should be organized. Here again, I understood the meaning of what they were saying, but I had no idea why they were saying it. I don't understand the motivation of the people who are making this assertion.

They are certainly not members of the Diet, and they have no reason to expect political contributions to roll in if they say this sort of thing; nor will it win them votes in the election. However, if they were merely saying it it would have to be called comical with strict social justice in mind. If social justice were the goal, there are many other phenomena about which they could be making pronouncements, and it would be incomprehensible rather than comical if they were to go around preaching loudly about the revival of prostitution and constantly engaging in serious debate with the people they call "menopausal old bags" with no concern about the time wasted.

I cannot believe that the popular writers and critics now urging the revival and organization of prostitution are so unthinking as to be unaware of this. If so, they are assuming this comic role only because they are being completely true to their own individual point of view. Even so, it cannot be that these people lack the opportunity and the money to buy women (this isn't a good way of putting it; please think of it as meaning buying the opportunity to be freely sexually intimate with women). Thus, if they are being true to their own point of view, in this case it is neither prosaic nor materialistic. Rather, we must surmise that it is more metaphysical—to their eyes, at least—that of a profound logic or sensibility based on the true nature of human beings, of men and women.

For a long time I didn't understand what exactly that was. But when I was making *Violence at Noon*, it suddenly dawned on me (please forgive me for constantly bringing up my own works; film directors only develop their ideas when shooting films). I felt that I really understood why my elders were speaking up for the revival and organization of prostitution, without caring about how it looked. However, I consider it somewhat cowardly to put forth my argument here based only on what I guess the psychology of others to be. Thus, if I were to speak only for myself here, and if I were to be in favor of the restoration and organization of prostitution, it would be for one reason only: that the prostitution system is really convenient for the relief of men's sense of shame and may be the only system capable of liberating them from it.

There must be men who are able to engage in sexual activity peacefully, without a sense of shame, only when they have purchased flesh with money and thus have before them an object rather than flesh. Now, when it is believed that there is complete sexual freedom, the lives of men like this will perhaps naturally be described only by the adjective "pitiful." But if you strip away the veils of everyday prejudice and common sense, this type of appetite must exist in all men who possess a sense of shame. And all men possess do a sense of shame!

The real-life Daylight Demon went on his spree just before the enactment of legislation to stop prostitution, so I am certain that the nights he was violent and stole money he always spent at a brothel. He would get up in the morning, drink some cheap Japanese distilled liquor, and once again take the field as the demon. His appetite was satisfied neither by the prostitutes nor by the women whom he forced into unconsciousness.

To satisfy desire, it is necessary to remove the sense of shame. Upon first feeling desire for an actual woman, all men feel themselves hemmed in by a sense of shame. Conversely, it may be that when they feel themselves hemmed in by a sense of shame, they desire a woman. It is usually said that such a condition first occurs after puberty, but it appears clearly even earlier in a more primitive form during boyhood or even infancy. When he is made to stand up and be scolded in his elementary school classroom, a boy must inevitably be conscious of the eyes of the girl he likes upon him. Moreover, he must be conscious of the fact that those eyes are staring at him unreservedly and indifferently. Or, when he is even younger, he must be conscious of the eyes of a young female relative remaining persistently on his body when they suddenly discover their anatomical differences one summer day at the beach, and he averts his eyes first.

These experiences accumulate, and when a boy enters adolescence and feels desire for a woman as a mature man, the feeling of shame hits him all at once. Then he suppresses his desire, and that suppression fans the desire. This is why adolescent boys are awkward and stiff like marionettes. They become bewildered and confused, hesitate, and fall down. This is because the stumbling blocks that constitute the sense of shame are scattered everywhere they go. So as not to stumble and fall, adolescent boys form groups and act in groups. They feel that they are only free of the sense of shame when they are in a group. Members of the group talk about their previous experiences with women and seek new experiences.

There are always people with experience in the group. The experienced ones become the center of the group. The inexperienced ones learn from them. Perhaps it is analogous to the relationship of respect between the leaders and the masses that occurs in groups the world over, but there is probably nothing that compares with the depth of the respect that the inexperienced have for the experienced in groups of adolescent boys. In such groups, the inexperienced become the experienced. This is a male course; in today's language, a playboy course.

The ultimate goal and result of this course is to remove the feelings of shame. The best playboys are those who have gotten rid of their sense of shame—or at least those who can pretend that they have.

Groups like this continue to exist as long as there are inexperienced people within it. However, when there are no longer any inexperienced people, or when the inexperienced begin to act like the experienced, the group's bonds slacken. The boys who believe they have become mature men must now separate from the group and confront women as men. It is at this point that true male-female relationships begin. It is also now that true love begins. Anything up to that point is merely sexual curiosity.

When one proceeds to this new stage, the first person to fall away is the original group leader, the playboy. Because he has rid himself of his feelings of shame, or believes that he has, he thinks little of women. Psychologically, he has fallen into a kind of sexual frigidity. Most of these men either enter into a dull marriage with a dull woman very early on or lead a meaningless life as a playboy who is unable to marry.

With the exception of these playboys, the men who have grappled with their sense of shame as they progressed from inexperience to experience now rush into a struggle with serious romantic love.

Before anything else, romantic love begins by one's considering whether the other has the same sense of shame as oneself. It begins with fantasies that the other does, and it ends when he finds out that she doesn't. He continues to have it, but she does not. Or, when he finds out that she has lost it, it is clearly a disappointment in love and a disillusionment. If each finds out that the other doesn't have it, that they have lost it, right before or after marriage, that marriage can immediately be called a graveyard of romantic love.

I believe, however, that for the woman the sense of shame is a passing feeling, while for the man it is an intrinsic feeling. Thus, women lose their sense of shame in the course of the maturation of romantic love, in the physical relationship, and in marriage, while men persist in their sense of shame even after this—permanently. While women's minds are turned elsewhere, men become daylight demons. Of course, even if they aren't actually manifested in actions like that, the resentments of men whose sense of shame is ignored and repressed must be prowling the earth as countless daylight demons.

Finally, why is the sense of shame intrinsic to the man? It is because he must always play the active role in the male-female sexual relationship.

Violence at Noon. 1966.

Feelings of shame or a sense of shame arise when one is conscious of being looked at by another. When the condition becomes more acute, it arises merely when the person fantasizes that he is conscious of being looked at. Every man must have experienced a sense of shame so strong that he stops dead in his tracks at something he has fantasized, blushing and violently clicking his tongue.

Feelings of shame like that would not arise if he did not have the active role. Even if you are looked at, if you are merely looked at, that is the end of it. Even if you are conscious of being looked at, if that is all, that is the extent of it. While being looked at and being conscious of being looked at, men must assume an active role. The feelings of shame start here. The struggle with the sense of shame starts here. The struggle is a hard one. It is unbalanced. There are those who struggle poorly, and there are cowardly struggles. There are those who struggle skillfully, and there are those who are unskilled. Whatever the struggle, a woman should at least know that there is this kind of struggle going on inside a man.

Because I am a pessimist about men and women, I don't in my wildest dreams think that women will fully understand the characteristic sense of shame that men have. But it probably is not meaningless for them to have even a vague knowledge of it.

(*Women's Opinion*, 1966)

To the Friends and Collaborators on
A Study of Japanese Bawdy Songs

This time we are going to begin shooting without making what is in the normal filmmaking process called a script.

When we start shooting, we will have at hand only a brief description that simply sketches the basic images of the characters and their actions. This should be called a script of images, because it consists of the conclusions reached about the images in the work by the director, the dramatist, the art director, and the producer. We believe that this will meet our needs as we begin shooting.

Accordingly, the concrete creation of each scene will be done during the process of preparation for shooting or during shooting itself, not only by the director and the dramatist, but by the entire crew and the actors as well. In other words, we will be creating what is usually called the script while shooting or, conversely, we will be shooting while creating the script. However, it would be more accurate to say that we will be attempting to combine into one unified creative process the two processes of filmmaking that are usually divided up and called scriptwriting and shooting.

Needless to say, we plan to apply this formula because we want the filmmaking process to be more creative. There are two reasons for our belief that we can be more creative by applying this formula in this particular instance. One is that the time allotted for the total production is short. When time permits, we first concentrate on creating the images in the script. When it is complete, our creative tension is temporarily eased and we are able to go into the shooting with a different kind of creative tension. This time, however, there isn't time for our tension to dissipate during the process. If we allow our tension to dissipate, time will run out before we are able to get into the next type of creative tension. Thus, this time we are going to try to complete the work in one burst while experiencing both types of tension.

The other reason is that we will have to include countless unknown elements in this work and in the creative process. We begin shooting in less than two weeks, but we still don't know what any of the actors will look like. It is likely that a lot of new performers and amateurs will be involved. It is sheer nonsense to think that it will be possible to say, "Okay, here are your lines," and have that be the end of it. For us to include them in our creative process, it is absolutely essential for us to force the people themselves to be creative. This is similar to the way that, when everything is done on location, the places themselves sometimes take on an active role and carve out a kind of identity within the work.

For these reasons, we are confident that by applying this formula, we will be able to bring off a freer, richer film production; at an even deeper level, however, there is the fact that we have great confidence in our abilities. We are confident that we are Japan's best film crew at this point in time. It is because we are Japan's best film crew that we are able to embark on an adventure that has never before been attempted in Japanese film. If we fail, it will be only because we lacked talent. We will simply need to develop our talent further and move ahead. There is no reason for us to fear a conscious lack of effort. However, if we lose our determination, that will be the end. We have only just gotten started; however, it is already certain that the future of the Japanese film depends solely on our adventure in freedom. We must fortify our lines of battle more and more. To those who have lost the willpower to enter into our adventure in freedom, I say: leave our lines of battle immediately. Only those who are able to plunge themselves resolutely into the unknown are our kindred spirits.

Okay, kindred spirits—we are taking off.

(January 1, 1967)

Today's Youth and *A Study of Japanese Bawdy Songs*

Each time I begin to make a new film, I struggle to find actors. Because the young people appear in a group in *A Study of Japanese Bawdy Songs,* it was even more of a struggle than usual. I had to interview them in groups of four or five instead of individually. In addition, I stopped asking them questions and told them to talk about themselves instead. This was quite successful. Everyone tells his own story splendidly.

But when it comes to telling one's own story, those who have nothing inside themselves fail. There were a great many young people who had a good storytelling style, but whose stories had no substance. I ended up choosing a pair who had their own theater company called Free Theater and a college freshman who had produced a student play. In other words, I chose people who taken an active role in something of their own. With the addition of Araki Ichiro, the quartet was complete.

Even now that the shooting is over, I think the group of four was a success. This time we made the film without a script, talking things over as we went along, and they contributed quite good ideas.

A Study of Japanese Bawdy Songs depicts the relationship between young people's sexual fantasies and reality; however, one of the four pointed out that there has to be a moment while one is pursuing sexual fantasies that their futility is perceived. Another said that there also have to be moments when one imagines something more exalted. We were able to incorporate these elements into the film satisfactorily. There are many places in which insights like these kept the film from becoming dirty, even though it deals with sexual issues.

Although Araki Ichiro is also popular as a singer, I convinced him to appear because I appreciated his humorous exploits, such as kidnapping his bride and quitting a television movie directed by Imai Tadashi. He was a character who exceeded my expectations. For one thing, he will never speak lines that he doesn't like. You

A Study of Japanese Bawdy Songs. 1967.

might think that that would be a problem, but he seems to think that he can express himself adequately without lines. In truth, even his smallest actions were imbued with a wonderful power of expression. I have been called "New Wave" for a long time, but I felt that I had met my first New Wave actor in Araki Ichiro.

This group of four represents what is best about young people today. In today's youth there is considerable power of self-expression and a good deal of self-possession. To me, however, that self-possession appears unbearably "reserved." I might also say that it is small or too complete, and that it is too self-contained. Although complete in itself, looked at within the context of society it is very much up in the air. And the youths themselves are unaware of this.

I made *A Study of Japanese Bawdy Songs* with the hope of making today's young people understand that state of being up in the air. But did I really get them to understand?

(*United News Service*, March 18, 1967)

To the Friends and Collaborators on
Japanese Summer: Double Suicide

Having completed *A Study of Japanese Bawdy Songs*, we are rushing headlong into the film entitled *Japanese Summer: Double Suicide*. We have the original script in front of us right now. In addition to the names of the three people on it—Tamura Takeshi, Sasaki Mamoru,[1] and Oshima Nagisa—the opinions of Nakajima Masayuki,[2] Toda Shigemasa, Nishizaki Hideo,[3] and Watanabe Fumio have also been incorporated.

Our films are usually films of premonition. We take a lot of our material from the past and present; however, we don't use it to explain the past or present. We take

1.   A scriptwriter who began working in the late 1960s with Oshima, Sasaki Mamoru's credits include *A Study of Japanese Bawdy Songs* (1967), *Japanese Summer: Double Suicide* (1967), *Three Resurrected Drunkards* (1968), *Diary of a Shinjuku Thief* (1969), *A Secret Post-Tokyo War Story* (*Tokyo Senso Sengo Hiwa*, 1970), *The Ceremony* (1971), and *Dear Summer Sister* (1972). He is now a very popular television writer.

2.   A noted producer of independent film and TV productions, Nakajima Masayuki was first recruited by the Shochiku Company in 1940. Drafted into the army in 1944, he was repatriated out of China in 1947 and began a career as an independent producer in 1949. He founded his own Palace Film Productions in 1961 and produced Oshima's *The Catch* (1961) immediately after Oshima's establishment of Sozosha. He then worked as a contract producer with Sozosha for a number of Oshima films: *Pleasure of the Flesh* (*Etsuraku,* 1965), *Violence at Noon* (1966), *A Study of Japanese Bawdy Songs* (1967), *Japanese Summer: Double Suicide* (1967), *Manual of Ninja Martial Arts* (*Ninja Bugei Cho,* 1967), *Death by Hanging* (1968), *Three Resurrected Drunkards* (1968), *Diary of a Shinjuku Thief* (1969), and *Boy* (1969). His collaboration with other directors includes *He and She* (*Kanojo to Kare,* dir. Hani Susumu, 1963), *The Dry Flower* (*Kawaita Hana,* dir. Shinoda Masahiro, 1964), *Silence Has No Wings* (*Tobenai Chinmoku,* dir. Kuroki Kazúo, 1966), *Crimson Clouds* (*Akanegumo,* dir. Shinoda Masahiro, 1967), *Double Suicide* (*Shinju Ten no Amijima,* dir. Shonoda Masahiro, 1969), and *Evil Spirits of Japan* (*Nihon no Akuryo,* dir. Kuroki Kazuo, 1969).

3.   A sound engineer who collaborated with Oshima in *Pleasure of the Flesh* (1965), *Violence at Noon* (1966), *A Study of Japanese Bawdy Songs* (1967), *Manual of Ninja Martial Arts* (1967), *Japanese Summer: Double Suicide* (1967), *Death by Hanging* (1968), *Three Resurrected Drunkards* (1968), *Diary of a Shinjuku Thief* (1968), *Boy* (1969), *A Secret Post-Tokyo War Story* (1970), and *The Ceremony* (1971).

material from the past and present only when it gives rise to our images of the future. At such times, the material already transcends its significance as material, becoming our images and projecting certain premonitions about the future to those who see the film. Thus, we are now trying to make exclusively premonitory films, and we consider all other films meaningless.

Because those of us who are making these films naturally share common premonitions, we depart from a common starting point. Thus, we don't need to include the slightest explanation in the script for ourselves. However, there are many people who think of films exclusively as explanations of the past and present. For these people, it is predictable that this time, too, there will be many misunderstandings. We have already come too far. But we have to go even farther. We don't want the distance that separates us to increase. We could take a break until they come closer to us, but we think that now is not the time to rest. As we continue to run, we think that giving them a bit of a hint in advance about our films would help to keep any increase in the distance between us to a minimum.

We believe that in our current film *Japanese Summer: Double Suicide,* misunderstandings are most likely to arise regarding the character Otoko.

Otoko is a person who suddenly gets the idea that he is going to die or be killed. Thereafter he becomes unnaturally sensitive to everything related to death and is moved only by those things. Being moved means not only being frightened; the things that move him also include the things that excite him.

One instance of this occurs in the context of his confrontation with Nejiko. Some may believe that Nejiko, who always wants to make love, is a symbol of life, and Otoko, who has a premonition that he is going to be killed, is a symbol of death. This is mistaken. Wanting to make love all the time is obviously evidence of life, but we were definitely not neglecting to point out that death soon comes into play where there is such strong evidence of life. Even more important than that, Otoko's premonitions of being killed (as a phenomenon, they take the form of a kind of delusion) are also evidence of life; in no way is this a sickness that can end in death. Otoko definitely does not want to die. He wants to live, and that is precisely why he has premonitions of death. In other words, in instances where Otoko appears at a glance to want to die, he actually wants to live, and that is beautiful. Insofar as Otoko's desire for life is convoluted, it is intensely beautiful—more so than Nejiko's straightforward desire to live. In this way, the two embrace two things that have something basic in common, and they are attracted to each other because it is manifested in polar opposite forms. It is absolutely incorrect to judge this work as a diagram that reads: Nejiko = Life, Otoko = Death.

A Japanese Summer: Double Suicide. 1967.

The second instance of possible misunderstanding is in the context of the confrontation of the characters with television, toys, ogres, and so on. When we said that we were thinking of making a film on the subject of double suicide, the two critics who are our closest friends laughed, saying, "Oh, you guys are finally going to try to draw us into a double suicide." Part of this statement was correct, but part was mistaken. The premonition that someone is making someone commit double suicide is correct. But that someone isn't us. We aren't the ones saying, "Let's commit double suicide." We ourselves have the premonition that someone is making us commit double suicide. That is precisely why we tried to create a character like Otoko, who has never before appeared in a film. Accordingly, Otoko doesn't take the initiative regarding his own death. Other people do take the initiative: some from intrinsic thoughts of symbols of death such as television, toys, and demons. Some, by thinking that they are living or that they want to live, head in the direction of life's opposite—death. Others start the march toward death because they lack an awareness of their own situation. Moreover, they never march together; they go forward while struggling with each other. Because of his premonitions, Otoko is dragged along; he also stands in the way at the front. Or he is dragged along while standing in the way. Without a single premonition, Nejiko is the reverse of Otoko and ends up sharing his destiny. The positions of Otoko and Nejiko in relation to television, toys, ogres, and other things must not be reversed. However, having given you a basic diagram so that you can understand, I will stop there; naturally, though, merely pointing it out has no meaning whatsoever. We must concentrate all our energies on how obscurely, intricately, and, above all, how beautifully we can mold these characters, not on how easily we can communicate their outlines.

For those of us who have set out thinking this way, it is the details that are at stake. Because we are all professionals in the positive sense of the word, our usual practice is to respect the independence of each department regarding details. This time we believe it is desirable to interfere with each other while respecting each other's independence. Our new slogan at this time is mutual interference even in details.

I believe total interference to be especially essential with respect to our actor friends, who constitute the point of intensity of expression. This time our actor friends must, above all, be a presence. The following words of Fukazawa Shichiro[4] articulate an efficient way of achieving this:

4.   A novelist and essayist whose novels have been adapted for films: *Wifeless Younger Brothers of the Northeast* (*Tohoku no Jimmutachi,* dir. Ichikawa Kon, 1957), *The Ballad of Narayama* (*Narayamabushi Ko,* dir. Kinoshita Keisuke, 1958), and *The Fuefuki River* (*Fuefuki Gawa,* dir.

Be expressionless.
Move sluggishly.
Have no emotion, only sensation.

These orders given by Fukazawa regarding a film with young people as its pro-
tagonists conforms nicely with what has come to be our objective.

How can we go far beyond naturalism and still permit each existence to stand
on its own? To what extent can time pass subjectively, or stop? Can our premonition,
expressed clearly as a framework in our script, take root as a film? Our work from
now on, which will decide this, can be boiled down to these two points.

(*United News Service,* April 20, 1967)

Kinoshita Keisuke, 1960). His novella *Tale of a Tasteful Dream* (*Hurryu Mutan,* 1960) appeared in
a monthly magazine, *Chuokoron,* in the midst of the political turmoil of 1960. The novella has a
dream sequence in which the severed head of the emperor tumbles to the floor. This infuriated
ultra-rightists, who dispatched an assassin to the home of the publishing company's director.
Although the director was not at home, his wife was murdered and a maid injured. The incident
drove Fukazawa from Tokyo to the countryside, where he led a quiet life as a farmer, writer, and
guitarist until his death.

On the Attitude of Film Theorists

Recently I have been feeling very skeptical about those who theorize film. I discussed one aspect of this in the *Japan Readers' Newspaper* last year, but I then thought that I should try to remain silent, no matter how skeptical I felt. Actually, last year I received a lot of abuse both during a symposium with Hanada[1] and Takei[2] and

1.   Critic Hanada Kiyoteru was the author of a collection of essays written after the war, entitled *The Overcoming of Modern Times* (*Kindai no Chokoku,* Tokyo: Mirai Sha, 1959). To develop contemporary audiovisual art and to counter the overwhelming dominance in modern times of printed language, Hanada proposed the exploration of medieval culture in which dance, song, speech, and theater worked on equal terms. This data was immediately criticized by Yoshimoto Takaaki for the theoretical fragility of its reasoning: language—spoken, sung, or written—permeates drama, and the theater and the audiovisual arts are no exception. Despite this fundamental critique, Hanada wrote "experimental" plays: *Cartoons of Birds and Beasts* (*Chojyu Giwa,* Tokyo: Mirai Sha, 1962) and *A Bombshell Journal* (*Bakuretsudan Ki,* Tokyo: Mirai Sha, 1963). *Everything Ends with a Song* (*Mono MIna Uta ni Owaru,* Tokyo: Shobunsha, 1964) is a musical Kabuki drama, a Brechtian exercise. Yoshimoto's bitterest critique of Hanada is directed at his theoretical/ideological texts, which involve an uncritical transposition of wartime "productionist fascism (social fascism)" to the context of a postwar "productionist Stalinism" dictated by Soviet Marxism. (See Yoshimoto Takaaki, "Problems of the *Modern Literature* Group," *Gunzo,* July 1964.)
2.   Takei Akio began his work as chairman of the National Federation of Students' Self-Government Associations (Zengakuren), and coauthored the *Wartime Responsibility of Men of Letters* (*Bungakusha no Senso Sekinin,* Tokyo: Awaji Shobo, 1956) with Yoshimoto Takaaki. This text is important for understanding the process of de-Stalinization among the younger Japanese leftists of the late 1950s. It deals with the issues of "conversion," coerced or spontaneous, of the writers of Marxist/leftist ideologies to nationalist/social nationalist ideologies under the enormous state pressure during wartime. Yoshimoto examined the crucially problematic nature of the idea of an "intelligentsia" that was embraced by leftist men of letters. To them it meant leading the masses to a political revolution through literature or, specifically, a proletarian literary movement methodologically armed with realist, "socially realist" criteria or with some tenets of avant-gardism. Yoshimoto had demonstrated the fallacy of these views; he argued that literature never makes contact with living reality through the transfer of knowledge to the masses by an intelligentsia, nor through any sort of literary or cultural movement, for it is an imaginative construct subtended by a complex and evolving accumulation of works of literature, national or international. It is sustained by the individual writer's or artist's consciousness and grasp of contemporary problems. Takei then

in Masaki Kyosuke's[3] critique (it doesn't deserve to be called that) of *Manual of Ninja Martial Arts,* but I even kept quiet about that. For I thought it was futile to respond to or get angry at those who, neither understanding nor trying to understand anything about the filmmaking process, make pronouncements based only on their own very narrow experiences of movements, life, and theory and who, moreover, bear ill will to begin with.

Matsumoto Toshio is of the same opinion regarding their lack of understanding of filmmaking. One group of Matsumoto's articles was a great stimulus for us because, while aware that he himself does sufficiently understand it, he still spoke from a broad perspective about how films ought to be. Nevertheless, after that he began to assume the stance of someone who does understand what filmmaking means. I'd like to ask him when he attained that understanding. At any rate, from that time on his writing went awry. It seems that the Ishido-Matsumoto debate will continue for some time to come, and inevitably, since it benefits our phantom journals commercially; however, it would be better if it were to stop now. Since it would be cruel of me to name a winner or loser, I will not do so, but I knew what the result would be from the beginning. Ishido Toshiro is speaking from the point of view of one who understands filmmaking. In comparison, Matsumoto spoke as if deceiving himself into thinking he knows something that he doesn't. This was not good, neither for Matsumoto nor for those of us who had been thinking that we would learn something from this debate. Matsumoto should have resolutely taken the position that he doesn't understand filmmaking, but that he would talk about the way films ought to be. I frequently hope that Matsumoto will return to this position as quickly as possible and spend his life educating us, as he did in the early days of our movement.

---

emerged to form a literary movement that was "progressive" to the extent that it was founded on the belief in an inevitable transition from capitalism to socialism. This transition, to follow a period of peaceful coexistence of the two major systemic blocs, was to be "democratic" insofar as it would engender a nonbureaucratic process of decision making in opposition to that of the old Japan Communist Party before Khrushchev's denunciation of Stalin. The organ of their movement was to be the magazine New Japanese Literature, issued by a group of like-minded writers and other artists. Yoshimoto regarded this as a farcical repetition of the postwar Modern Literature group, because it retained its faith in the role of intelligentsia at a time when the masses had no need of one, and it still gave credence to the role of political ideology in literature's relation to reality. It developed into a diminutive version of the Modern Literature group because it had eliminated the "anthropological" approach introduced by *Modern Literature* along with the political ideology nurtured by the bitter wartime experiences. Oshima had been a contributing member of the *New Japanese Literature* group.

3.   A critic who contributed articles to *New Japanese Literature,* and whose theoretical position was similar to that of Hanada.

Manual of Ninja Martial Arts. 1967.

Obviously, I am not saying that people who are not familiar with filmmaking shouldn't talk about films. They must talk about films. However, I would like them to always have a keen understanding of the point of view from which they confront the film. If they do that, we will probably be able to discover the personal angle from which they are theorizing about film. Texts thus written will probably be educational for those of us who make films because they will inevitably include things that cannot occur to us. Now there are too many instances in which the opposite takes place. Too many statements are made by people who act as though they understand the film-making process despite the fact that they do not. To give a familiar example, there are the statements on the problem of directors who don't make films. Those who deceive themselves into thinking they understand the filmmaking process confine all problems to the director's company and other external circumstances. The problem, however, lies elsewhere, both inside and outside the director—for the most part inside. There were three years during which I was unable to make films—a short period, as I think about it now. You could say that there was no company that would hire me to make a film and leave it at that, but I don't think that was the whole story. If there had been a film that I was sure I wanted to make, I could have taken it around to companies. I also could have gone around looking for someone to put up the money. But I didn't do that. Psychologically, I was not in a position to make a film. I think I would like to make a film about this inner state sometime (Federico Fellini's *8½* alludes to it, but doesn't seem to me to capture it perfectly) and so I won't go into detail about it here, but this is something I can speak of with confidence, having experienced it personally. Insofar as non-productivity is a psychological problem, there is no need for anyone to sympathize with directors who aren't making films. Nor does this mean we must scorn them either. In a director's long life, it is completely natural for him to have three, five, or even ten years during which he doesn't make films. There is no need for the director himself to feel shame or fear. This, at least, ought to be obvious, even to people who don't know how films are made—if they are aware of their ignorance. However, with superficial knowledge and they like to make guesses about mundane problems such as those in the relationship between the director and the company, they lose touch with the basis of the problem. If they decide on their point of view resolutely and think about it in a disinterested way, the significance, for the Japanese film, of the fact that none of those considered to be master directors made a film last year, for example, will become quite clear.

Here, I really should stop, but because it would trouble me if readers were not able to surmise the rest, I will state it clearly. The problem of the silence of masters should not be considered chiefly as the crisis of the decline of a film industry that cannot let them make films. It must be understood as follows: as a group, the masters cannot, for internal reasons make films and that this is a sign of changing artistic trends in the Japanese film. Looked at in this way, it will become clear that the greatness of Shindo Kaneto,[4] which enables him to continue his creative work furiously in the midst of this, does not depend on his business acumen or organizational skills. Rather, his greatness shines through because of the creative flame that burns brightly inside him.

It is said that the Japanese film is bad now, that it is no good. It is said that there is no decent work. I don't agree. I think that the Japanese film is good. I think that it is changing. I think that it will improve even. Those who say that the Japanese film is bad can see only the films of the past. They can't see the films of the present. Their opinions, dominant in mass media, have even come to penetrate the hearts of the people in the film world. We have to fight this. We also have to fight those who put on progressive and artistic airs and say that the Japanese film is bad and those within the film world who decry today's Japanese film. Beginning around the fall of last year, my desire to confront this problem suddenly increased, and since then I have been arguing and fighting night and day, everywhere, from public forums such as symposia and interviews to private drinking parties. I'm not likely to change my position next year, either.

4.   Shindo Kaneto is an internationally known filmmaker and scriptwriter. Arriving in Kyoto from Hiroshima, he went to work in 1934 in the film-processing laboratory at the Shinko Kinema Studio. In 1936 he moved to Tokyo to become an assistant in the art department of the company's newly constructed studios for modern dramatic films in Oizumi, Tokyo. He worked under the art director Mizutani Hiroshi while writing one script after another. After winning prizes for his scripts, he was able to move to the script department. Hearing that his artistic mentor, Mizutani, was to go to Kyoto to work for Mizoguchi Kenji's *A Tale of Loyal Retainers of the Genroku Era* (*Genroku Chushingura,* 1941–42) at the Koa Film Studio, he rushed off to follow him and study Mizoguchi's filmmaking. Mizoguchi proved to be a very severe master. Shindo directed the construction of the full-scale set of the interior of Edo castle. Shochiku bought out the Koa Film Studio and Shindo moved to the script department of the Shochiku Studio. Upon his return from the war, he wrote Mizoguchi's *Woman's Victory* (*Josei no Shori,* 1946) and *My Love Burns* (*Waga Koi wa Moeru,* co-scripted with Yoda Yoshitaka, 1949). His real success came with his collaboration on Yoshimura Kimisaburo films: *A Ball at the Anjo's* (*Anjoke no Butokai,* 1947), *A Brilliant Day of My Life* (*Waga Shogai no Kagayakeru Hi,* 1948), and *Costumes in Deception* (*Istuwareru Seiso,* 1952). He made his directorial debut with *The Story of a Beloved Wife* (*Aisai Monogatari,* 1951) for which he wrote the script. At the end of the U.S. occupation in 1952, he tackled a subject unapproachable until then, the atomic bomb, in *Children of Hiroshima* (*Genbaku no Ko,* 1953), which was extremely successful. *The Barren Island* (*Hadaka no Shima,* 1960), composed with no dialogue, established his international reputation. He founded a long-lasting independent production company, the Modern Film Association (Kindai Eiga Kyokai) together with Yoshimura Kimisaburo. Upon Yoshimura's death, Shindo became the sole representative of Kindai Eiga Kyokai. He is still active and has written several books on the cinema.

However, this fight is inherently one that should be fought by those who theorize film. The task of those of us who make films is to provide our work ammunition for them. Thus, our fervent desire is that the ammunition we provide be used effectively to strike the enemy. However, because we are always trying to make new kinds of ammunition, they often don't know how to use it. There will probably be those who say, "What are you talking about? The ammunition you send us rattles, and we don't know where the bullets will be coming from." There are those who will say, "Your ammunition is always the same. We're tired of it already." I think, however, that the reason they say such things is that their position on film is not clearly defined. It is possible to fight whether or not you understand arms manufacture. However, it is obvious that if you act as though you know what goes into making them when you don't, your attitude when dealing with weapons will be irrational.

With this in mind, I intend to spend some time here correcting, one by one, the principal mistakes in attitude of critics and theorists. So far I have outlined my basic views.

I also plan to spend some time writing about what goes into making a film. However, speaking frankly, I can't say that I fully understand what does go into making a film. Thus, I plan to explore the question as I write. Moreover, I would be troubled if anyone thought that he or she understood filmmaking immediately after reading such a text. In any event, understanding the filmmaking process is extremely difficult. (There were two or three things I wanted to write on the subject of *Manual of Ninja Martial Arts* and *A Study of Japanese Bawdy Songs,* but I have already exceeded my allotted space.)

In writing about the attitude of those who theorize about film, I raised the question of understanding. My main point was that I cared not at all whether they understood it, but that they must have a clear self-awareness of their stance on that issue. Reactions to this appeared immediately.

In a symposium in the May issue of *Scenario,* in response to Ogawa Toru's[5] presentation of my views, Hayashi Tamaki[6] says, "I gave up the notion of trying to understand films from the inside." I understand the seriousness of Hayashi Tamaki, who has expressed his concern about the position to take when reviewing films for the newspapers. Therefore, although I don't want anyone to give up "trying to under-

5.   A critic and longtime editor of a monthly magazine, *Film Art* (Oshima refers to this kind of film journal as the "phantom journal"). Limited readership makes it very difficult to sustain monthly publication. He has had, on occasion, to feature eye-catching articles or debates, inviting popular artists or controversial ideologues to the journal.
6.   Critic and contributor to *Film Art, Film Criticism,* and *Scenario.*

stand films from the inside" that easily, I accept his statement because so few critics are now serious. I was surprised at the following statement by Onchi Hideo:[7] "In order to really understand, you have to make one or two films as an assistant director."

What on earth is he saying? When I said that it was difficult to understand film-making, in no way did I mean that understanding required you to be present at the scene of a film's production. It is absolutely untrue that you will understand what goes into making a film by being present at the production of one or two films as an assistant director. Far from it: there are those who have tried making five or six films as a director and still don't understand it. Conversely, some understand after working as assistant director on just one film. There are probably also critics who understand even though they have never observed a film production. They are the exceptions, however.

What I am trying to say is that only those who have participated actively in the making of a film can understand what goes into making a film. "Making a film" must not be construed narrowly as meaning being present at a film production. That is why I chose the words "making a film." For example, even if one is a film director, this is not necessarily a guarantee that it is he is who makes films. This is even truer of the crew and the actors. On the other hand, by supporting some work and negating others, it is obviously possible for a critic to make films. This does not mean giving absolute support to one particular group of actual work. It means having an image of the ideal work and supporting works that approach it. Of course, if you have only two or three works that you consider ideal, that cannot be called having your own standard. Critics of that sort don't understand what goes into making a film. As stated above, their understanding does not matter; however, they must speak from an awareness of their position. Because he is an old friend, I can say the following without anxiety: The time is coming when Onchi Hideo will have to consider seriously whether he himself understands filmmaking.

At the end of the symposium, Onchi Hideo says, "Recently I saw *The Battle of Algiers* and was very deeply impressed. . . . In the future, I too would like to make *The Battle of Algiers*." When it comes to this, I feel he is pitiful. In my view a film such as *The Battle of Algiers* should not be praised by those who know what filmmaking consists of.

7.   Onchi Hideo joined Toho in 1955 as an assistant director. His first film, *The Young Wolf* (*Wakai Okami,* 1961), did not impress the company executives. He is rather good at program pictures dealing with topics and themes of contemporary youth.

Film magazines and other areas of journalism have been in an uproar about *The Battle of Algiers* over the past two or three months. Nearly all have expressed the kind of vehement admiration you'd expect from people cheering for their own racial independence. Furthermore, several would-be politicians have interpreted the contents of the film as promoting their own interests and they used it for their own political ends. This is a total farce. Films can't be used for political purposes. A film can be truly political only when it deeply moves the individual spectator. A film speaks only to the individual. In Japan today, cheers—whether for racial independence or for terrorism—are nothing more than emotions that are already at hand. There are already many kinds of melodrama that appeal to these emotions. Nevertheless, the fact that Japanese film critics as a whole are praising *The Battle of Algiers,*—which is for the most part merely a melodrama—to this extent is enough to convince one that they are experiencing a temporary stoppage of thinking. This must not go unlamented. (The director of *The Battle of Algiers,* Pontecorvo, was also in charge of writing the music. What is it about that music, which doesn't make you think of anything? It is the epitome of melodramatic music.)

As Ishido Toshiro has rightly observed, the biggest problem of *The Battle of Algiers* is the three-year gap between the death of Ali, the leader who remains at the front lines of the people's struggle for liberation, and the sudden uprising of the entire people. The narration of the film doesn't reveal a single reason for the uprising and says that no one knew the motive for it. Nearly all of the reviews of *The Battle of Algiers* have naively swallowed the narration. "No one knew." Of course, they also naively believe that the makers of this film didn't know. Can we leave it at that, however? If we do, this film is utterly ridiculous. If "no one knew" is the current view of the Algerian public, or of a majority there, there is no point in making the work without some personal statement. Of course, there are those who make films that merely go along with public or majority opinion, and naturally, some praise those films, but even those who are usually critical of that sort of thing admire *The Battle of Algiers* unreservedly. Here lies the essential weakness of this work; however, since in spite of everything, I don't think that the people who made this film are fully responsible so I would like to consider it further.

I cannot believe that the creators of *The Battle of Algiers* prepared absolutely no response about the reasons behind the uprising. As Ishido Toshiro points out, the reason is contained in the structure of the work. It begins with Ali a moment before his death, goes back to the fighting that took place earlier, and then returns to Ali a moment before his death, showing it. That the uprising of three years later is placed directly after Ali's death is clearly intentional. If that is the case, one naturally has to doubt the statement, "No one knew." One has to think that the filmmakers had prepared another response. But in Japan, this occurred to practically no one.

Naturally, Ishido Toshiro, who understands filmmaking, has made a correct analysis to this point, but he then falls into sentimentality (saying, for example, "We are somewhere in this three-year gap") and doesn't pursue it further. I would really like to take this up with Ishido sometime. My feeling is that we aren't in the three-year gap at all. I think that we are living in a different kind of time. I am also opposed to Ishido's toying with political arguments such as those of the left wing that say that a general strike is a means of negating terrorism. I can't bear to see Ishido, who is first class when he writes about the arts, drop down suddenly to third class when he theorizes about politics. We must strictly avoid talking about art and politics as a unit whenever we feel like it.

Matsuda Masao[8] (in the April issue of *Film Review*)[9] has offered a solution to the problem presented by Ishido. This is the best piece that has been written about *The Battle of Algiers*. Matsuda poses the question, "Is the reason that the entire populace staged a demonstration three years after Ali's death really an insoluble riddle?" He seeks the answer from the meaning of Ali's silence inside the wall. Matsuda says, "The silence of Ali, who refuses all conversation with the French *colons*,[10] who symbolize intellectual ascension, is paired beautifully with his subconscious dependence on violence. . . . The silence of the lower classes, who constitute the overwhelming majority (a silence with no possibility of communication and which may be termed a nonpolitical consciousness) can be politically organized." And he says that "The pulse of his emotions beats unsteadily in the depths of Ali's consciousness as he is silent within the wall and, three years later, transcends time and space to transmigrate to the insurrection of the lower classes at the Casbah." These words are so fine that I want to agree with them in almost every respect. Moreover, I feel that I have seen not only Omar, the youth mentioned by Ogawa Toru, amidst the insurgents, but Ali as well.

---

8.   Critic and a compassionate leftist ideologue, Matsuda Masao, like Adachi Masao, played in Oshima's *Death by Hanging*. He launched an openly leftist film journal, *Film Review* (*Eiga Hihyo*), in the late 1960s.

9.   This is a new *Film Review* (*Eiga Hihyo*) in a format different from that of the earlier publication of the same name, which was discontinued early in 1959. This new journal was founded by Adachi Masao, Aikuro Hisato, Sasaki Mamoru, Hiraoka Masaaki and Matsuda Masao in the later 1960s. By this time, the editor-in-chief of *Film Criticism* (*Eiga Hyoron*) had been changed. Sato Tadao was replaced by Sato Shigeomi, who was interested in avant-garde cinema and introduced New American Cinema and the Underground Cinema to Japanese readers.

10.   Immigrants of European descent in Algeria.

How wonderful if *The Battle of Algiers* were the work Matsuda Masao says it is. But I don't think it is. I think that the revelation that Ali's silence is linked to the uprising is merely that of Matsuda, who saw the film, and not that of the film's authors. Matsuda, a talented man, extracted this from the film by his extensive consideration of this question. The creators of *The Battle of Algiers* fall far short of that.

Why, then, did they fall short of Matsuda Masao? This question implies another. What intention lies behind *The Battle of Algiers*?

The first, most basic idea that comes to mind is that they were trying to make a record of the people's struggle for racial independence. Nearly all of the critics in Japan stop here. The most important question, however, is at the next level. Why make a film just then about the people's struggle for racial independence? "Because a people's struggle for racial independence is a good thing" is an irrelevant response. No film is made in isolation from the question of why it is being made now. There always has to be a purpose.

I know nothing of the production history of this film. Nor do I know anything about the political situation of Algeria after independence. One thing that can be gleaned from watching this film, however, is that it was made in a form that would obtain the cooperation of the government. Which means that the government (that is, the present system) intended to make a film about the people's racial independence now. To what end I don't really know, but it is certain that it was to support the present system. Were the filmmakers in complete agreement with the government's intentions? Did they, too, make this film in support of the present system? I can't help feeling that the Algerian filmmakers had another intention. One indication of their intent is the structure. The structure is too unusual for it to be saying "all hail" to the people's struggle for racial independence. I daresay that the Algerian filmmakers might have been planning to include a criticism of their present system somewhere. I feel that, for example, they might have wanted to say something like "the spirit of the revolution has been lost." But they also had a weakness: they had to make the film with the cooperation of the current system. For that reason they couldn't come out with their theme clearly so that they were unable to do anything other than make a film that could be understood only by those who wanted to understand it. Along came the foolish Japanese intelligentsia, who thought, like the Italians, that as long as it was a people's struggle for racial independence it was a good thing, no matter where or how it was portrayed. They smeared the nectar of melodrama all over it. Thus, it wasn't understood even by those of good will. And thus the trashy *Battle of Algiers* was born. Venice gave it an award, and everyone in Japan praised it.

Moral: don't fret if you're not successful at festivals. For every wise man there are a thousand fools: that is as true abroad as in Japan.

If we make films that take the past as their subject, they must also contain premonitions about the future. In *The Battle of Algiers,* for example, there is not a trace of such a premonition. It may be only natural that those who continue to make films full of premonition—in an age when films without any are praised—are treated as lunatics. We must move forward, however. For me, as I move forward with my next films, *Japanese Summer: Double Suicide* and *Murderer's Encyclopedia,* Matsuda Masao's words are greatly encouraging.

(*Film Art,* April–June 1967)

The Error of Mere Theorization of Technique

I think that what set apart the summer of 1967 in Japan was the movement to make war an everyday thing.

All of the conspicuously showy newspaper advertisements for publishing houses were for war chronicles. It would probably not even be an exaggeration to say that they constituted over half of each day's advertisements. In response, the books most visibly displayed in bookstore windows were also all war-related.

The same was true of the film world. Although the number of war films did not increase, they attracted a larger public. *Ah! The Cherry Blossoms of Those Days!*[1] having shown the way, *Japan's Longest Day*[2] was that summer's biggest hit.

What does this state of affairs signify? Although this tendency had begun emerging gradually several years ago, why in the world has it suddenly become so dominant?

At this time the United States returned the documentary films of atomic explosion that had been seized, and paintings depicting the war were also coming back. A television director said that he would like to use these paintings as the basis for a project of some sort. Even in these paintings, which at first glance appear to justify blindly war, resistance is clearly present in the brushstrokes. He wondered if he couldn't make some use of that. I don't doubt his good intentions. But what meaning does that resistance have now? Why would anyone think that this discovery would accomplish something? We have to search for a larger meaning.

The return of the war paintings, to be sure, and even the return of the atomic bomb film—which in itself is generally thought to have positive significance—are

1. *Ah! The Cherry Blossoms of Those Days* (*Ah! Doki no Sakura,* dir. Nakajima Sadao, Toho Production, 1967).
2. *Japan's Longest Day* (*Nippon no Ichiban Nagai Hi,* dir. Okamoto Kihachi, Toho Production, 1967).

probably part of a movement to make the people of Japan accept war as an everyday matter. Otherwise, there would be no reason for their having been returned at exactly the same time that war-related works were suddenly dominating the mass media.

In this way, our environment is now overflowing with war images that clearly have one intention. It matters very little that among these images are depictions of tragedy, pain, and meaninglessness. These overflowing images of war—including the tragic, painful, and even meaningless ones—are intended to penetrate our consciousness so that they will be processed with our everyday sensibilities. Once they have become the stuff of every day life, we will probably accept the tragic, the painful, and the meaningless just that way. Then the state of affairs in Vietnam will become commonplace inside us as well. If that happens, we will be just one step away from taking the stage as direct mass murderers, guns in hand, of the Vietnamese people.

What are we to do in this situation? What can be done by those who have some responsibility for the images inside us? Almost nothing, except to become accomplices to the state of things?

It was precisely this that angered me about Nihon Television's "11 PM" show of August 21. I used the rudeness of the imbecilic director, a certain Tsuzuki, as an excuse for anger, but it was merely an excuse. In actuality I was angry at the irresponsibility of the television people, who are largely responsible for the images we see. Of course, not all television people are irresponsible. However, it is obvious that unless television, which is controlled by a state licensing system, establishes a critical nucleus in response to this state of affairs, it will immediately be swept away and become irresponsible. The best directors, producers, and writers of Japanese television's short history have been embroiled in a bitter struggle over this very point. Nevertheless, things are just about as bad as they can get, and young directors have emerged—a new type of infinitely inferior person who thinks that irresponsibility is an example of a good attitude, a new technique—who will not carry on the tradition of that bitter struggle.

They can be generally characterized as follows: first, they are interested in something. However, because they are mostly of low intelligence, they are unable to become interested in something before someone else has. Usually it is after the newspapers or weekly magazines or one or two leading television programs have introduced it. Moreover, they don't have their own opinions, since they aren't capable of thought. They arm themselves with, at most, a commentary from a weekly magazine. Beyond that, the most they are able to do is go to the scene or assemble people at a television station and aim the cameras and microphones. "It'll work out as I go along." "Something will probably turn up while I'm looking." These are their basic thoughts. But nothing happens, of course. Nothing turns up. That's because there is nothing inside them to begin with. The program ends in the midst of this indefiniteness. "Thanks for your efforts." "It was pretty interesting, wasn't it?" "Yes, it was interesting." Inane self-satisfaction. Even if it was, by some coincidence, interesting, it was only because the material was interesting. If the material is fairly interesting, it will even be interesting the first and second time it is rebroadcast. The material keeps changing. They follow along joyfully. The current state of affairs continues to develop. They will probably continue on nonchalantly in a Japan that has been transformed into a battlefield. "Thanks for your efforts. It was pretty interesting, wasn't it?" Can it possibly be a good thing to leave guys like this alone?

Especially intolerable is their claim that they are innovators, that this irresponsible, passive way of doing things is one form of documentary, an application of "happening-television."[3] This is neither innovative nor anything else—and not worth being described as a documentary or a happening. Ultimately it is passive, uncritical, affirmative of the present situation, and beautifully consistent with television's direction in the current political climate. That is why it is tolerated. Being unashamed, however, young directors are totally unaware of this. In reality, the imbecilic director Tsuzuki Somebody appears to be a man who thinks that he is innovative insofar as he has requested scripts from Tamura Tsutomu and Sasaki Mamoru. I patiently tried to explain this, but I wasn't able to make him understand. That is why I call him an imbecile. However, the situation is truly frightening. Can human beings afford this blindness as things change?

I would offer a warning to the present and future critics and artists of Japanese film. Long ago—I think I can call it that—in April 1961, NHK started a program called "You Are the Jury." It was a courtroom show that took social problems as its theme, with a lawyer taking the supporting stance and a public prosecutor taking the opposing stance; witnesses, evidence, and supporting arguments were presented by both sides. Although stiff, it was an early version of today's talk shows. Thinking about it now, I can't help feeling emotional about it because the theme of the first episode was "war chronicles"—the boom was just beginning at that time. Actually, rather than a boom, it was more that people were merely discovering that these things existed, but by then—one year after the anti-Security Treaty riots—the seed had already been planted for the overwhelming boom in war chronicles that is taking place now.

3.   The English word "happening" is used in Japanese to indicate a film or television program that is produced using "Candid Camera"-type techniques.

Mitarai Tatsuo, who defended war chronicles, is alive and well, and so am I, who was the public prosecutor. Considering that war chronicles have gone beyond the boom stage to become an everyday thing, my superficial defeat was inevitable; however, because I am, needless to say, a person who will fight through an infinite number of losing battles, that in itself doesn't sadden me. What I want to mention here is the exceptional farsightedness of the directors at NHK who were in charge of planning this project six years ago. They predicted the future successfully and for that reason sent me off to a battlefield where I would inevitably be defeated as a fighter on their own side. What is a fighter on your own side?

Two months later I was asked to appear on "You Are the Jury" for the second time, as a defender of "young people of recent times." The public prosecutor was a member of the National Public Safety Commission, Obama Ritoku. I was reluctant to appear. If I appeared, I would naturally have to defend the National Federation of Students' Self-Government Associations. I would have to defend a certain neighborhood party. I would have to attack the Defense Academy students. As my personal opinion, this was nothing to be ashamed of in itself, but I naturally felt weighed down by the opposing view, held by NHK as well as the majority of the Japanese public. Of course, there are probably people with more vehement opinions than mine who don't appear on television; my reason for feeling that way, however, was that it is a rather heavy burden for those who do appear on television to have to express opinions that always border on the vehement. In response to that, the directors, who were about my age, coerced me into appearing by saying, "If you won't speak up, who will?" It was clear that they wanted someone to speak in their place. That moved me. In them I saw an activism that was diametrically opposed to the attitude that says, "It will work out as we go along," or "Something will turn up while we're shooting."

That program ultimately went off the air after less than a year. I was shooting either *The Catch* or *Amakusa Shiro Tokisada* at the time and don't know the details of its demise. And I have no way of finding out why it ended. However, I can't believe that it was completely unrelated to the activist stance of the directors. At any rate, they ended their battle there and moved it to a new location. As long as one is active, the battle will continue. The significance of the battle, however, shifts a little each time. This is frightening. I am now trying to grasp the significance of that fear. To what did they transfer their battle, and how? No, before I deal with that, I must explain the battle from which they came. They had been members of "The True Face of Japan."

It is difficult to theorize about television programs that are constantly disappearing. I didn't have a television when "The True Face of Japan," one of the pioneers of the television documentary in Japan, was originally broadcast (from November 10,

1957 to April 5, 1964), and although I later watched tapes of it for a lecture at Tokyo University's Newspaper Research Institute, I can't really discuss it in great detail. Fortunately, however, there was a written debate about it called "The True Face of Japan Debate" from 1959 to 1960, between Hani Susumu[4] and NHK's Segawa Masaaki and Yoshida Naoya, who agreed to respond to his criticism. The debate has a lot to teach us about the problems that confronted "The True Face of Japan."

In his critique, Hani Susumu said that "The True Face of Japan" had two key strengths. One was that the amateur producers sought unique subjects, which caused the camera to come up with curious images in the course of its struggle with their conceptual intentions. The other was the fact that it succeeded as a totally new kind of televised social criticism by avoiding explanations through the use of a nontraditional documentary narration that competed with the image. However, Hani Susumu continued, these methods had now been adopted by cinema so that the effects of old documentaries, which terrified spectators by this direct grasp of reality, has been lost.

Hani's critique is truly accurate. The responses written by Segawa and Yoshida are not direct rebuttals. In many respects they are merely explanations of their position. That can't be helped. The critique is saying that the program was better before, but the producers must have had *some reason* for changing it. We should not expect their response to be satisfactory. But what is the reason for the change? The response doesn't speak clearly to that either. At most it merely says that although the techniques used may not be new to film, they're new to television, and many aspects of television are undiscovered as yet and will be explored through tireless experimentation. These things do not constitute a response, however. One must conclude that the reason the techniques of "The True Face of Japan" were changed in midstream will remain obscure.

In my view, the whole reason for this change in technique is political. Political pressure, both direct and indirect, compelled them to change their technique. Even

---

4.   Filmmaker who joined the Iwanami Film Company (Iwanami Eiga Sha) in 1948 and made many innovative documentaries: *Life and Water* (*Seikatsu to Mizu,* 1952), *Snow Festival* (*Yukimatsuri,* 1953), *Town and Sewage* (*Machi to Gesui,* 1953), *Children in the Classroom* (*Kyoshitsu no Kodomotachi,* 1955), and *Children Who Draw* (*E o Kaku Kodomotachi,* 1956). Iwanami produces educational and industrial films as well as public relations films. Hani's first feature film was *Bad Boys* (*Furyo Shonen,* 1960), a drama in which he directed the boys of a juvenile delinquents' reformatory. It maintains the documentary form and method. His other notable films are: *A Full Life* (*Mitasareta Seikatsu,* 1962), *She and He* (*Knojo to Kare,* 1963), *Bride of the Andes* (*Andes no Hanayome,* 1966), *The Poem of a Fairy* (*Yosei no Shi,* 1971), and *A Timetable in the Morning* (*Gozenchu no Jikanwari,* 1972). Hani founded his own production company, Hani Productions, in 1961. He is the author of several books on cinema.

if narration that is so strong as to compete with the image does not necessarily go so far as to negate the current state of affairs, it clearly prompts doubts and criticism of it. If you look at the subjects of the episodes that Hani Susumu cites as having impressed him, "The National Federation of Students' Self-Government Associations," "A Haven for Drunks," and "The Korea inside Japan," it is clear that all of them have strong political significance. Did that sort of thing come to be prohibited? The excellent producers and directors then thought: "Why couldn't we express our intentions through the exclusive use of images, without depending on narration? Because compared to words, which can easily be checked, images can be interpreted in a variety of ways." As I have discovered, this is how the episode of "The True Face of Japan" aired at the height of the anti-Security Treaty riots, came to emphasize film techniques.

Were these conscientious producers aware that their shift in technique was deeply connected to politics? What about that outstanding critic? I can't believe that both were completely unconscious of that fact. If they were conscious of it, did they hide it, repressing their bitterness? "The True Face of Japan Debate" ends in a very gentlemanly fashion. There is, however, an important lesson to be learned from this.

When there is a change in technique, when there is a lot of theorizing about technique, there is an obvious change—particularly a political change—in the circumstances surrounding one's autonomy. The lesson, whether one is aware of it or not, is that this is when the maintenance of autonomy really becomes an issue. This is when many people lose their autonomy. What must one do to avoid losing autonomy? I shall briefly now address this question.

Unfortunately, the transformation of "The True Face of Japan" was unsuccessful. After the Asanuma incident that autumn, the names of the producers of "The True Face of Japan" disappeared from the screen. In the face of political power that strong, their transformed technique was almost powerless. Thus they changed battles again and again. To "You Are the Jury" and "Chronicle of Today." And, after the end of "The True Face of Japan," to "Images of the Present Day." But ultimately the change in technique was only that. To triumph over circumstances even temporarily, the establishment of new techniques, rather than just a change in technique, is necessary. How can new techniques be established?

Those who, like myself, find writing unbearably disagreeable, tend to want to stop writing whenever they find an excuse to do so. This morning, too, I sat down at my desk, knowing that I had to fulfill my obligation to *Film Art*. Just then *New Japanese Literature* came in the mail. I flipped through it absently. There were the so-called film reviews, which I had to skim, thinking that there would probably be an unfavorable review of one of my works. As usual, there was bad-mouthing that constituted neither a review nor anything else. It merely said that my writing was unpleasant, and ended with the cliche that the decline of Oshima's work must lie in the decline of his critical sense. The writer was Masaki Kyosuke. I first heard his name a long time ago, but I don't really know what it is that he does. I know only that he is someone who has always managed to hurl nothing but abuse at me and my works. It isn't only Masaki: the person previously in charge of film reviews, Kitamura Yoshinori, was the same way. The film reviews in *New Japanese Literature* have hurled only abuse at all of my work since I started at Sozosha (while not even bothering to review a work like *The Diary of Yunbogi*).[5] I don't want to read this type of thing, but they send it to me and ultimately I can't help reading it. I think the literary movement of *New Japanese Literature* once was very significant, but since it was toppled by just one individual, Yoshimoto Takaaki,[6] it has become meaningless. (I can't understand

5.   This entire film is composed of still photographs of boys, enlarged to normal 35-mm format. The photographs were taken while he was traveling in Korea, and the soundtrack was composed of Oshima's script and the fragments of diary entries written by a Korean boy. Published in Japan, the diary was a best-seller at that time. The dramatic structure of the image track owes much to the film's editor, Uraoka Keiichi.

6.   Perhaps the most influential critic and thinker of the past three decades in Japan. Oshima seems to imply that the axe of Yoshimoto's critique fell upon only Takei Akio and the literary movement of the New Japanese Literature group. It was, however, directed at Oshima as well. (See Yoshimoto Takaaki, "What is the inversion of the value of the post-war thoughts?" in *The Contemporary Eye* (*Gendai no Me*, February, 1964). Oshima says, "I think that formerly the literary movement of *New Japanese Literature* was very significant, but since it was toppled by just one individual, Yoshimoto Takaaki, its existence has become meaningless." However, the *New Japanese Literature* was, from the beginning, a diminutive reprise of the *Modern Literature* movement (see note on Takei Akio). Yoshimoto further claimed that all literary and artistic movements are arbitrary and gratuitous and that they should never command the masses with a set of political or artistic ideologies like an "intelligentsia" or a group of cultural bureaucrats. In the December 1963 issue of *The Contemporary Eye*, Takei wrote "The Dissolution of the Sentimental Autonomist," which was meant to be a critique of Yoshimoto's thought. Oshima's "The leader of the Cultural Movement," advocated an artistic or cultural movement with a group of creative artists at its core, so that it could exist free of the logic of capital or capitalism. This position incurs the objection, however, that no artistic movement can be free of the logic of capital in a capitalist world. Moreover, artistic movements and practices flourish and grow through the mediation of capital and its logic. Takei's logic, on the other hand, reflected that of a cultural bureaucracy's belief in the "inevitable transition of capitalism to socialism." Yoshimoto predicted in "What is the Inversion of the Value of the Post-War Thoughts?" that it would take at least a decade for his point to be understood. Although Oshima's filmmaking cannot be interpreted as the enactment of the "ideal" of an art movement proposed in 1963, it was, ironically, just ten years later that Oshima dissolved his Sozosha. Yoshimoto soon completed a major work, *What Is Beauty for Language?* (*Gengo ni totte Bi towa Nani ka*, 2 vols, Tokyo: Keiso Shobo, 1965). His latest publication is *Theory of the High Image* (*Hai imeeji Ron*, 2 vols, Tokyo: Fukutake Shoten, 1988–90). For his theoretical writings on cinema, see "About the Cinematic Expression," in *Kinema Bi-weekly* (*Kinema Junpo*, the latter issue of March 1960) and "What is the Cinematic Expression?" in *Kinema Bi-weekly* (*Kinema Junpo*, the latter issue of May 1960).

why people like Ogawa Toru, Ishido Toshiro, and Saito Ryuho remain members of the *New Japanese Literature* group. Indeed, because those people joined the group as recruits when infighting with the group's communist faction prompted an effort to increase the membership—I was also invited to join by Takei Akio, but refused—they may not take their membership too seriously.) Because I didn't want them to send it to me any longer, I didn't send in my subscription money at the end of last year, as I had at the end of the previous year. They continue sending it to me anyway, but with this year coming to a close, I hereby request that they kindly not send it to me next year.

The existence of insincere people like Masaki destroys my will to write. Making films is enjoyable, though it is at the same time like a hard spiritual exercise, but I think of writing as a kind of obligation. The reason I think I must fulfill my obligation is that others are seriously fulfilling theirs, even if it is painful for them. So when I encounter someone who is insincere, I feel sad and empty. That is why I start to feel like not writing.

Masaki will undoubtedly reply that those are Oshima's "nationalist ideas." Masaki really did say something like that in a symposium in *Perspectives*. In that symposium on film theory, "The Degeneration of the Critical Sense," Masaki's attitude is, by the way, obvious. He is, for example, unable to respond to Iijima Koichi[7] and to Sato Tadao's criticism of "The Opinion of the Movement Generation" by Hanada Kiyoteru and Takei Akio. In spite of the fact that Ijima and Sato are both expressing their own opinions, Masaki alone is unable to depart at all from the type of formulaic view that one might call a *New Japanese Literature*-type opinion.

Some ten years have passed since they first started advocating composite art, or artistic synthesis, but I don't know of a single artist or work that has emerged as a result. Notwithstanding, they still bandy those words about as if they were holy writ, criticizing me, who doesn't make films that way, as being a member of the party group rather than of the movement group. Hanada Kiyoteru may be the Oya Soichi[8] of the world of artistic movements, but naturally I took no notice of the fact that he categorized me in that way; that I am somehow able to continue producing meaningful work is partly because I was not deluded by their absurd sermons on "artistic synthesis." One other thing about his point that my film movement and my ilk are exclusionist and that I belong to the party group because I'm not a part of what they

7.   Critic and scholar of French literature.
8.   Social critic Oya Soichi (1900–1970) commented on the coming of the television age as the cretinization of 100 million (*ichioku sohakuchika*), the figure for the Japanese population at that time.

call the synthesized mass art movement: I think that movements are exclusionist by nature. They thereby display strength. Consider the October 8 riot at Haneda by the National Federation of Students' Self-Government Associations. They were able to strike that big a blow against an approximately equal number of riot police only because they divided themselves into a number of factions and fought in a decentralized way. What would have happened if there had been reciprocal communication horizontally, a vertical chain of command, and so on? If they had been watching the moves of their comrades on either side and waiting for orders, they undoubtedly would have lost their timing. Because the movements of each faction were independent, the opposition was unable to discern the movement of the whole and became confused. I think of artistic movements as the same sort of thing. An artistic movement emerges when a small number of people who are able to talk directly about creation in a day-to-day manner do something in common. Because art is, in that way, based on the special symbols of each of the small things in our daily lives, artistic movements arise only in the context of personal relationships. These people must split off into a number of individual artistic movements that produce outstanding work (including criticism).

Will the synthesized mass artistic movement that the *New Japanese Literature* people talk about really come about? I don't think so, but even if you give them the benefit of the doubt, will they be able to do anything more than politicize art? "Politicize art" is a strange expression, but the fact that *New Japanese Literature* fought the rulers of the Communist Party bureaucracy is one example of the politicization of art; that in itself is an example of something significant. It was an effort to protect art from the outside, which is different from generating art from the inside, however. I am not a narrow-minded person, so I won't say that there is no need to protect art from the outside. But it is natural to think that the basic problem of art lies in its generation from within, and artistic movements are inevitably movements of artistic creation. Protecting art from the outside and fostering it are, at best, merely artistic politics. I would like to say something for the benefit of those who can't live without calling themselves artistic political movements and movement groups, but I will omit it because artistic politics are always getting in the way of our artistic movements. That the formerly anticommunist *New Japanese Literature* group now has the same psychological makeup and mode of operation as the communist faction clearly shows the traps into which artistic politics can fall, does it not?

I have written for *New Japanese Literature* in the past, and I have felt it to be a strong presence in artistic politics. Also, at the time of my debut and now, Takei

Akio, with a sycophantic giggle, has fallen in line with Hanada Kiyoteru's criticism of me, but he was my strongest champion from the time that *Night and Fog in Japan* was banned through the movement to get it shown again. I am still grateful for that. (Now that I think about it, at that time Takei was also fighting a fierce battle with the communist cultural bureaucracy. He was able to see a variety of things clearly then. Later, while banishing that bureaucracy from *New Japanese Literature,* he ended by becoming a cultural bureaucrat.) *New Japanese Literature* still has many outstanding artists and critics, including the three film people I have been discussing. Out of respect and friendship for those people, I would suggest that the *New Japanese Literature* group dissolve as soon as possible and that the independent artistic movements reform themselves. (For the same reasons, I would like to suggest exactly the same thing to all of my friends in the *Film Images Art* group.)[9]

However, with rare exceptions, those who join these groups probably don't understand the groups' objective positions (which, moreover, they think are movements). If I were to add one last thing for the benefit of those people (knowing that it is an extra word, which will incur extra resentment), I would say, "Compare the existence in Japanese film of the small independent production companies Kindai Eikyo and Sozosha with the existence in literature of *New Japanese Literature.*" If you exclude the work in Japanese film produced by each of the small independent artistic movements of the past several years, such as Kindai Eikyo, Sozosha, Teshigawara Productions,[10] Gendai Eiga Sha, and Immamura Productions,[11] almost nothing remains.

How does *New Japanese Literature* compare to Japanese literature? (It goes without saying that the condition of Japanese literature as a whole is bad. Film is gen-

9.   A group of filmmakers and film theorists, notably Matsumoto Toshio and Okada Susumu, whose writings deserve theoretical investigation.
10.   Teshigawara Hiroshi's film production company. His first film was *Hokusai* (1953). The second was a documentary about a boxer, Jose Torres (1959). Teshigawara's first feature film was an adaptation of a television drama by Abe Kobo, *Pitfall* (*Otoshiana,* 1962), followed by *Woman of the Dunes* (1964), and *The Burnt-Up Map* (*Moetsukita Chizu,* 1968). All are based on Abe's novels and lauched Teshigawara's international reputation.
11.   Immamura Shohei's production company. Immamura first joined the Shochiku Studio as an assistant director in 1951 and transfered to Nikkatsu three years later. His first film, *The Stolen Desire* (*Nusumareta Yokujo,* 1958), was received as the work of a major new filmmaker. Almost all of his following films have stirred interest and discussions when screened: *Pigs and Battleships* (*Buta to Gunkan,* 1961), *The Insect Woman* (*Nippon Konchuki,* 1963), *Intentions of Murder* (*Akai Satsui,* 1964), *Pornographers: An Introduction to Anthropology* (*Erogotoshitachi yori,* 1966), *A Man Vanishes* (*Ningen Johatsu,* 1967), *The Deep Desire of the Gods* or *Kuragejima: Tales from a Southern Island* (*Kamigami no Fukaki Yokubo,* 1968), and *History of Post-war Japan as Told by a Bar Hostess* (*Nihon Sengo Shi: Madam Omboro no Seikatsu,* 1970). He made several important documentaries for television. He is the director of Yokohama TV Broadcasting and Film Production School.

erally considered bad now, but I think that literature is far worse.) Even if you subtract the works produced by *New Japanese Literature* (no, what should you subtract,
anyway?), Japanese literature remains exactly the same, doesn't it? Bad work (including criticism) should be compared with *Film Art. Film Art* is sometimes marred by
foolishness, such as symposia with Hanada and Takei. (This is probably commercialism, but a bad habit of this magazine is the gathering of somewhat famous middle-
aged artists and scholars from other journals for interviews and symposia. If they
want to theorize about film, let them write. It's not that they don't write, but that they
can't. I don't want people without the passion to theorize about film.) This, however,
is the mainstream of Japanese film criticism, and it holds sway over an overwhelming
majority of young students, in particular. Are the young people who are interested
in a literary career seriously reading *New Japanese Literature* now? And *Film Art* certainly doesn't constitute a synthesized mass artistic movement. Of course, the contributors probably rush to the assistance of these journals, but what's really
supporting them is the strong will and direction of the several editors who run things
on their own. I feel this in the selection of contributors and in the way things are
arranged as well; however the outstanding thing, not generally realized is the way
still photographs from films are collected—their selection, cropping and layout. I
was so impressed by the layout of stills that accompanied last month's special collection of reviews, "Japanese Summer: Double Suicide," that I thought it was a kind
of review in itself.

   Given the context of a magazine like *Film Art,* which is an artistic movement,
what is the point of seizing on some film artist or another and saying, "Hey, he is in
the party group," or "Hey, there is no activism in his films"? The movement which
includes Hanada and Takei is not an artistic movement—it is merely artistic politics.
Moreover, their labeling themselves a movement merely proves them to be artistic
politicians. This is exactly what is meant by the phrase "throwing one's weight
around without knowing one's real ability."

   I tried to explain this gently to Hanada and Takei so that they would understand, but they are not only indifferently unashamed, they continue as always to make
shameless pronouncements. So it has come to this. It is a case of reaping what you
sow.

   Now, to return at last to my original subject. . . . As is already clear, my conclusion is that there is a close relationship between technique and political pressure,
and changes in technique take place under such pressure. Furthermore, these
changes represent an effort by the artist to firmly establish his autonomy. When this
new technique, which is almost inevitable for the artist, is merely imitated by others,

and when critics theorize about technique in isolation from its basic roots, the result is an endless fall.

I had a reason for basing my argument on documentaries in particular. The artists and critics who were trying to create while taking part in politics considered the advocacy of documentary techniques in postwar Japan to be a way of avoiding political pressure, on the one hand, while allowing them to restore their atrophied fiction-creating abilities, on the other. (I realize that by saying this sort of thing I am inviting those who call themselves documentarists to lash out immediately, inviting the accusation of a dualist theory of documentary and fiction. The best fiction and the best documentary would probably coincide, and there is also probably such a thing as creating fiction in the spirit of the documentary. However, I think that nothing is gained by trotting out that kind of generality in the context of original creation. When the artist chooses a technique, it is a most certain, and inevitable thing in that he feels that he absolutely has to do this at this time. And that in itself was by no means either good or bad. The artists whose true selves were riding on it probably did good work, at least. However, because documentary technique regrettably became a fad, in that people paid lip service to it, those for whom the selection of that technique was in no way inevitable called themselves documentarists, which led in many cases to whole lives being wasted. Compared to that lot, the producers and directors of "The True Face of Japan" and "Nonfiction Playhouse" were placed in the position of being unable to make a show unless the documentary technique reflected their true selves, whether they liked it or not. Forced, moreover, by political pressure into becoming conscious of their technique, they established, at least temporarily, a documentary technique for "The True Face of Japan," as opposed for example, to a general documentary technique. As mentioned earlier, they had to transform that technique even further, but that does not constitute a lessening of their accomplishments.

Thinking about it this way, one can say that the outstanding environment for the postwar Japanese documentary was chiefly television, and that the people in film proper didn't produce outstanding work in which technique reflected their true selves, nor did they make theoretical contributions. Matsumoto Toshio may reply, "What about my stuff?" With all due respect, however, he unfortunately had only a basic theory of documentary to begin with, and he claims by mere application of these techniques the status of author and creator of films. Amazing! If there had been no documentary films, would Matsumoto have become an author?

Director Immamura Shohei's *A Man Vanishes* was flung just as it was into the midst of the Japanese film world, and that was sufficient to provoke debate. I was shooting in Kyoto at the time and so wasn't able to participate in the debate, but read later what had been written, and I sensed danger. Everybody was talking only about technique. And their way of debating was to say that technique exists a priori and Immamura either had used it well or hadn't. In particular, most pointed out that he had used it well, which will probably give rise to many imitators. Of course, imitators don't usually get as far as the filmmaking stage, but I can easily imagine many spiritual imitators coming into being. This will exert a bad influence on young people who are interested in film. Even if it doesn't, now is the time to flee. People start to avoid discussing theme. At such a time, the dominant tendency is to want to discuss technique only. The discussion of *A Man Vanishes* on the basis of technique alone intensified this tendency. I would therefore now like to discuss the significance of Immamura's technique.

What did Immamura think would emerge from the pursuit by his fiancee of a man who had disappeared? Had he known, he could have written a script and made it into a dramatic work. He didn't know what would come of it. Or, if he did know, he felt it would be dangerous to draw a conclusion based on it. He felt that it wasn't quite enough. One of these two motives, probably the latter, caused Immamura to start using the documentary technique. (He later said that tis was fiction, but it is a fact that he started by using the documentary technique and nothing can change that.)

Next there is the problem of theme. Was there a theme from the beginning, was it anticipated to some extent, or was there none at all? I think that there was hardly any theme.

If you combine the above two points, the result is that Immamura had, to a certain extent, assumptions about how the situation would evolve, but he couldn't anticipate the type of theme that would result. But isn't it likely that Immamura set out with thoughts along the lines of "We'll probably find a theme as we go along," or "At any rate it seems like a situation that will get interesting," or "Let's get on with it"?

This is the crudest starting point for a documentary. From the perspective of today's television documentaries, it is probably about five years behind the times. Of course, stupid directors influenced by the experimental "happening underground" might proceed this way. (In the future some fools will probably attempt to imitate *A Man Vanishes.*) Superior television documentarists, at least, wouldn't start out like this. However, there must have been a strong inner tension in Immamura as he dared to use the documentary technique, which he had never used before, even if it was a crude technique. I don't know much about Immamura's relationship with politics, nor can I be sure about the kind of pressure that forced him to change his technique. However, there was no likelihood of his being able to produce the film he had been wanting to do, *Kuragejima: Tales from a Southern Island,* and he was probably driven by his reputation as an erotic artist. It may not be possible to ascertain the reason, but something in Immamura made it inevitable that he choose a new technique. Once he got started, Immamura showed great tenacity. It is only his inner tension that makes the first half of *A Man Vanishes* worth seeing. If vulgar artists and imitators had set out from the same starting point, it would be impossible to sit through ten minutes of their work.

But, but . . . It is totally untrue to say that a documentary's theme is discovered in the process. Immamura realized that, of course, midway through the film. A decisive change in direction takes place there. It turns toward fictionalization. After that Immamura's inner tension changes qualitatively as well. His desperate effort as a professional artist who has to make the story consistent at all costs comes to the surface in the way he gropes simultaneously for technique and theme. (Mori Kota's *The River: Poem of Love*[12] contrasts with this. Mori also set out thinking that he'd discover a theme along the way, or that it would at least become clear, and although he despaired of this during the process, he brazened it out. The freshness of an amateur is there, but there is a limit.) The relationship between the fiancee and the older sister becomes interesting, and Immamura focuses on them persistently. However, this turns out to be a vicious circle, and no theme is discovered there. At that point the concept is brought out high-handedly for the last time: "I don't understand the truth."

"I don't understand the truth": is that the theme? I put this question to the many reviewers of *A Man Vanishes.* This is neither a theme nor anything else, since this type of conclusion can be drawn from any work. Also, it has no connection with the themes of any of Immamura's other films. An abstract theme like "I don't understand the truth" may be of interest to would-be essayists who find it clever, but if true authors make it an issue, it should always be argued in the context of the specific truth that is not understood. If he has no general understanding of the truth of facts, an artist should just give up writing. It would be distressing if a fraudulent concept of this type were to pervade the critical world like a form of mass hysteria. *A Man Vanishes* is a film that started off with the very mistaken notion that a subjective theme would emerge midway through, failed marvelously, made a tremendous effort to redeem itself, and had charm in that great effort. Although most of those who

12.   *The River: Poem of Love (Kawa Sono Uragiri ga Omoku,* dir. Mori Kota, 1967).

reviewed *A Man Vanishes* should see this mistake in technique, they see a triumph of technique. Actually this must be considered a film that exemplifies the failed documentary.

Immamura probably said that he doesn't understand the truth because he thought he doesn't understand "truth in the documentary." Thus he declares his revocation of the documentary technique that he had once used. Conceivably, people will differ as to whether they view this declaration of revocation and the high-handed way of redeeming the work as sincere or not.

In any case, Immamura will probably come to see the error of his ways and cease making work depicting truth. Immamura does not worry me, but those, fascinated by his example, who consider only technique are the ones who distress me. They demean themselves and lead others into error. For their benefit, I wanted to talk about how strange it is for technique to be debated in isolation from the artist and his theme.

This time I have shot too many arrows of criticism, both directly and indirectly, at too many people, but nevertheless I think that all the targets of my arrows are basically in the same camp. As I wrote earlier, I will be very dismayed if the situation is such that, when those who are trying to normalize war come in proudly displaying their theme, we are debating only technique. To repeat, the most interesting changes in technique always take place because of political pressure. For those who carry this out subjectively, it is inevitable, which gives it a certain charm. That immediately becomes a fad, then crashes, so that people unconsciously lose their ability to confront politics. This situation is most distressing.

(*Film Art,* November–December 1967)

"If Evening Comes"[1] is a thirty-minute play for television that I wrote four years ago, in the spring of 1964, with the idea of producing it myself for Channel 12. It was politely rejected, however, on the grounds that the subject matter was subversive. In its place, I hurriedly wrote and produced something called "Our Revered Teacher."[2] That was the only television studio drama I ever produced, so the project left an impression.

I naturally felt more attached to the rejected "If Evening Comes," and I was surprised to see Tokyo Broadcasting System (TBS) director Jissoji Akio with a copy of the script, which had been published and abandoned. Jissoji was a member of Waseda's Third Film group,[3] and a member of TBS's dA group.[4] I think that Third Film is

1.   *If Evening Comes* (*Yoiyami Semareba,* Jissoji Akio, 1969). With his own funds Jissoji set up his company, Production Danso (Fault). Directed *If Evening Comes* with A.T.G. as a coproducer. He had worked for TBS (Tokyo Broadcasting System) in the assistant directors' and the directors' production department, but resigned in 1968. His following film was *This Transient Life* (*Mujo,* 1970) with a script by Ishido Toshiro.
2.   "Our Revered Teacher" ("Aogeba Tootoshi," TV drama, dir. and script, Oshima Nagisa, 1964).
3.   The Third Film group was housed in the students' cinema studies club at Waseda University. They were opposed to both the Japanese modernist directors and the "old masters" against whom the modernists were in rebellion. With students from other universities they published a journal, *The Third Film,* from 1957 to 1960.
4.   A play of inversion on "assistant director." Six assistant directors—Jissoji Akio, Murak Yoshihito, Imano Tsutomu, Namiki Akira, Nakamura Toshio, and Takahashi Ichiro—who joined the Drama Direction Department of the TBS TV Production Division. (TBS also owns, among other properties, a national radio broadcasting network and a publishing house.) In 1959 they formed an association in order to produce innovative works based on their own original scripts. They published three issues of a journal, *dA,* which presented scripts, essays, and criticism. Some of these scripts were in fact adapted for production. After working for some time as directors, in 1970 they formed an independent television directors' organization "TV Man Union," together with like-minded colleagues from other production studios. The initial membership came to twenty-five. Jissoji Akio did not remain with them, but turned to filmmaking.

a bad group (at some point I will be writing a long piece about my reasons for think-ing so), but I nevertheless feel positively toward Jissoji because he always makes progress in his own work within the context of a movement of some sort.

Jissoji said that he had a chance to make a film and was going to do "If Evening Comes." Actually, I had had it printed as a film script after I returned from a month of traveling in the Soviet Union and Europe. It was one of my earlier works, intended for television, and I was a little ashamed of it, but under the circumstances I had to accept. I had handed it over to them exactly as it was, and it was up to Jissoji and his crew to decide how to present it. I had got over the fact that Jissoji's work to date seemed to be a bit lacking in self-assertion (the epitome of Third Film) compared to work by other members of dA—such as Imano Tsutomu's, whose work was some-what bogus but smelled, nonetheless of a strong ego, and Muraki Yoshihiko's, whose work was a bit weak, although he uses that to his advantage by forcing himself into difficult situations—and I hoped that Jissoji would take this opportunity to establish a new sense of self.

Naturally, this Jissoji film was an independent production, and it seemed that independent productions would be at their best that fall. I needn't go into detail about Ogawa Shinsuke's[5] tremendous efforts here. Kuroki Kazuo[6] had finally reached the level of *Kyuba,* and groups like the Cinema Nascence Group and Vision were embarking on independent productions all at once. The new works by Takechi

---

5.   Ogawa Shinsuke worked at the Iwanami Film Company (Iwanami Eiga Sha) and made mostly public relations films. His first feature film was *The Sea of Youth: Four Correspondence Students* (*Senen no Umi: Yonin no Tsushinkyoikuseitachi,* 1966). The second was *The Forest of Choking Death* (*Assatsu no Mori,* 1967), which dealt with students' hopeless struggle against a university administration that was determined to suppress its own dishonest handling of entrance examina-tions. Ogawa's persistence in documentation confirmed the students' efforts. The film was in great demand by students in other universities. After this success, he founded independent Ogawa Pro-ductions. Working with a team, he produced over seven years (1967–1974) a series of six films about the Sanrizuka Struggle of Farmers and students against the construction of the new Tokyo-Narita International Airport. Their involvement in both the struggle and in film production surpassed any preconceived idea or method of documentary filmmaking. Their recent effort has involved a ten-year research project for a documentation of rice farming life in the far north of Japan.

6.   Kuroki Kazuo joined the Iwanami Film Company in 1954. He made a one-hour documentary, *The Seawall* (*Kaiheki,* 1958), and many public relations films. The last PR film at Iwanami was *Hok-kaido, My Love* (*Waga Ai: Hokkaido,* 1962), which did not please the administration and led to his departure from the company. Four years later he distinguished himself as a difficult and poetic film-maker with *Silence Has No Wings* (*Tobenai Bhinmoku,* 1966). He flew to Cuba and made *Cuba's Lover* (*Kyuba no Koibito,* 1969). His other films are *Evil Spirits of Japan* (*Nihon no Akuryo,* 1970), *Ryoma Assassination* (*Ryoma Ansatsu,* 1974), and *Preparation for the Festival* (*Matsuri no Junbi,* 1975).

Tetsuji and Yoshida Yoshishige were independent productions, and, if you include Imai Tadashi's *River without a Bridge*,[7] Ito Daisuke's *Gion Festival*,[8] and Okamoto Kihachi's *Human Bullet*,[9] you would have to say that the principal artistic current of the Japanese film had completely divorced itself from the Big Five film companies. Our Sozosha's *Diary of a Shinjuku Thief* was another strong representative of this trend.

Several years earlier, Wakamatsu Koji had soared onto the scene like a comet, and Adachi Masao[10] of student films and a genius named Yamatoya[11] began getting involved alongside the Big Five, I strongly felt that the idle complaint of film directors inside and outside of the industry—that even if they wanted to make films, they couldn't—which they had been making for many years, had become completely meaningless; if you wanted to make a film, you should do so. I had been emphatically asserting that it was possible to make films. I didn't even write one-tenth of what I thought about the Matsumoto Toshio attack, but the reason I continued the attack to the extent I did was that, as a former comrade, I deeply lamented the fact that the Matsumoto was completely insensitive to this change in the film world and that he, having become a member of the Art Theater, was moving further and further away from actual production. (The other night, while drinking with Matsumoto, I teased him by saying, "Hey, you've really gone downhill since you became a member of the Art Theater." I was reprimanded by the president of the Art Theater, Izeki, who said,

7.   *River without a Bridge* (*Hashi no Nai Kawa*, dir. Imai Tadashi, 1968–70).
8.   *Gion Festival* (*Gion Matsuri*, dir. Ito Daisuke, 1968).
9.   *Human Bullet* (*Nikudan*, dir. Okamoto Kihachi, 1968).
10.   Adachi Masao started a meteoric career as a student filmmaker at the film production department of Nihon University with *The Sealed Vagina* (*Sain*) and *The Wooden Bowl* (*Wan*) in the early 1960s. They show a penetration of the Underground Cinema within Japan. He published a few arcane scripts prior to collaborating with Wakamatsu Koji as an aesthetic/political advisor and scenarist. Their collaboration includes: *When the Embryo Hunts in Secret* (*Taiji ga Misturyo Suru Toki*, 1966), *Violated Women in White* (*Okasareta Byakui*, 1967), *Jin Pang Mei* (*Kin Pei Bai*, 1968), *Study of a Mad Double Suicide* (*Kyoso Joshi Ko*, 1969), and *Sex-Jack* (*Sex-jack*, 1970). His last film venture was the documenting of the training camp of the PFLP, the faction of the Palestinian resistance that was not fighting as an ally of Arafat's Palestine Liberation Organization. Wakamatsu edited the footage into *The Red Army-PFLP: Declaration of the World War* (*Sekigun-PFLP: Sekai Senso Sengen*, 1971). Adachi was cowriter of Oshima's *Three Resurrected Drunkards* (*Kaettakita Yopparai*, 1968) and *Diary of a Shinjuku Thief* (*Shinjuku Dorobo Nikki*, 1968).
11.   Yamatoya Jin became well known as the coauthor of Suzuki Seijun's *The Brand of a Kill* (*Koroshi no Rakuin*, 1967). He joined the Nikkatsu Studio in 1962 as an assistant director, but left in 1966. He joined Wakamatsu Productions in the same year and directed *The Season of Betrayal* (*Uragiri no Kisetsu*, 1966). After directing several more films at Wakamatsu Productions, he turned to writing scripts for various young directors.

"Why is it going downhill to become a member of the Art Theater?" Of course, I don't
think that becoming a member of the Art Theater is in itself a step down. Far from
it—I think it is a good thing. But for Matsumoto, I think it is a drastic step in the wrong
direction.) Matsumoto, however, convinced that he was being attacked unreasona-
bly, wouldn't lend an ear to these friendly words. He put on the airs of a critic and,
after becoming absorbed in the assignment of ratings to my films according to an
absurd system ("This one was so-so," "This one was no good"), he ended up looking
lonelier than ever.

I wonder what a Matsumoto thinks of the surge in independent productions
this fall. I would like to hear his observations as a responsible activist. In this connection, here is part of an appeal regarding the Suzuki Seijun problem[12] by a Sozosha
comrade and laborer in film art who joined forces with Sozosha to participate in film
creation: "To all who intend to make films: Make them freely and independently.
These days it is a crime to intend to make films and not make them. We consider
those who don't make films as the enemy."

Particularly when I begin thinking like this, the significance of the progress
being made by the movement—through their logical and sensual understanding of
this on a scale unprecedented in the film world—centered on meetings of the Joint
Conference Struggling to Resolve the Suzuki Seijun Problem, becomes clear to me
for the first time.

At first the Suzuki Seijun problem was nothing more than a movement of minimal influence taken on by the Cine Club research group. For the first time, the Japan
Film Directors' Association decided to get involved in this type of issue as a group,
but only to a limited extent. Suzuki Seijun filed a complaint, and, in response to the
call of the Directors' Association, the Photography Directors Association and the Film
Actors' Association indicated their intention to be supportive; however, the movement still didn't gel. After June 12, when the Cine Club's research group—which has
persevered in its uncompromising battle, albeit with its minimal strength—spon-

12.   Suzuki Seijun was fired by the Nikkatsu management after he made *The Brand of a Kill* (*Koroshi no Rakuin,* 1967), allegedly (as in the case of his other films) because of its unintelligibility. His
modernist imagery and nonlinear montage converted a banal script into a visual whirlwind, whose
visual extravagance and mysterious lyricism were not to the management's taste. The problem of
the firing of Suzuki Seijun, however, should be just twofold: 1) The loss of his livelihood; 2) The
impossibility of his continuing to make films or for audiences to see his new work. Oshima's arguments, insofar as they derive from a productionist ideology and are unsupported by an analysis of
Suzuki Seijun's films, are open to debate. The initial cine-club organizers had embarked on such
an analysis.

sored a demonstration, the movement became a distinct force overnight. With this demonstration as its turning point, the movement escalated rapidly. There were meetings after the demonstrations, and incorporators appeared spontaneously to form the movement's union. There was a planning meeting on June 20, with about fifty people in attendance, and fourteen were spontaneously appointed as planning committee members. There was a general planning meeting on July 6, attended by about 150 people, and a meeting of more than thirty organizational representatives as well as individuals at which an executive committee was appointed. A mass organizational meeting on June 13 was attended by approximately 500 people. Each activity was an astonishing expansion of the last. The strength that sustained these gatherings came from the young students and film youth. (I hate the term "film youth." Please forgive me for having to use it here.) They propelled this movement passionately, tenaciously, and faithfully. They were inexperienced in many respects, and that led to mistakes, but their passion and will enabled them to overcome mistakes. This movement should continue for a long time, and I want to refrain from hasty criticism, but I must articulate certain things so as to clarify the essence and disposition of this movement.

Why was this movement able to mobilize so many young people? It was, of course, because the Suzuki Seijun problem was essentially a combustion point, revealing in a single stroke the structural contradictions of the Japanese cinema. However, that is merely a pretense. Human beings don't act on the basis of pretense alone. Something is needed to gain people's sympathy. What is that?

The Japanese film is losing its ability to accommodate the young people who aspire to work in film. For the past several years, that tendency has made rapid headway, and now it is completely impossible for young people to penetrate the Japanese film world. Those who didn't lose their will to make films—even if they couldn't get into the Japanese film world—resolved to make films on their own. A series of events, beginning with the rise of the student film and culminating in the establishment of the underground cinema, was clearly the challenge as well as the answer directed by young people at the Japanese film world that wouldn't admit them. Those young people naturally sympathized with Wakamatsu Koji, who quickly rose as someone making films outside the Japanese film establishment (the Big Five film companies), and they empathized with Suzuki Seijun, who, despite being given material far inferior relative to his talent, was making a tremendous effort. (I feel that Suzuki Seijun is being thoroughly persecuted. His fee for directing, mentioned in the complaint, is extremely low for his age and experience. I surmise that it is even low compared to that of younger people at Nikkatsu, such as Urayama Kiriro[13] and Esaki Mineo.)[14]

However, I do not say that the young people initiated their movement out of empathy and sympathy for Suzuki Seijun. They must have started it because they knew it would give them an opportunity for to express their ambitions. These ambitions, which cannot be satisfied merely by making independent films, thus made a huge breakthrough. They had to raze the current Japanese film system. They became the driving force for this movement. Kawakita Kazuko,[15] surprised at the way this movement, which started out small, rapidly expanded and intensified, has continued to serve splendidly as its nucleus. Her judgment that "the young people who gathered here are all potential filmmakers" is completely correct.

The executives of the Japan Scriptwriters Association, which refused to participate in the joint conference, are completely ignorant of this situation. In other words, they are insensitive. That insensitivity is a sin; it is even a crime. Not only are they closing their eyes to the fact that a majority of the students of the Script Research Institute are participating in this struggle, but one of the association's board members even said something to the effect that participating in such a conference is bad for one's future as a scriptwriter. The complete text of the statement of the Cooperative Association of the Japan Scriptwriters Association reads as follows:

> From the beginning, when the Suzuki Seijun problem was caused by Nikkatsu, this organization, in acknowledgement and awareness of itself as a professional group, has been carefully monitored by its board of directors and others. Accordingly, it voiced an independent objection to Nikkatsu in the past.
>
> However, regarding the disposition of the Joint Conference that is to be formed soon, it is thought that the groups participating in it are too varied and that there is an aspect inconsistent with the idea of a joint conference consisting solely of professional groups, which is the goal of this

13.   In contradistinction to the directors of the "Shochiku New Wave," his viewpoint on contemporary youth was positive. He became another representative filmmaker of the 1960s. His first two films produced at Nikkatsu were *A Town of Cupolas* (*Kyupola no Aru Machi*, 1962) and *Bad Girl* (*Furyo Shojo*, 1963). Since *The Woman I Abandoned* (*Watashi ga Suteta Onna*, 1969) he has had difficulty working because of his refusal to produce the pornography to which Nikkatsu turned.
14.   Esaki Mineo's first film, with a script by Tamura Takeshi, was *The Bride Is 15 Years Old* (*Hanayome wa Jugosai*, 1963). Although then considered promising, he has made only program pictures ever since. Once Nikkatsu changed its production line to pornography, he quit the studio.
15.   Very active cine-club organizer and a founder, together with her husband, Shibata Shun, of the French Film Company.

organization. Accordingly, our board of directors has decided not to participate in the Joint Conference to be organized on the 13th.

This organization considers this problem as one professional struggle, and there will be no change in its plan to deal with this problem from an individual standpoint in the future. At the same time, we would like to be a positive part of the interactions regarding their issue with the Committee of Five Associations (centering on the Japan Film Directors Association, to which Suzuki Seijun, who raised this problem, belongs; the other members are the Japan Film Photography Directors Association, the Japan Film Actors Association, the Japan Film Art Directors' Association, and the Japan Scriptwriters Association).

As an officer of the Directors' Association, I will continue to promote the activities of the Committee of Five Associations, including the Scriptwriters Association. However, apart from the joint struggle with the Scriptwriters Association, I want to preserve my individual freedom to continue to follow up on the attitude and responsibility of the executives of the Scriptwriters Association. Depending on the time and circumstances, I will use my name as an individual.

As soon as this statement was published, the Nikkatsu Writers Club (an assembly of Nikkatsu scriptwriters), which had until then planned to join the Joint Committee, canceled its membership. Did they perhaps mean to say that they had something to lose by joining the Joint Conference?

I am confident that the future of the Japanese film lies with the young potential filmmakers who gathered to form the Joint Conference. If people remain blind to this, how can they entertain hopes for the future of Japanese film? The insensitive are subject to disaster. Your offenses have been noted. You have only to wait for the day that you are overcome.

(*Film Criticism,* September 1968)

An artist does not build his work on one single theme, any more than a man lives his life according to only one idea. Foolish critics, however, want to think that works have just one theme running through them. Then when they find something that contradicts that one theme, they immediately say that they don't understand the work. Our work has nothing to do with these foolish critics. We want to put into it everything we are thinking and experiencing now. If we didn't, creative work would have no meaning for us. Of course, that also applies to *Death by Hanging*.

It is true, however, that *Death by Hanging* had as its starting point the events set in motion by the criminal Ri Chin'u, perpetrator of the Komatsugawa High School incident. In my opinion, Ri Chin'u was the most intelligent and sensitive youth produced by postwar Japan, as demonstrated by the collection of Ri's letters edited by Boku Junan, *Punishment, Death, and Love*. Ri's prose ought to be included in high school textbooks. Ri, however, committed a crime and was sentenced to the death penalty.

I had been thinking of devoting a work to Ri ever since he committed his crime in 1958. I wrote one script in 1963, the year after the execution. During that period I continued to depict the Korean problem in "The Forgotten Imperial Army," *A Tombstone to Youth, The Diary of Yunbogi,* and *A Study of Japanese Bawdy Songs*. I further explored the problem of crime more and more deeply in nearly all my work. Needless to say, both crime and the Korean problem are ultimately national concerns.

The two contexts in which the nation believes it is permissible to kill people are the death penalty and war. We say no to the death penalty and to war. We object strenuously to their existence. However, our objections will carry no weight unless articulated by an ideological level that transcends the nation. Based on Ri Chin'u,

Death by Hanging. 1968.

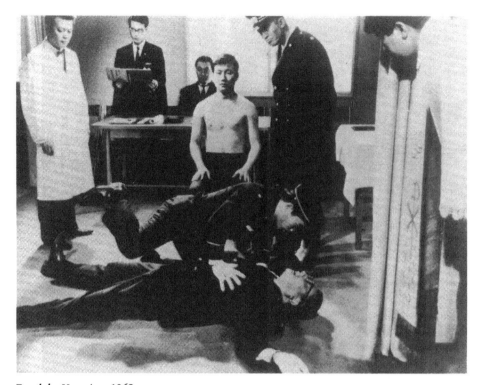

Death by Hanging. 1968.

who came close to achieving that, we created R, a character who did not die after execution.

The character R—and the work *Death by Hanging*—owe a great deal to the strength of the countless people who are interested in Ri Chin'u. Another way to express this is to say that I am indebted to the strength of all who have a deep interest in the Japan-Korea relationship—even if those people represent a whole range of opinions. Also, our ability to construct a realistic execution site and to realistically depict execution is due to the good offices of Mukae Yoshiteru and others in the penitentiary system. We would like to take this opportunity to express our deep gratitude to them.

Based on this solid foundation, the scriptwriter, location crew, actors, and everyone else once again participated in the making of the film from the beginning. Recently film productions dependent on the Art Theater[1] have been in the news, but we pride ourselves strongly on the fact that the original method that we have been carving out for ourselves for some years is now coming to fruition. Matsuda, Adachi, and Ishido offered their generous, joyful participation in work outside their true occupations. I don't know how to express my gratitude to them for their generosity.

I will continue to engage in bold film production with my fellow Guevaras; there is no doubt that *Death by Hanging* is one of our milestones.

(Film Scripts of Oshima Nagisa, 1968)

---

1. A company engaged in producing, importing, and distributing films, established in 1961.

As those who see it or read the "plot summary" will readily understand, *Boy* is based on the case of parents who taught their son to pretend to be hit by a car so they could collect damages and "conscience money." The events took place in Japan in 1966. The incidence of this type of crime, in which a pedestrian purposely runs into the path of a moving car and then claims to have been hit, first occurred in postwar Japan when, after the Korean War, the country experienced a period of high growth during which the number of cars on the roads increased. This crime received particular publicity around 1960, when it occurred frequently in the Kamagasaki section of Osaka. By then the number of cars had increased so dramatically and the roads had become so crowded that, even if so trivial a crime had been committed, it probably would have been absurd even to mention it. It was then that the incident of the child's being hit by cars suddenly occurred. When all is said and done, the most remarkable thing about this case was the fact that a child was being used to accomplish the objective. The other remarkable fact was that this one family had traveled all over Japan making their living at this.

Only three days passed between the time the incident was first reported in early September 1966 and the time of the arrest, but during that time the newspapers gave it extraordinary coverage, and the following week nearly all of the weekly magazines made it their top story. I think that both the newspapers and the weekly magazines were strongly attracted to the two remarkable aspects of the incident. The headlines of some of the weekly magazines of the day were: "Accident-Faking Couple Uses Child" (*Shukan Asahi*), "The Criminal Journey of the Demonic Accident-Faking Couple" (*Shukan Sankei*), "The Private Life of the Accident-Faking Family Who Travels around Japan: The Past of the Demonic Couple Who Make a Living Using Their Ten-Year-Old Darling" (*Shukan Bunshun*), "Five Months of Strange Devotion in the Parent-Child Accident-Faker Scheme" (*Asahi Bungei*). However, in spite of this sud-

Boy. 1969.

den commotion, the incident didn't remain in the news for long. Two weeks later the only thing published on the subject were notes written by the child's natural mother; they appeared in a women's magazine, but after that there was basically nothing else. Probably because people thought that, as a crime, accident faking was too petty and that the two unique aspects of the incident were too outlandish.

At that time, I had completed *Violence at Noon* and was devoting all of my energy to editing *Manual of Ninja Martial Arts,* but this incident shocked me so much that I felt shaken to the depths of my soul. I thought that the incident was something I should write about. By "should write" I meant that I should apply my powers of imagination more often to plotting this type of incident, to constructing this type of crime. I felt that the reality of the incident lay in a place far beyond my imagination, and I realized keenly that, as Yanagita Kunio[1] says, "The world of reality is far more profound than the world we read about in books or hear about in stories."

Since my first release, *A Town of Love and Hope* (original title, *The Boy Who Sells Pigeons*), in 1959, my films have all had some connection to crime. I finally became consciously aware of this after I conceived my 1966 work, *Boy,* and followed it with *A Study of Japanese Bawdy Songs, Japanese Summer: Double Suicide, Death by Hanging, Three Resurrected Drunkards,* and *Diary of a Shinjuku Thief.* Several astute critics also pointed it out to me. It was at this time, after I had grappled with a born criminal in *Violence at Noon,* that I thought that this crime of accident fakers who use children was something I myself should plot: you might say that it was a point of self-awareness for me.

It is now said that, along with crime, "youth" is also a consistent basic theme of my works. You might agree, considering that "youth" appears as the hero once every two or three years, starting with *The Boy Who Sells Pigeons* and continuing through the wartime children in *The Catch,* the wandering infants of the public relations film *A Small Adventure,*[2] and *The Diary of Yunbogi,* which is based on the writings of a ten-year-old Korean boy, but as an artist I haven't always necessarily been aware of this. I first realized it when the critic Tanemura Suehiro[3] mentioned it to me, but I don't remember whether that was before or after I published the script of *Boy.* At any rate, it is true that I was first strongly attracted to this "accident-faking boy"

1.   Founder of Japanese folklore studies, 1875–1962.
2.   *A Small Adventure (Chisana Boken Ryoko,* 1964); a Nippon Seimei (life insurance company) project. The original idea was conceived by Ishihara Shintaro. Scripted by Ishido Toshiro.
3.   Critic and translator of German literature.

because his image overlapped with that of the hero of *Yunbogi's Diary,* which I had made the previous year, the year of the Japan-Korea compromise settlement.

Although I hadn't anticipated it, the incident of the accident fakers was truly an incident with my own theme. This may sound presumptuous, but that is the only way I can describe the feeling that struck me when I read the newspaper reports.

The first person with whom I discussed the idea of using this as the basis for a film was Watanabe Fumio. When Watanabe came running into the Sozosha office eager to discuss it with me, I was staring at a newspaper containing an article about it. It seemed as though the images were already totally formed in the mind of Watanabe, that outstanding "idea man," who said, "It's great. Absolutely. All you have to do is shoot the kid's face; you only need to get the father and mother from the waist down."

Nakajima Masayuki concurred right away. The producer, a true Tokyoite, said brightly, "Yes. It may sell surprisingly well as a sensational piece." After that, when I returned to the *Manual of Ninja Martial Arts* editing room, I telephoned Tamura Takeshi. "I think it'll work. Let's do it from the boy's point of view. How about doing the narration in the form of the boy's letters?" These were two responses unheard of from the stubborn scriptwriter.

Some oppose our method of making films in a group. "How can a disparate group of people get together and create a unified thing?" they argue. Those who say such things understand nothing about people. You have to be able to share a common image of some kind with others. Of course, there may be some who say they have images that they absolutely can't share with anyone else. In such cases, however, if someone else says, "I have the same image," then that is that. I myself am not so arrogant. I always want to work with several people who share my images. Even if two people merely want to make a film about the case of the accident fakers who exploit their child, they have a common image at the most basic level. If one doesn't believe in shared images, how can one make a film to show an audience of hundreds of thousands or millions of people? To make a film and show it to people is, ultimately, to search for people with whom one has images in common.

One day, fewer than ten days after the accident, four of us closeted ourselves in a hotel in Akasaka and mapped out our plan. In the case of this work, we had the most common images possible, at the highest possible level. One indication is that, on the first day, all of the basic images jelled. We decided to conform to reality in terms of the sequence of events, the basic facts about the characters, and their attitudes toward the incident. But if that were all we did, we would be no different from the weekly magazines. We had to create the parts that were buried between the incident and the superficial actions. It is there that the characters first diverge from the real people and become characters created by us, with no relationship to them. That was our first basic task—and, in particular, determining what was going on inside the boy's head. In the midst of that analysis, according to my notes of that day's discussions, the following images emerged: "adaptable/his imagination is developed/he wants to be someone other than himself. Ultraman, spaceman/he talks to his younger brother/he has beatific visions in vast fields of clouds." These refer only to the boy, but our images of the father and mother steadily expanded in the same way.

On the next day, things also went along smoothly as we traced the story from the beginning, establishing the details. We didn't have quite enough to fill in all of the details of the second half, but I thought it was okay and left the rest to the writer, Tamura, as I returned to the *Manual of Ninja Martial Arts* editing room. To my surprise, five days later Tamura finished writing and brought the manuscript to the editing room. "Nabe stayed right by my side and saved the day," Tamura said, his face a bit flushed with the joy of finishing. It seemed that Watanabe had been conferring with Tamura the entire time the script was being written. How did he have the time to do that? "This time 'Nabe was in good form from start to finish," Tamura said— meaning that this time was different from the usual process during which Watanabe Fumio, the idea man, contributes good ideas at the beginning but as time goes on tends to come up with only long-winded, ridiculous ideas.

For these reasons, the completed script was very highly regarded. In the monthly *Scenario,* Yajima Midori kindly said, "I feel a dark excitement," and Hayashi Tamaki took the trouble to write a piece praising it in *Film Review.* However, no company would let us make it. At that time I was doing a lot of work with Shochiku, and the producer seems to have tried to approach them about it, but there was no satisfactory response. Later, the script received a special prize from the Scriptwriters Association.

In February 1967, Sozosha's independent work *Manual of Ninja Martial Arts* was distributed by A.T.G. and its commercial success in the entertainment industry was unprecedented. As a result, there was talk of a cooperative production with A.T.G., and *Death by Hanging* was produced, which was also a success. After that, when *Three Resurrected Drunkards* was completed, I traveled to Moscow, Warsaw, Prague, and Cannes with *Death by Hanging,* which received favorable reviews abroad as well. Heartened by that, we decided to do an independent production of *Diary of a Shinjuku Thief* and a cooperative production of *Boy* with A.T.G. In September 1968, exactly two years after the completion of the script, *Boy* was finally able to go into actual production.

As the production began, I decided privately that this film would commemorate my tenth year as a film director. I seriously thought that I wanted to return to the psychological state of a novice. Ten years before, in 1959, I was quietly making my first film, under the title *A Town of Love and Hope,* which had been changed from the more significant *The Boy Who Sells Pigeons.* At that time it was not customary in Japan for the first film of a new director to receive attention, so there were no visitors to my set or my location. The noted actress Mochizuki Yuko was kind enough to appear in that film, but all the others were unknown young amateurs, along with Watanabe Fumio and Chino Kakuko. I worked away at the shooting, consulting with assistant director Tamura Takeshi about the script as we went along. At that time, too, Watanabe was a helpful confidant, and he instructed the amateurs in acting. For the next ten years, I made film after film, all of which were painful for me, but during that time I earned, in spite of myself, something of a false reputation. People came to view me and my works in the light of that false reputation and with preconceptions. The eyes of those people must have influenced me to some extent. I always felt a certain constraint when making these films. Paradoxically, I continued to make films so that I could become free. The sadness and anger I felt when making each film must have been passionately incorporated into each one, into every theme. There is no work that I regret, but I think the incorporation of those kinds of feelings occurred too frequently. When I said to two or three people that in making *Boy* I wanted to return to the heart of a novice, I meant that I wanted to make a break with the works I had done up to that point. But I didn't want people to be aware of this; I wanted to avoid journalistic sensationalism.

As we began shooting, the biggest problem was organizing cast and crew. There was practically no problem gathering the crew, which consisted of the familiar members present since *Death by Hanging.* It was a decidedly small group and we were in for a long journey, so we wouldn't consider admitting even one unfamiliar person. For that reason, I included two assistant directors and one actor in the photography department. The two assistant directors also acted as drivers, steering the vans all over western Japan to our locations. On location we ended up with a total of fifteen people: one director, three assistant directors, a seven-member photography department, one art director, one recording engineer, and a two-person production department. There was no lighting department because of my cherished view that photography and lighting should be one department: the photography department as a whole would take responsibility for the lighting. Because three members of that department were amateurs, photography director Yoshioka Yasuhiro faced the demanding task of having to teach them everything, beginning with how to plug in an electric cord. But the crew became extremely close, and we were able to conclude the four months of travel without a single fight (although the younger members sometimes came in looking as though they had had a run-in with the local hooligans). Because understanding was so close, there was even a time when I yelled at them for not being competitive enough.

When I decided to embark on the actual production of *Boy,* I chose Watanabe Fumio and Koyama Akiko to play the parents. The choice was made taking into account the fact that they would have to work as crew members in addition to their acting duties. Watanabe, who had been in on this work since the planning stages, was of course thrilled to accept the part, but Koyama was somewhat hesitant to play a "bad woman." Needless to say, that hesitation was nonsense, and she ultimately took the part. These two worked hard, not only as actors but as crew members as well. They went all out, doing everything from schooling the boy and the little brother in acting to taking care of daily details and helping out with crew meals and entertainment. I even left to the two of them the task of translating the script, which was written in standard dialect, into Kochi dialect for the father's and the son's speeches and into Osaka dialect with a bit of Kochi for the mother's.

Casting these two and selecting Tsuyoshi, the two-year-old only son of Kinoshita Toshimi of the production section, to play the little brother was easy, but casting the main role, the boy, was tough going until the end. Finding actors is always the work of one of the producers, Yamaguchi Takuji. It is typical of him to bring around all kinds of strange girls, but this time he seemed to be at a loss, bringing around only twenty or so little boys and saying that he had been to all of the juvenile drama groups in the Tokyo area. We narrowed it down to three and I thought we would decide on one of them, but when we thought about it seriously there always seemed to be something missing, and we ended up having to start all over. The date on which we would begin filming was fast approaching, and Yamaguchi ended up flying to Kochi and looking there. I had instructed him to find an animated child who was really living, rather than the type of overprotected child one finds in a juvenile drama group. I told the assistant directors to start by combing the fifty-odd children's homes in Tokyo. Naturally, though, a great many places refused to allow us to carry out our search for a child. Also, when we actually looked at the children, there was the problem of the sensitivity that comes from living in a group, and for a time we thought that we wouldn't be able to expect much. However, three days after that search began, assistant director Ogasawara Kiyoshi telephoned and asked me to come right away because he had found a good child in Meguro's Wakaba Dormitory. I immediately went for a look with the other assistant directors, and I saw that he was undoubtedly a good child. His upturned eyes impressed me more than anything. It seemed that Ogasawara had gotten to see him during the dormitory's rehearsal for class day, when he was playing the role of a girl. He was the nine-year-old fourth grader Abe Tetsuo.

Even though one look convinced us he was right for the part, it wouldn't be possible to use him without the permission of the dormitory and the school. Fortunately, we received an understanding response. I was especially touched by the words of the dormitory supervisor, who said that it would be a good experience for him because getting to work and tour the country was an opportunity that Tetsuo wouldn't be likely to encounter in his life.

The facts of Abe Tetsuo's life, as he gradually came to relate them to us, were complicated. To put it simply, his father was dead and he had lived briefly with a mother who was not his natural mother; his life history was almost identical to that of the boy in the film. No one could have been more appropriate. When traveling by train to a location, he would hold tightly onto his luggage with one hand while clinging tenaciously to the clothing of the crew member next to him with the other. And for some time before we reached our destination, he would persistently ask if everything was still all right and why we weren't getting off yet. When we asked him about it, he said that a number of times as part of the process of changing parents he had been left on trains. I'd call him a fool, laugh, and tell him to calm down, asking him how could we do the film if we left him behind, but this brought tears to the eyes of some of the crew. Among the crew, Ogasawara, Kurata, Ueno, and Osa acted as "Tetsu's" home tutors so he did not fall behind in his schoolwork. Senmoto and Ozeki announced that they had come along to teach "Tetsu"—who was always being reduced to tears at the dormitory—to fight, and they did their best to teach him, but I think the degree of their effectiveness is altogether questionable. At any rate, it can be said that finding "Tetsu" was our biggest piece of good fortune in the entire film production. We intend to watch his long future closely to determine whether appearing in the film was a good thing for him.

With the "Tetsu" decision, the long journey of *Boy* was finally about to be launched. I set out for Kochi on October 13, shooting began on the 15th, and we traveled to Kochi, Niihama, Onomichi, Kurashiki, Kita Kyushu, Matsue, Shirosaki, Tango Jinya, and Fukui. We returned to Tokyo on November 26 and spent the three days beginning December 10 in Takasaki, heading for Yamagata on the 14th. After that we went to Akita, Wakkanai, Otaru, and Sapporo and then returned to Tokyo. On January 18 we went to Osaka, finishing shooting on the 26th; we finished the reshooting of some minor scenes on February 4. The entire trip was 7,400 kilometers—three and a half times the distance between Kagoshima and Aomori.[4] The first half of the shooting in western Japan and the second half in northeastern Japan took twice the scheduled amount of time, which really upset one of the producers, Nakajima Masayuki, who was left alone in Tokyo.

If we had worked in a studio during the golden age of the Japanese film, it probably would have been enjoyable. We would have enjoyed the views in each place, eaten delicious food, stayed at hot springs, received the cooperation of the theater in each town related to the company (there probably would have been one), done the shooting in a leisurely fashion, and shot the indoor scenes without haste, using sets when we returned to the studio. In contrast, we were shooting the entire film on location, so it was really tough. Except for the minimal lighting equipment we had brought along, we had to arrange for everything—even electric generators—on location. Under those conditions, indoor and night scenes were lost causes. Before we left there was even an argument during a meeting when the cameraman said, "It won't come out at this distance," and the producer said, "If it doesn't come out, it will just have to not come out," but we somehow managed to push the shooting through and return home. The art director believed that even though not a single yen had been budgeted for art, it was necessary to somehow reconstruct the scenes personally; he urged the assistant directors to walk around the towns with him, borrowing things with which to decorate. The hardworking Osa Takamichi laughed, "The easiest thing to borrow is the Japanese flag." We also bought all of the actors' costumes on location. I bought the deep red sweater and plaid accordion-pleat skirt that Koyama is wearing when she first appears at a Sunday market in Kochi for 800 yen. Koyama put them on, looked in the mirror, and said she felt nauseous, and the things the sightseers on location whispered about her made her feel even worse: "Koyama Akiko's taste is really terrible." Although in a certain sense cars had a major part in the film, we never spent money borrowing one; all of the footage was of cars that happened to come along. Between coordinating with the cars, keeping the little brother in good humor, and dealing with the sightseers, everyone was worn out.

All these difficulties, however, were linked to the creative work, so everyone bore them calmly. What was difficult was the quality of our lives. We had decided that

---

4.   Kagoshima is a city to the extreme south on Kyushu, the southernmost of Japan's four main islands, and Aomori is a city to the extreme north on Honshu, the largest of Japan's four main islands.

the budget for each person's daily lodging with breakfast and dinner should be less than 1,000 yen. The production department's struggles to implement this system were extraordinary, but you must also appreciate the struggles of those who had to live under those conditions.

Even reducing expenditures to that extent, we had so little money, excluding lodging and transportation expenses, that we had almost nothing to spend on location. Other than the little we did have, we were completely dependent on local goodwill at all of the various sites. We turned to those with whom we had connections for everything—loans of cars, care of the actors doing scenes there, contrivances to reduce lodging fees, loan of art materials. At times we even imposed on people with whom we had no connection, making brazen requests. If we had not had the warm goodwill of the people upon whom we relied at each location, this film would never have been completed. Our only way to repay these people's kindness was to bow in gratitude.

Cooperative production with the A.T.G. involved a total of 10 million yen, with the A.T.G. contributing 5 million and the production side contributing 5 million. Even before production began, we knew that *Boy* would be impossible to make under those conditions, and even though we reduced expenditures to the absolute minimum, the film still ended up costing about twice that much. However, that was merely the cost in actual yen. If you add proper payment of the guaranteed minimum for the producers, the playwright, the main crew, Watanabe, Koyama, and me, and if you calculate the materials and labor that were supplied to us free of charge on location, the total would probably be twice that again, or 40 to 50 million yen. At any rate, we were able to do it for only 10 million because, apart from my strength of will, there were the incredible efforts of the on-location producer, Yamaguchi Takuji; the utter dedication of the crew, including the actors; and the sincerely appreciated support of all kinds that we received at each location. Whenever I think about the fact that I was able to make this film, I am filled with all kinds of feelings and don't know whether as an individual I should be proud or ashamed.

Before leaving on location, I gathered everyone together and said, "We are going around the country on a journey of crime with a family of accident fakers. Spend all the time on location feeling like criminals." But actually it was more like a journey of beggars. We went along stealing the sights and sounds for *Boy*, sometimes quietly, sometimes violently. And during the trip, "Tetsu" and "Tsuyoshi" grew up. "Tsuyoshi" in particular grew up before our eyes. During the latter half of filming he came to understand the concept of work. I had insisted that the film be shot with the scenes progressing in chronological order, and my desire to capture the growth of the two children on screen enabled us to do that. I think it comes across clearly in the film. As the two matured, the crew came to love them deeply. By the end of filming, several people said they wanted to adopt "Tetsu."

We spent New Year's at Otaru. It was an unusual experience for everyone to spend New Year's on location, and we pounded rice and celebrated enthusiastically. Around that time I judged that everyone's love for the two children was becoming a bit indulgent. So I made a declaration: "From now on, no one should speak to those two except as the work requires." People were really dissatisfied with this pronouncement, and we had just drunk New Year's sake together. Even now I remember the reproachful looks that I received. Watanabe, drunk and looking demoniacally unkempt with the beard he had been growing since Takasaki, said, "Okay. It's better that way," and fell asleep looking sad. Alone, Toda Shigemasa and I piled up the sake cups dejectedly, saying, "Everybody's got to be a damn humanist!" But I thought that the crew's altruistic attempt to bury their inner emptiness by becoming attached to the children was unforgivable. And in order to do the important scene after Otaru, in which the boy becomes isolated and independent, I thought that "Tetsu" had to throw away dependency and become able to stand on his own in reality as well.

I had the same basic attitude overall toward the making of *Boy.* As far as possible, I wanted to shoot the boy and the family of accident fakers with detachment. I had been thinking this even before the script was written, but my original resolve was intensified when another Sozosha writer, Sasaki Mamoru, who had been in Africa during the writing of the script, returned and, after one reading, said, "Isn't this a bit sentimental?" No matter how this material was treated, there was no reason for the result to be sentimental. Thus, I thought that a script that could, upon a first reading, give an impression of just *slight* sentimentality, was a good script, and it was with confidence that I was able to make the film in a detached manner. At one point Tamura seemed to think that we ought to reconsider the Hokkaido section, which Sasaki had called sentimental, although he later changed his mind. The three of us had a meeting in Tokyo after we completed the first half, but rather than tamper with the momentum of a script that had been written in one breath, the opinion emerged that we should not fix it and that we should leave further elaboration of the details entirely to what happens on location. I wanted there to be more explanatory scenes and speeches, but we concluded that this would be a mistake; shooting the whole film with detachment would cause the meaning of the existence of the boy and his parents to weigh more heavily on the viewer. And so I was able to shoot with detachment to the end, in accordance with my original plan. Although I provided no expla-

Boy. 1969.

nation whatsoever, the sharp editing of Uraoka Keiichi[5] and the overall composition and placement of sound by Nishizaki Hideo, including the music of Hayashi Hikaru, were in complete harmony with my design. Consequently, after about a month of editing and recording following filming, we were able to see the first print on March 18.

I feel now that the boy, little brother, father, and mother whom I filmed with such detachment appear readily in my mind's eye. Is this what is called a delusion? Yes, I made this film with detachment on the one hand and prayer on the other. What kind of prayer? A prayer for the people who have to live like this. The tear that the boy sheds at the end is the same. In that sense, for me this family was a holy family. After coming back from location, "little brother" was said to be spending his days playing with his parents and making them recite the speeches he had been made to recite. "Big brother!" "The Andromeda nebula." And then "little brother" is said to order "Action!" I wonder if directing appealed to his two-year-old mind. Now, feeling deeply the cruelty of a director's work, I lay down my pen. Before the people with whom I made the film, those who supported us, and everyone who sees the film, I can only hang my head in silence.

(Sozosha pamphlet, June 1, 1969)

---

5.   A film editor who was an important long-standing collaborator on Oshima's films: *Cruel Story of Youth* (1960), *The Tomb of the Sun* (1960), *Night and Fog in Japan* (1960), *The Pleasure of the Flesh* (1965), *The Diary of Yunbogi* (1965), *Violence at Noon* (1966), *A Study of Japanese Bawdy Songs* (1967), *Manual of Ninja Martial Arts* (1967), *Japanese Summer: Double Suicide* (1967), *Death by Hanging* (1968), *Three Resurrected Drunkards* (1968), *A Secret Post-Tokyo-War Story* (1970), *The Ceremony* (1971), *Dear Summer Sister* (1972), *In the Realm of the Senses* (1976), *Empire of Passion* (1978).

The other day I had the opportunity to see ten films made by high school students. Technically, of course, they were all terrible, and the projection of the 8-mm films, in an auditorium so worn out that pigeons had built nests there, was extremely poor. I, who rarely watch films, ended up thoroughly tiring my eyes because, unlike most films, it was always impossible to predict what would happen in the next scene. In one sense that is really great, but it causes the viewer to spend every second on edge, so my eyes burned late into the night. On the other hand, the auditorium, located on the third floor of a gymnasium, is extremely cold, and I, who don't even wear an overcoat in the winter, found my teeth chattering in time with the sound of the film projector. Despite the poor conditions under which I saw them, the films were extremely interesting and, in many ways, enlightening.

Among the films I saw, there was one protest film of a campus demonstration, but it wasn't very interesting. Instead, the many works in which the students looked within themselves were of greater interest. Surprisingly, their modes of self-examination were frighteningly similar: they saw themselves as bad people, people with nothing to do, who don't know what they should do. Consequently, the actions of the heroes in these films, which accurately project the thoughts and emotions of the artists, were indescribably humorous and sad. A cigarette-smoking scene was common to nearly all of the works, which probably indicates the importance that the violation of this mild taboo holds for them. It brought back vivid memories of the dusky four-and-a-half-mat potato store next to school where I smoked my first cigarette.

In this way, the manner in which they examine themselves often becomes, when expressed, a song of self-tyranny and self-scorn, particularly so when it takes the form of a film of themselves making a film, or merely their making a film of themselves. That has apparently been the most popular form since the Sogetsu Festival the year before last, when the high school student Hara Masataka's[1] *Sad Parade Tinged with Comedy* was in the spotlight. But to someone as lazy as I, who hadn't even seen Hara's film, it was very interesting, and it even seemed to be a method of great significance. In these films, they don't know what they should be shooting, so they start by shooting the most boring things. They themselves, who are shooting boring things, are the heroes of these films. You might say that they are the true heroes of all of these student films.

Just now, I used the word heroes. They are not, however, the brilliant heroes of the military. Nor are they the heroes of grand human tragedy. At most they are no more than rank-and-file soldiers using cameras as weapons in their battles with illusions. One of their cherished patterns is for the mighty enemy with whom they were fighting to turn out to be nothing more than the detached leg of a broken mannequin. However, I feel a truly fresh surprise and awe that the self-examination of these high school filmmakers is taking this form. This type of self-examination seems completely different from that of youths in the past who aspired to becomes novelists, poets, and dramatists. Among the young people who aspire to be poets, for example, are probably those who feel impatience and despair that expression of their thoughts doesn't take the form they desire. However, even if at times they have basic doubts about their own poetic talent, their pride in being a poet remains all the more intact. And this is probably equally true of aspiring novelists and dramatists. It seems that young filmmakers are completely different, however. Why?

These young student filmmakers start by confirming that they are powerless. The following two things confirm their powerlessness for them. First of all, if they don't have a camera in hand, they can't even begin. Don't they feel their powerlessness overwhelmingly with respect to the taking in hand of the camera? Next, they don't know what to shoot. However, this not knowing what to shoot must not be analyzed as meaning only that the subjective conditions for creation aren't met. It is due, perhaps, to a specific aspect of cinema, one absent in literature: an economic aspect. The question of what to shoot becomes restricted by economic conditions. When young filmmakers finally hold a camera and raw film in their hands, they have nothing in their pockets of their dingy jackets—zero. When they say they don't know what to shoot, they are probably talking about this poverty.

When I begin writing this way, I suddenly become emotional. The tears well up. My own situation is essentially the same. I had a three-year period when I couldn't make films. When normal people would have said they didn't have the opportunity

1.   Hara Masataka coscripted Oshima's *A Secret Post-Tokyo War Story* with Sasaki Mamoru.

to make a film, I merely maintained that I didn't know what to shoot. Some critics even praised me, saying that this was daring. However, the words saying I didn't know what to shoot were also saying that my pockets were empty.

When student filmmakers say they don't know what to shoot as a way of expressing that their pockets are empty, they inevitably begin making films of themselves making films. Their works are at the same time colored deeply by self-tyranny and self-scorn. This in itself proves them to be the legitimate heirs of the future of film.

I am confident that only these student filmmakers and others trying to get started under the same conditions can be the filmmakers of the future. When I said this last year, criticism that must be termed abusive was directed to me. These critics maintain that artists attempting to start from zero don't produce strong work, and that artists cannot ultimately emerge from among those starting from that position.

Making films starting from zero is definitely an extremely difficult task. However, difficult is not impossibility. With the lies of commentators pretending to be well informed, these critics use the words "difficult" and "impossible" interchangeably, slamming their door right in the faces of those who are trying to carve out a future—while they themselves turn their backs on their difficulties and run for easy cover. Unlike them, I try to place myself in the dead center of the difficulty. What, then, is the key to overcoming the difficulty of making films starting from zero?

I have not prepared a possible response to that question. If, however, if one could say just one helpful word to these student filmmakers, I'd say that they should intensify the criticism both from within and without.

At present, Japanese film criticism is in a definite decline. Putting aside journalistic criticism in the newspapers, I am talking chiefly of what is written in the monthly film magazines, where the only things printed are chatter completely unrelated to film and gossipy items that reflect likes and dislikes in ugly human relationships. Those who are beginning to make new films starting from zero must make a decisive break from the world of "criticism." They need to establish that genuine criticism is completely unrelated to this "criticism." The zero position can only be strengthened once one's works and one's inner self are met by that kind of real criticism. The self, submitted to criticism, can then attain strong cinematic expression.

The filmmaking method that consists of shooting oneself, with its inherent criticism, is definitely the most appropriate method for a first departure. It is probably the turning point with respect to whether you can establish your own criticism. But how far can you really go from there? How deep and how far can you go?

The history of film is not long. And the history of those who try to make their way as filmmakers, starting from zero, amid the conditions of Japanese society and of the Japanese film, has only just begun. I am conscious of being at the forefront of that history, so to speak. As an inheritor of the old cinema, I feel its burden, its servile blood coursing through my veins. I have tried, gradually, to shed that burden and, drop by drop, to rid myself of that blood. To the leaders of the cinema still to come, I can offer only a few words drawn from my modest experience. You must ceaselessly formulate and sharpen your critical views, both of others and of yourselves. The world of cinema now faces a situation of extreme complexity. How is new work to be shown? How is it to be seen? But the really fundamental question is the following one: how are the new filmmakers, those who will make the great films of the future, to come into being.

(pamphlet written for the festival of Akita University, May 5, 1970)

The Man Who Left His Will on Film is the subtitle of my film *A Secret Post-Tokyo War Story*. This subtitle conveys the entire content of the film. One day last fall, I was possessed by the vision of a man who leaves his will on film. My visions are always films, and this film was conceived in this way.

From time to time I am asked where in the world such conceptions come from. It is absolutely impossible to respond to this question. They just appear suddenly in my mind on some days, at some times. In a manner of speaking, I see and hear the voice of a phantom. I can say for certain, however, that I am an artist only by virtue of seeing these phantoms and hearing their voices. And the people who see my phantoms and hear their voices with me are my crew and my audience.

However, the phantoms I see and the voices I hear must have their origins within me or in my interactions with the outside world. The word "origins" may be a bit strange, but there is absolutely no reason that a phantom completely unconnected to my inner life would appear before me. Therefore, even if it is impossible to explain why I was possessed by a vision of "a man who leaves his will on film," I can probably piece together and explain something of the psychological states in which I am possessed by that type of vision.

Actually, it is up to critics and film lovers to investigate and analyze the psychological state of mind at the source of a film director's work; it probably isn't something the director himself should discuss. Although this task is an integral part of criticism in other artistic disciplines, in today's film world it is almost never done, and film directors are constantly and mercilessly having to shield themselves from incessant attacks by journalists (at times even the critics take part) who ask "What is your reason for making this film?" "Why did you make this film?" and so on.

The Man Who Left His Will on Film. 1970.

Nor can I go completely against that custom. But because I am incapable of explaining the conceptions themselves, I will improvise an explanation of my psychological state, which can be thought of as the probable basis of my conceptions.

As far as this film is concerned, two questions arise: to what does making films mean to me, and how are able people to terrorize themselves? I will omit the former, both because it doesn't require explanation and because, in the sense that it is a private thing, it is impossible to explain. I will say a word about the latter because it relates to the title *A Secret Post-Tokyo War Story*. Last fall, during the "Tokyo War" (as the Red Army faction called it), the peak of which was the barring of Sato's visit to the United States, I was deeply moved that, although each sect challenged the other, saying that they were determined to fight to the death, the curtain was drawn on the struggles of the 1960s without a single fatality in the midst of what looked like a defeat for the demonstrators. I too had roamed the Haneda area, camera in hand, but of course I wasn't able to die either. For me, the question, "How can one die in the 1970s?" is the answer to the question, "How can one live?"

(*Outstanding Films:* Monthly Film Review, July 1, 1970)

It is raining. It rained yesterday, and it continues to rain today. I don't want to think about the past, but it was raining the same way ten years ago. Is June the season of memories?

On June 15 ten years ago, I stayed up all night walking. From the Diet building to Yurakucho, rain and blood and mud, torn flags, broken flagpoles. That was immediately after *Cruel Story of Youth* was released.

You love all your work, just as you love all your children. However, some works are happy and some are not. Just as there are happy children and unhappy children in this world, there is nothing one can do about the characters in the works one creates. *Cruel Story of Youth* was a happy work. Although the backlash it generated was substantial, the good will extended to this work, trying to assimilate something new, prevailed. You might say that this was because, in the midst of their rebellion against authority during the upheaval over the security treaties, many Japanese were discovering a surprising newness inside themselves as well. I will never forget June 3, the day *Cruel Story of Youth* was released. In a quiet bar in the East Ginza, some journalists who covered film were giving me a party. It was a party to encourage a new director, given at their own expense. Has there been a new director since then who has been as fortunate as I? People were so generous! It was a good season.

That day. On that day, however, the main topic of conversation was not film, but the general strike scheduled for the next day, June 4. Some of the journalists said passionately, "Let's go to the Japan National Railways office in Shinagawa." Political views were not in agreement. However, the night deepened, and, for the brief moment when goodbyes were said, everyone prayed in their hearts for a good fight by all. Prayed for a good fight!

Although we didn't know what the good fight was against.

The Man Who Left His Will on Film. 1970.

Ten years. Has my fight been a good one? It has supported me through my rec-
ollections of that night and of the year 1960. That day I believed in the whole world
because of those people.

The tenth year. I make the tenth year's *Cruel Story of Youth*.

A Secret Post-Tokyo War Story

Last September's Osaka War, as the Red Army faction proclaimed it. And the
Tokyo War in November. They were illusions, however. Each sect was exclaiming,
"We'll fight to the death," but ultimately there was not one death. Of course, I too was
roaming the Haneda area, camera in hand.

A Secret Post-Tokyo War Story is the answer to the question, "How can one die?"
At the same time, it is a requiem dedicated with deep emotion to the many young
people who were killed, without thinking they were going to die, in the peaceful
Japan of the quarter-century since World War II—the victims of that postwar
adolescence.

It is raining. June 15 of the tenth year. Rather than staying up all night walking,
I return to my lodgings and write this.

(United News Service, June 20, 1970)

Second Interlude: Some Fragments of My Life (1969–1974)

My Adolescence Began with Defeat

When does adolescence begin and when does it end? I wonder if one can know when one's own adolescence began. That seems almost impossible—at least so far as I am concerned.

I think that I am still in adolescence. I wonder if this is because I am involved with films.

Those who watch films are mostly young people. Surveys indicate that the peak age of Japanese film audiences is from seventeen to twenty-two. Young people see films fanatically. I wonder if they see life itself in them. They talk about them feverishly. Nearly everyone has one or two films he has seen and felt passionate about during adolescence. And he probably has a memory of a coffee shop where he sat around talking about a film for hours.

At some point, however, people stop seeing films. Once they have jobs and families they practically stop seeing films altogether. They say things like, "Oh yes, films. I want to see them, but I don't have the time." I had a televised confrontation with a large group of housewives who talked like that. "What do you do about this kind of person?" the moderator asked. I said that I don't make films for people who say they don't see films. It's fine if they don't. What bothers me is the air of intellectual superiority with which they say it. As if to say, "We don't see that sort of thing." I said, "You're lying. You don't see films. In fact, films don't interest you. I'm sure you don't read books, either. Other than passively taking in the images projected from the nearest television set, you don't absorb a single thing. You've fallen into a state of total intellectual idleness."

I don't know about other countries, but in Japan this happens to everyone after adolescence. In the midst of that Japan, I am independent. My films are independent. Fifteen years ago I had a career as well. Ten years ago I started a family. For better or worse, however, because it was the career I chose, I didn't have the leeway to fall into intellectual idleness. It may have been inevitable, but during that time, along with some friends, I had to continue reading and thinking. As a result, I am independent.

The only people who see my films are young people. The friends who went through adolescence with me fifteen years ago say, "The old films were good, weren't they?. . .By the way, what are you making now? Lately I haven't even had time to see your films. Sorry about that. I'll see the next one. Let me know when it comes out, okay?" Thank you, thank you. There's nothing to say. People say the old films were good. However, a person is able to see a film and be moved by it only because he or she has a certain degree of sensitivity. People saw films and were moved by them during adolescence, that time of acute sensitivity. Even if they were to see a film now, their sensitivity has dulled, and they wouldn't be moved. They have lost even the sensitivity that causes them to want to see a film.

When I am among those people talking to them, I feel that I myself am still in the midst of adolescence. I am independent, and for that reason I am positively full of rebellion. Rebellion is a sure sign of adolescence. You could even say that it is the surest sign. I couldn't possibly stop rebelling yet. When I talk with young people, I think to myself, "They too will soon have an occupation and a family and become like the average intellectually idle Japanese. And l will remain, remain, remain. I have to remain. I must remain in an adolescence that takes the form of independent rebellion."

I wonder when my adolescence began. I can't discern it for myself. However, I probably have to mention the things that happened that day—although I am reluctant to do so because too many people, all kinds of people, especially the intelligentsia of my generation, have said too much about that day.

By that day, I mean that hot summer day when a strange silence gripped Japan. I was thirteen years old, an eighth grader. I was playing Japanese chess with a friend in a dusky house in the traditional commercial section of Kyoto. At noon, leaving the chess pieces as they were, my friend returned home, about ten houses away, to eat. In those days, it was unthinkable to eat a meal at someone else's house or to be treated to food by them. After eating, my friend came back. Then we continued our chess game. The afternoon was no different from the morning. The hot sun continued to beat down, but the old Kyoto house was dark. We continued staring silently at the chessboard, which was the bottom of a wooden box onto which drawing paper had been pasted, lines drawn in ink, and varnish carefully applied.

During that one game, however, the whole world changed. "It" happened. What we had been taught could never happen, what we had believed would never happen, had happened. I don't know whether I won that chess game or lost it, but it wouldn't have mattered if I had won. My stouthearted mother was already getting dressed to go meet my younger sister at the evacuation camp. And then she was probably hanging out of a railway car into which people had been packed like sardines. If that is true, I spent the night alone. I wonder if I prepared my own supper. No, there was nothing to eat, so I probably spent the whole night cowering.

Looking back, I think that that day—August 15, 1945, the day on which the Emperor conceded, on the radio, Japans defeat—was probably the beginning of my adolescence. If so, I would have to say that it was a strange adolescence, in the true sense of the word. The reason my adolescence began on the day is that I learned that there was nothing of which one could say that it could never happen. I had been thinking that adolescence would be more full of hope because my father, who died when I was six, had left me so many books, and by that time I had already read most of the classics. I had even scanned a few pages of a very old edition of *Das Kapital*. According to the knowledge I had gleaned from those books, adolescence was something that began with innocence and hope and ended with heartbreak and frustration. My adolescence, though, began with frustration. There was nothing resembling hope.

The next day, remembering, I dug up the garden. The garden, although small, was the traditional Japanese type with a pond and stone lanterns, but it had been converted into a sweet potato field, and I had buried some books there in a large pot. We had sent things like encyclopedias and old books to my younger sister's evacuation site, but I had put the familiar books that were particularly important to me in the pot. But that was a careless idea. The pot had absorbed water, and the books were half rotted. A strange odor emanated from the book remains when they were exposed to the daylight. Among them, I felt that I, who had loved the books, was ugly. For the next five or six years I read nothing but textbooks and *Baseball Magazine*. Nor did I have the money to buy books. When I went to bookstores, it was to shoplift. A best-selling dictionary of the time was the easiest book to steal and resell.

I wonder when the word "frustration" became as popular as it is now. Certainly the word was heard frequently after the anti-Security Treaty riots of 1960. It was said that the youths and students who fought then suffered from intense feelings of frustration. All three of the films I made before and after those riots—*Cruel Story of Youth, The Tomb of the Sun,* and *Night and Fog in Japan*—were tales of the frustration of adolescence.

At that time, when you made a film with a company, you were made to write something called a production plan. It was printed at the beginning of the script. It didn't always indicate the artist's plan; instead, at times it contained words couched in euphemisms to single out points of compromise with the company. Let's say, however, that production plans can be trusted to some extent. In the production plans for *Cruel Story of Youth,* I wrote, "This is the story of young people who were only able to show their youthful anger in a perverted way. This distortion drives their adolescence—which could have been beautiful—into cruel defeat. Through that tragedy, I expressed my intense anger at the conditions that dominate modern-day adolescence."

In the production plan for *Night and Fog in Japan,* I wrote, "All men have responsibility. Those who created the current situation must change it. Those who should become the nucleus of reform but remain embedded in their lives; those who once stepped forward as the nucleus of reform but became frustrated and now impatiently wait for reform to come from outside themselves; and those who preserve the stagnant conditions in spite of their unceasing belief that they are the nucleus of reform—I strongly denounce the corruption, depravity, and mistakes of such nuclei."

In one plan I write of defeat and in the other I write of frustration. Viewing the matter in this way, I am sure that when I treat adolescence in my films, I maintain strong images of frustration, defeat, which continues to haunt me. This is even clearer when you see the films, and several outstanding critics have pointed it out immediately. The funny thing is that just after I made these films, when I first met Masumura Yasuzo, who is a bit older than I, he said, "What is this? You, with such a serene face, what do you have to be frustrated about?" Certainly, there is truth in that. I have almost never shown a sad expression in front of anyone, and even when I'm not with people, my countenance isn't that sad. And I've never had the experience of being unable to eat because of some disappointment. Moreover, I have never considered suicide. It may seem strange to people that my stories of adolescence are based on images of frustration, but the opposite is true. It isn't strange at all.

Frustration is natural. Once you understand that there is nothing that absolutely cannot happen in the human world, everything is ultimately wasted effort. Even if one decides on some goal and tries to accomplish it, events completely unrelated to one can determine whether or not the goal is accomplished. When you look at it this way, there are a lot of opportunities for disappointment during adolescence, when the human heart burns passionately. I made up my mind about this long ago. So I go on grinning. I am not surprised by a bit of frustration.

When did I make up my mind about this? I wonder if it was on that day. I stopped reading books after that day. I sweated it out as the worst player on a sandlot baseball team. I dabbled in student theater and, although my acting was poor, I flattered myself that I was second best. When I went to college, I chose law rather than literature. I vainly avoided thought and reflection. I thought that I wanted to be just a lump of flesh.

However, the moment I entered college, I was attacked by a strange feeling of disappointment. I suddenly felt that I was at the end of my adolescence. This was strange because I sensed that adolescence was ending at the time when it usually begins. The lectures were dull; I had no money. Having entered the law department, I had no idea of what I wanted to become in the future. I didn't have a beautiful girlfriend, and, although I had been hoping I was a genius, it somehow became clear to me that I wasn't. The fact that I had lived apathetically for the five years since that August day exploded all at once. Finding no place for myself on the large campus, I had nowhere to turn. And I was intensely worried about the fact that my adolescence was over.

In that frame of mind, I became involved in student theater once again and also participated in the student movement. The student movement became a struggle to be won or lost. Many of the struggles ended in defeat. At those times, the leaders still said we had won. They searched for reasons to justify their saying so. I wasn't able to believe it, however. Defeat is defeat. What's wrong with that? When I thought that, I felt my destiny and the movement overlap. To put it grandly, I felt myself overlap with history. By that time, my feeling of disappointment had already disappeared. I decided to yield to the selfish desires of the moment and let my destiny take care of itself. I was no longer afraid of defeat or frustration or independence. I became involved in the student movement merely because I wanted to; I didn't join the faction to which the leaders belonged. In that respect, I thought, I was yielding to the flow of history.

At that time, I encountered a book and a phrase. The book was Camus's *The Myth of Sisyphus,* and the words were those of Akashi Kaijin, a poet stricken by leprosy: "If you don't glow like the fishes in the depths of the ocean, there will be no light anywhere." These words and the image of Sisyphus continuing to push the boulder up the mountain, no matter how many times it rolled back down, described my feelings exactly.

The student movement accumulated its defeats, and I made repeated mistakes in the student theater; before I knew it, four years had passed. While listening to the school president's inane address, I thought to myself, "Like being pursued by a boulder. . ." Perhaps the only thing I had gained during four years of college was an image of what frustration was.

I entered the studio with only that. There my second adolescence began. What happened after that is a very long story. I have been defeated time and again; those who know me, however, know that I am fine all the same.

(Reading for Youth, August 1969)

My Father's Nonexistence: A Determining Factor in My Existence

What can parents do for their children? They can't do anything. Would not the most they can do for them is to die at an early age?

I think outrageous thoughts such as this in spite of myself.

According to the method now used to calculate age, my father died when I was six; it was around the time I received my report card at the ceremony marking the end of first grade. Recently my homeroom teacher from that time told me that, when I received word that my father had died and I was told to go home, I didn't go immediately. What was going through my little mind at that time?

My father was a government official, so as soon as he died we lost his official residence and had nowhere to live. My maternal grandfather's house was in the traditional commercial district of Kyoto, so we ended up living there. In the entrance a nameplate bearing my name was hung next to the one bearing my grandfather's.

My grandfather died soon afterward, and until I graduated from college I lived in that house with my mother and younger sister. For my mother it was always a struggle, but I think that my sister and I lived rather luxuriously and self-indulgently. The psychological pressure that comes from not having a father, however, was considerable.

And so I feel that it was my father's nonexistence, rather than my mother's existence, that determined my mode of existence. I had all kinds of feelings about my dead father, including resentment and longing, and I thought a lot about the meaning of those feelings. But I didn't really think often about my mother, who was right there with me.

During a certain period after I had finished college and gone to work, I began to wonder what would have happened if my mother had also died during my childhood. Of course, I wasn't so lacking in filial piety as to wish that she get sick and die. But I wonder what would have happened if Kyoto had suffered the kind of air raids during the war that other cities endured and our family had been split up. I can't help having regrets about the kind of totally different future that might have opened up for me. I resented having the protection of my mother's existence: it made my life merely average, relatively speaking, as opposed to extraordinary.

Therefore, if there is anything not average inside me, it is because of my father's nonexistence. I didn't realize this until I got a job. Because of my father's death, I had absolutely no idea about how to interact with older men. I am 99 percent submissive to older men and exceedingly courteous. However, the 1 percent in me that can't possibly be deferential is resolutely rebellious and impolite. By the time I found out, only recently, that this way of behaving toward older men was inadvisable, I had already gotten myself into trouble many times. The goodwill they felt toward my submissive self merely intensified their exasperation at my rebellious side.

It is clear that this behavior works against me in life. Conversely, though, accumulating these handicaps helped make me at least slightly out of the ordinary. Therefore, this behavior pattern, which gets me into trouble, is important in itself, and insofar as my father's nonexistence was the basis for it, I should probably be grateful for his nonexistence.

As most people do, I got married and had children. When my oldest son was born, I wanted to try to live for him until he was six, the age at which I lost my father. He is already far older than that. I can die anytime.

We must discard the notion that parents must live for the sake of their children. If we live, we live for ourselves. Conversely, we can die anytime.

What can parents do for their children? Nothing. Thinking that they can do something is merely a feeling on the part of the parents. It is the same whether they do something or die having done nothing. It is merely a matter of how the child assesses the situation. Outstanding children will always feel dissatisfaction and rebellion at what their parents have done for them.

A parent who is resigned to the fact that there is nothing he or she can do, but who must nevertheless live with his or her children, can at least clearly articulate the fact of his or her nonexistence in their presence. In concrete terms, the parent must create time away from the child. That is true discipline and education.

Today, however, when parents closely examine all of their children's homework assignments, most homes exist in an entirely different realm from that of true discipline and education.

(Techniques for General Education, August 1973)

There Is No Youth without Adventure

Does the fact that I have been asked to write something about adventure mean that I am thought of as an adventurer?

The image one initially presents to the world doesn't readily disappear and is nearly impossible to change later.

Because I was fortunate enough to be able to exhibit my work to the world while I was young, my existence inevitably seemed treasonous to the previous generation. Furthermore, just as I made my appearance in the film world, I was forced to leave the company with which I had been associated, which probably made my conduct seem combative. Also, some of the opinions I expressed in the process decorated the pages of the weekly magazines in words that were more sensational than those I had used. Moreover—and for this I am solely to blame—in the midst of that irritation I even caused a minor violent incident. There was probably nothing I could do about it if people thought I was vulgar and violent physically as well as rebellious and combative psychologically. My wife tells me that even now people sometimes say to her, "You certainly do a good job living with that frightening husband of yours." Perhaps that image of me is consistent with that of the adventurer.

In reality, since childhood I have thought of myself as someone with absolutely no connection to adventure.

My childhood took place during the war, so "adventure" was happening all around me. In my early youth, however, adventure took the form of stories like "Dankichi the Adventurer"—a lone hero who fights natives and animals in the South Sea Islands. In the middle stage of my youth, the adventure story was transformed into the tale of a hero who encounters Japan's militaristic policies; toward the end of my youth, it was the story of a hero who follows Japan's state policies to the letter and heads for unexplored regions.

I read all these stories with the same interest as most youths, but I didn't become wildly enthusiastic. At no time did I pattern myself after these heroes or think I wanted to be like them. Privately I thought that this was because my body was weak.

The word "adventure" meant to me just what the Chinese characters used to represent the word imply: "to defy danger." I did not have nearly the physical strength needed to defy danger. Adventure meant that there were people from whom strength gushed, and that such gushing strength drove them to deserted islands in the South Seas and to the wilds of Manchuria and Mongolia. Realizing that I didn't have that kind of strength, I secretly resented those friends of mine who seemed to be endowed with it. Along with that resentment and hatred, I harbored an unnameable dissatisfaction with the militaristic era that allowed my stronger friends to enjoy a certain superiority. I may have felt that I was compelled to "be adventurous" by those around me.

Thus the end of the war was a kind of liberation for me: I was no longer compelled to "be adventurous." The friends of mine who had worn triumphant looks for being endowed with the strength for adventure were ruined: the Japanese people were confined to four small islands for the second time, exactly as they had been before the Meiji Restoration.

There is no youth without "adventure," however. Or, youth discovers its own "adventure" as a matter of course. That in itself was not unique. It simply meant that the same two roads to "adventure" that tempt youths of any era were open to us. However, because until then any "adventure" not conforming to the national goals was forbidden, the freedom of the "adventures" that now opened up before us was dazzling.

One of the new "adventures" on which we could embark was women. Another (and the issue of women is included here) was the desire for a more ideal depravity—a desire which, if pursued, led to suicide.

One of my friends heroically embarked on an "adventure."

Actually, it was nothing more than a little high spirits. Even now I can still see before me the face of one of my friends, carefully checking the crease in his trousers as he went off to a coffee shop forbidden to students. The shop was a favorite haunt of the delinquent schoolgirls who wore their sailor blouses tight, which was also forbidden. I also remember one of my literary magazine colleagues on the second floor of a roast sweet potato shop near the school—another store that was off-limits to students—taking amphetamines by injection and finally holding up the syringe and glaring at me, walleyed, saying he was going to commit suicide by injecting air into his veins. At that time I discovered once again that I was not "adventurous."

This time it was clearly not a problem of physical strength, nor did it seem to be a matter of psychological strength. Inside me, thoughts about the body of the opposite sex were burning more briskly every day, and my desires for suicide were making my many sleepless nights unbearable. In the midst of those days and nights, I finally found my way to an idea. The idea was that the reason I couldn't be an "adventurer" was not because I lacked the inner willpower or the external strength but because the strength that checks that impulse is too overpowering. In a word, I was a coward. During the war there were many pallid youths with dreams of "adventure" who were actually inferior to me in terms of physical strength. Since then I have become accustomed to living in the company of my characteristic cowardice.

The life I have lived isn't worth a detailed chronology, however. Let's skip ahead a step. Having studied law in college, I took a job with a film company, and almost as soon as I became a young director, I rushed out of the company. At the time, it was thought to be impossible to make films outside a film company. For the next twelve years, however, I made independently produced films. Now that producing independently has become common, I have disbanded my independent production company and am groping for a new road that will once again allow me to be a complete individual. So, at first glance my external actions may make me look like a man of "adventure" or an independent pioneer.

However, even if I were really an adventurer or an independent pioneer, it was simply because I was cowardly, not because I was rebellious and combative, let alone vulgar and violent.

I entered a film company for the simple reason that it was difficult to find a job at that time and, partly because I had been active in the student movement, I couldn't find anything else. Because my mother had raised me by herself, I thought that I ought to graduate from college without taking any extra time and that I ought to make my own living when I did graduate, so I took a job simply so that I could eat. I merely went about things in a cowardly, modest way.

When I caused trouble at the company and resigned, I had just married, and I don't know how many times I tried to resolve things with the company harmoniously. I also wrote an apology to the company, thinking that if they would let me travel to a foreign country for a year of study, the storm would blow over and I would be able to work there contentedly. However, I ultimately decided to resign because I thought that if I remained under those conditions, I would be a failure. It was not because I was bold or courageous but merely because I was a coward frantically trying to protect himself.

Ever since that time in my youth when I realized that I was a coward and weak, my main concern has been how a weak person like myself can continue to protect himself and survive in this world.

The frantic effort to protect one's weak self takes the form of bold actions; this may have given me the appearance of an "adventurer."

"Adventurers" are people who head for unexplored regions and unknown territory. The world's popular "adventurers" are people who challenge the remote corners of the earth, the unexplored regions. If I were to qualify as an "adventurer," it would be only on the basis of my being a person who challenges unexplored psychological territories.

Frankly, the first time I made a film, I myself didn't know what kind of film I would make. I merely possessed one exceedingly small image.

It was a very, very dark image, in which I face the world, and try to express myself, and am decisively punished because that act conflicts with the rules of the world. When the film I made based on that image was treated coldly by the company, I knew that my image had not been wrong; and at the same time, I had been given a clue as to the type of film director I was. Since then I have gradually come to understand myself more each time I make a film. To put it another way, each time I make a film, I have also gradually come to understand myself less. In any case, I still don't understand myself completely.

Consequently, I may be an "adventurer" because I challenge unexplored psychological territories, but clues to that search are found only by searching the unexplored territories of my own psyche.

Perhaps I do deserve the title "adventurer" in one respect: I have used the film only to explore territory that is unknown to me as an individual—the same film that has been completely popularized as a medium and, has been established as a skillful telling of circumstances are already basically known. Of course, a few great film directors of the past have achieved this in their films, even if unconsciously.

Beginning in the latter half of the 1950s, film directors who recognized this emerged to create work based on their decision that the film was not a medium for skillfully narration of things that are already generally known, but rather that it should be a medium for the exploration of unknown territory. Their numbers are few, however, both throughout the world and within their respective countries. "Adventurers," however, are always few—just as in our old junior high school class, "adventurers" confronting girls and the desire for depravity were, ultimately, few in number.

I tell you now why I bear the glory and tragedy of being an "adventurer" and solo pioneer in international and in Japanese film.

Of course, film is not the only medium in which one probes the unexplored regions of the human psyche, for outstanding artists have traditionally done this, even though some of them may not have done so consciously. However, they were normally loners and few in number. Today, when all art is placed on the conveyor belt of mass communication and artists treated like overprotected children, it has become difficult for fresh art that explains the unknown regions of the human psyche to emerge. In that respect, the film is still not established in society as an art form, and, far from being overprotected, film artists are put in a situation where they can't produce a work without a struggle. Therefore, there is perhaps a stronger possibility that, using the situation to their advantage, more "adventurers" will emerge in film than in other situations.

Although the world has become somewhat smaller, outer space is gradually being explained, and, for the first time, unexplored geographical regions are becoming fewer, there will never be a lack of unexplored territory for the human being: for the human being, the last unexplored region is himself.

Accordingly, whether or not like an artist of stature, he makes public the substance and traces of his investigations, every human being is an explorer of the unknown regions of the human psyche, an "adventurer." The qualifications for being an "adventurer," however, are not boldness and bravery, as is customarily thought; rather, they are knowledge of one's own cowardice and weakness.

For a long time I resented the type of geographical "adventurer" who crosses the Pacific Ocean alone in a yacht. But it is not their physical strength or boldness or bravery that drives them to "adventure." They may be people just like me who are trying to discover for themselves the meaning of living by putting their weak selves in such situations.

(Supplementary fall issue of *PHP, Peace, Happiness, Prosperity,* a revue of general culture, founded by the president of Matsushita, October 1974)

The first time I made a film in color—my first film was in black and white and my second was in color—I imposed a small taboo on myself.

It was to never shoot the color green. It's easy to avoid green costumes. There probably isn't a lot of green furniture. You need only remove any green signs. The problem is the green of trees and plants. That film was set in a city, and so there were no green fields. In the end, the problem boiled down to the green of the shrubbery. I didn't have a garden made to go with the house on the set, and while shooting on location I took care to see that the camera angle excluded trees and shrubs.

I took a job in a studio not because I liked photography but because I needed a job—I took a job in a studio only as a way to eat. Those were days when it was extraordinarily difficult to get a job, and you couldn't pick and choose. I absolutely could not stand the films that were mass-produced by the studio in which I worked: tear-jerking melodramas and flavorless domestic dramas in which imbecilic men and women monotonously repeat exchanges of infinitely stagnant emotions. The places where these exchanges, which can only be called artificial, unfold are gloomy, decaying eight-mat drawing rooms and four-and-a-half-mat living rooms that contain such symbols of family stability as tea cabinets. In the background there was generally a totally commonplace garden. I hated such characters, rooms, and gardens from the depths of my soul. I firmly believed that unless the dark sensibility that those things engendered was completely destroyed, nothing new could come into being in Japan.

Just then, there began appearing in the actual cities of Japan scenes that differed from these. I remember vividly even now the excitement I felt the first evening I visited the clusters of high-rise housing built by the Japan Housing Corporation on the huge area of reclaimed land along the coast. The concrete walls cut across the sky in acute angles. The dreamlike lines of mercury lamps began to light up here and there. The long, long uninhabited corridors reverberated with a metallic clacking sound that was an echo of something I couldn't identify. Ah! With this the sensibility of the Japanese will change! Japanese with a different sensibility will be born!

I visited a young official of the housing ministry at that government-built high-rise development. He was a friend from my student-movement days. He spoke passionately of his conviction that the founding of these dwellings would change the lives of the Japanese people for the better. By that time I had already stopped believing that the lives of the people could be changed for the better by a plan imposed on them by a government agency, so I wasn't in complete agreement with him. However, because I was naively convinced that our sensibilities would probably be changed by these types of buildings, I responded to him cheerfully. It was an inspiring evening.

Seizing on the excitement of that evening, I spent about two and a half years in a fifth-floor studio apartment in government-built housing located right in the middle of a poor suburb on the outskirts of an industrial city. I don't know whether my sensibilities changed while I lived in that three-mat concrete room. The view of the street from my fifth-floor window was sad—especially in the evening, when the matchbox houses bathed in the twilight appeared all too clearly to be more and more artificial. When I thought about the lives being led by the people in those little boxes, a scream that life is meaningless pushed upward from deep within my breast. I desperately resisted the temptation to throw myself out the window, and instead I decided to scorn the people leading those meaningless lives, myself included, with all my heart.

When I began shooting films, I decided to smear my films black with the feelings of scorn I had for those people and the simultaneous feelings of anger I had as one scorned. As far as possible, I made my heroes characters independent of their houses. Although you can say that essentially human beings are not separable from their dwellings, I tried to first establish my characters as individuals by choosing those who could actually exist separately from them. On a very technical level, I tried to eliminate completely all scenes with characters sitting on tatami while talking. It is difficult to shoot a composition with one person sitting on tatami and one standing, and if both are sitting down it becomes completely static. Also, it takes about twice as much time for a person sitting on tatami to stand up as it does for a person sitting in a chair. So, even when I did feature tatami rooms, I used chairs unmercifully.

At that time, the green of shrubbery was, for me, the root of many evils. No matter how severe a human confrontation you are portraying, it immediately becomes mild the instant that even a little green enters into it. Green always softens the heart—

well, I don't know about foreigners, but at least it does in the case of Japanese. This was definitely true, at least as I have observed it in frames on movie screens. For that reason, I banished all green.

The green of pines is particularly bad. When that irregularly shaped green comes in, everything becomes ambiguously neutral. The sky above the green of the pines isn't good either. The blue sky in itself is by no means a bad thing. The blue sky above the brown earth is sufficient to teach us the terror of human life. The blue sky beyond the green of the pines, the blue sky that you can just catch a glimpse of beyond your neighbor's fence: those are the bad ones. They give the small satisfaction the feeling that this is good enough, the small sense of relief. In that film, therefore, I didn't shoot the sky over the roofs of the houses or the sky outside the windows at all.

I don't know whether or not the results were good. The film aroused a maelstrom of praise and censure and became popular anyway. No review, however, noted that I had repeatedly done the unnatural by banishing green and not shooting the sky.

Nearly fifteen years have passed since then. It is almost twenty years since my evening of excitement about a high-rise development of reinforced concrete. The sensibility of the Japanese people is far from changed. Instead, as if to ridicule the excitement of an ignorant youth, they are burying every room of reinforced concrete in every possible mass synthetic chemical product, transforming these dwellings into the set for a truly mild new domestic drama.

My friend, formerly a young official at the housing ministry, returned to university-level research and is beginning a basic reexamination of the homes of the Japanese people.

If a film director on the threshold of old age thinks about the road his own work has traveled, he sees that with each new project the tendency to deny reality and play inside his own fantasies has grown stronger.

The destiny of the camera, however, is that it captures scenes of the real Japan. If so, to what extent can the landscape be modified as landscape? And to what extent can the artist, using the camera as a medium, convert the landscape into fantasies?

The film director approaching old age will soon no longer have the cheek, as in former days, to banish green and negate the sky. But he will strive to make his way into the endlessly minute aspects of reality, to discover and abstract his own fantasies there. And he will try to use the fantastic to thoroughly negate reality.

The film director on the threshold of old age must impose this sort of difficult task on himself because scenes that decisively negate reality do not exist in Japan today. Ambiguous Japan, where the instant that anything is made it seems to be completely buried in reality. This is particularly true of modern-day Japan. Is that really the nation's destiny?

I have a definite distrust of the architects and others who create Japan's scenery, particularly because they have not created even one place with scenery that adequately negates reality. But perhaps this is only the occupational resentment or prejudice of a film director who is trying to travel a difficult road and is getting tired.

(*Kyosenzui,* a periodical on flower arrangement, September 1974)

From My Diary

Prison

Suddenly I think about the people who are locked in gaol. Gaol is such an old word. But somehow I feel that the words "jail," "prison house," and "prison" describe it perfectly.

It isn't that I think of any people in particular. I just think vaguely about the cold and dampness of the prison and of the dark gleam in the eyes of the prisoners. I think of the prisoner in solitary confinement who suddenly thinks about death. I think about the execution ground I toured as preparation for the film *Death by Hanging.* With its salmon pink walls and sash windows, it was like a civilized residence.

They talk about revising the penal code. Loud voices clamor against recognizing a larger range of criminal activities and instituting heavier penalties. Opposition will no doubt come into being. But I think silently, alone.

Is the destruction of the prisons forbidden? Is releasing all prisoners forbidden? When did we lose the ability to exert our imagination in the direction of destroying the prisons?

Are we not all prisoners now? Do we have any freedom? Are our houses not cold like prisons? Is the gleam in our eyes not dark like a prisoner's?

The movement against the revision of the penal code, which doesn't have the power to see its way clear to destroying the prisons, looks to me like a festival outside the prison walls.

In ancient times, revolutions began with the destruction of prisons. No, history called the uprisings that were strong enough to destroy the prisons "revolutions."

(*Asahi News,* May 20, 1974)

Dignity

A human being risks his entire existence in an antagonistic confrontation with those around him. To the aroma that exudes from that person at that time the word "dignity" can be applied.

Our days are passed in a place that is all to far removed from that type of human dignity.

Rather than being our own, the labors of our days are merely a series of things we are made to do by those outside ourselves. We live lives that are even more evanescent that the bubbles floating along the stream—and even more meaningless.

The reason we show an abnormal interest in crime and scandal is that a life, which usually drifts by, thereby appears caught up by a pole in the river's flow. A drowning man grasps at straws. For we find, in crime and scandal, a tiny trace that reminds us of human dignity. Crime and scandal, however, are also merely parts of life that are external to ourselves. Thus, for the person concerned and for the observer, they weather and disappear in time.

The path to human dignity lies through the act of one who, having been previously involved in a crime or scandal, chooses that option for himself once again, in the very midst of the flow.

Only a very few are able to accomplish this. I believe that the majority of them is now in jail.

(*Asahi News*, May 21, 1974)

War

"Let's wage war against the government and public corporations," said Koizumi Yone, who died in the Sanrizuka "war."[1]

Her age, her place of birth, her childhood, even the name of her husband— she remembered none of these things clearly. She devoted herself single-mindedly to the act of living. Her "war" began when "the government and public corporations" clashed forcefully with her life.

For her, to live meant to wage "war," and not waging "war" meant death.

I see living proof of human dignity in the great diversity of victims in modern Japan who rose up, defying death.

---

1. Confrontations that occurred when local residents and students demonstrated against the construction of New Tokyo International Airport (Narita) in the 1970s.

For me, the most memorable of the accounts of Koizumi Yone concerns her return home from the hospital several days before her death. It said that she kept screaming, "I don't want to go to a nursing home. I don't want to!"

What was it that made her scream so?

She had lived out her life with absolutely no connection to the modern history of the Japanese nation and had fought a "war" with that nation at the end. Did the nursing home, a product of modernization, seem like an enemy prison camp?

If so, one would have to say that in the streets and fields of Japan there are piles and piles of corpses—dead and living—of anonymous warriors who are unable to cry out as Koizumi Yone did.

(Asahi News, May 22, 1974)

The Corpse

For the past five years there has been a corpse before me, and I don't know what to do with it.

It is the corpse of a woman, who, like Koizumi Yone of Sanrizuka, died refusing to go into a nursing home.

She had been living alone as she grew old, and although she had sold her house and donated a large sum to a nursing home and was steadily making plans to live in the room that had been built with the money (or so it seemed to those around her), she was found dead one day, wearing burial clothes, in her futon. The cotton inside the futon had recently been willowed. She had cleaned her room until it was spotless, made decisions about the disposition of all of her belongings and labeled them accordingly, and laundered everything down to her only set of undergarments. She was found by a relative who had received a telegram from her that said, "Seriously ill. Come immediately."

This death gave me a shock that chilled my soul and moved me.

At the same time, though, it confused me. This splendidly noble way of dying is evidence of the fact that she had lived her whole life based on the idea that one must clean up after oneself. It is evidence of a life in which depending on someone else was unthinkable. When I think about that, the nobility turns to tragedy.

The fact is that she was one of the Japanese women who went to Southeast Asia to work as prostitutes after the Meiji Restoration of 1868.

(Asahi News, May 23, 1974)

Misery

I think I have a case of manic depression.

One day, my emotions flow unimpeded, becoming a thick, enveloping vapor, and I am one with the world. The next day the air around me is thin and my chest is as heavy as if I had drunk lead. At the same time, though, I am listless, as if in a world without gravity. All I do is drift in a faint blue funk.

I have lost track of the way leading to the discovery of human dignity.

I don't have the life of certainty of those locked in prison, criminals who are on the way to committing their second crime, or of those who had to lead lives of direct confrontation with modern Japan.

For that reason I have always created work when in contact with such people, and I intend to continue doing so. But has making those works increased the certainty of my life? I have to say no.

Instead, whenever I make a work, my faint bit of inner certainty blends into the work, and my own life becomes less and less certain. Does this mean intensification of doubts as to certainty?

Is this type of misery a sickness of the age in which we live, floating like jellyfish in a controlled society? Or is it just that as we grow older we go from certainty to uncertainty? If we can't even be certain of the answer to that, the misery cuts deep indeed.

(*Asahi News,* May 24, 1974)

The King

When I attended, for the first time in thirty years, the reunion of my junior high school classmates, we reminisced about one teacher in particular. He was our Western History teacher, and what was engraved on our minds was his response whenever he thought we had lost interest in the lecture: he would close his textbook and tell us stories.

The Greek tragedies scared us even more than the ghost stories. The mere sound of names like "Agamemnon" and "Oedipos" (as he pronounced it) reverberated ominously, and our hearts froze with the fear of what oracle might be in store. I wonder if that was because this happened during and just after the war, when our own fates were being trifled with by the gods as if we were merely leaves on a tree.

One question has remained with me during the intervening thirty years. The titles of Greek tragedies are often proper names, and yet, despite the fact that both were kings, it is not *Agamemnon the King* but only *Oedipus the King*.

Perhaps that title signifies that someone who was not supposed to become king had done so. However, I now understand that Oedipus was indeed a king among kings. His tragedy lies in the fact that he knows that he has killed his father and married his mother. Because he exerted all of his efforts to find out who he was and, as a result, had to endure tragedy all alone, Oedipus alone is worthy of the title "King."

(*Asahi News,* May 25, 1974)

The People inside Her Head

I met a strange girl.

She says that the voices of four or five people are always inside her head. And she says that they restrict her activities. She says that for nearly five years she has been ruled by the voices and cannot live freely. I understand why she is pale and lacks vitality despite the fact that she looks younger than she is and has a pretty face.

"Why did you come to me?" I ask. "Isn't this the way it's done in the entertainment world?" She stares at me with eyes tinged with the color of insanity. She appears to want to think that the people inside her head (as she puts it) actually exist and are controlling her.

I answer soberly that it isn't possible. Directors do sometimes suggest this to young actors, but there is no way that people you have never even met can control you for five years.

"What is it you want to do?" Although she can't respond too well to my questions, I learn that she has taken the examination of a club for models. She has a strong need to expose herself. But something inside her tries to stop her. It is "the people inside her head." So, why did she come to me? Is this an aspiring actress? Making up my mind that she was, I suddenly started thinking, "Perhaps, 'the people inside her head' do actually exist."

(*Asahi News,* May 27, 1974)

The Balsam

In a bar.

It is the kind of bar where they indiscriminately shove a microphone in the patrons' faces and make them sing. One woman sang "Ferryboat of Tears," first in Japanese, then in Korean. She's probably Korean.

What would be an appropriate follow-up? "The Balsam" in my dimly remembered Korean.

"The Balsam" is a song that was greatly loved by the Korean people before the war. The gist of it is that when the balsam is blooming beautifully in the hedge, a cool wind comes, scattering the blossoms and causing the children to disappear too. The wind represents Japanese imperialism.

Whether she found my faltering Korean pathetic or planned to correct me, the Korean woman, whom I had never seen before, came over and sang along with me. Ten years had passed since I had been to Korea and learned that song.

Few Japanese make an effort to learn the history of the Japanese oppression of peoples. Only a very few young people are groping to find their way with that history in mind.

Whether or not those young people are conscious of it, they are joining with the formerly oppressed peoples, sensitive to the fact that they are now rising again.

I am ashamed of myself for singing "The Balsam" half sentimentally, in spite of my theoretical belief in the rising up of the oppressed.

(*Asahi News,* May 28, 1974)

The Weaklings

I received a letter of thanks. That is extremely rare.

Her personal story was, "I want to separate from my second husband." The reason? "Because I want to marry my third husband." Why? "Because I love him." It is truly simple.

Both her first and second husbands had a wife and children. "Because she loved them," she made them divorce and marry her. Why did she decide to leave? "Because I had an affair. I am the guilty one."

It is rare for a woman who comes seeking advice to say that she is guilty. Why does she have affairs? "It may be beautiful when the man says that he will leave his wife and child so that your two hearts can live as one, but as time goes by and life settles into a routine, he gets bored, doesn't he?" I asked. For the first time, she began to cry, nodding her head.

She is forty-eight, her new man is forty. But what totally shocked me was hearing that he had a seventy-year-old common-law wife. "That seventy-year-old has ended their relationship, and she is happy for us. I plan to look after her forever," she said, beaming.

She had won. She was a strong person.

But this is an exception. People who come for personal advice are weaklings. In this world, the weaklings are always troubled. They all come for personal advice about how to dispel their troubles. I have nothing to say in response. I don't receive any letters of thanks for them.

(*Asahi News*, May 29, 1974)

Films

Shopping in a department store takes courage. Standing in the street with packages from a department store takes even more courage. Having bought my children some games, I was waiting for a taxi, carrying a big package.

A young woman walking by glanced at me, took several more steps, and then stopped. Staring at me, she walked toward me as if by a reflex reaction.

"When will you be making a film?" Her face was full of curiosity. She was wearing a light green suit. Her hair was short and curled. I gave the usual excuse. Then I said, "You are . . . ?"

"Just a fan." She blushed and walked away.

Films are a product of industrial society. The dreams depicted in films were industrial society's dreams of prosperity and unending progress. And the films themselves were symbols of industrial society's prosperity and unending progress.

I wonder why I have to make films now that industrial society's dreams of prosperity and unending progress have shattered.

You, in the light green suit. Do I have to make films in spite of that? What thoughts do you have about films and me?

The most that I can create is a reverse utopia. And I don't want to lead you there. Hey, you. Still, do I . . . ?

(*Asahi News*, May 30, 1974)

Education

"There are men to whom women want to show only their good side—not their bad side. You're one of them," a woman said.

The words really tickled my vanity, so I made them known to people on another occasion.

"You're the type of person about whom even men feel that way," another woman said.

All things considered, one balances out the other. And I wanted to be that way for women only.

Am I an educator, a believer in enlightenment? In any event, I have an abnormal tendency to think that those around me are good, or to think that I want to make them good. I think these things without the least hesitation. Nevertheless, I have felt skeptical about myself since I was a boy. This is the basis for the clarity of my speech and the abstruseness of my films.

Enlightenment and education are appropriate as objects of passion when a nation is a period of vitality. Even when under foreign domination, vitality lies in trying to free itself of domination. The Japanese are not now in a period of vitality.

Education cannot exist in the absence of popularizing passion. The reason that those who chatter about education seem comic is that they are fundamentally lacking this passion. Even if they had it, however, they would still be comic.

(*Asahi News,* May 31, 1974)

Beggars

"Mom, when I grow up, let's live together as beggars, okay?" my child says.

"Uh, why?"

"Beggars really make money."

"There are other ways to make money. If we were beggars, I'd be sad."

Hearing this absurd conversation at the table, I'm suddenly dubious. "Have you ever seen a beggar?" I ask. The child coyly refrains from answering.

"He's probably seen one on TV or somewhere," his mother says nonchalantly.

Today, no beggars are to be seen in the cities and villages of Japan.

Long ago there were beggars all over the outskirts of the cities and villages. Along with them were handicapped people. Children played with them and teased them: that was the beginning of their knowledge of the depths of life.

Now beggars seem to have been shut up somewhere. Since the time of the Tokyo Olympics, they've become a rarity.

Then where did our child get an image of a beggar? What made him think he wants to become one? It makes me think strange thoughts. Did he see freedom in being a beggar?

Give him freedom. Give him the freedom that allows beggars to exist. Aren't all people beggars to an extent? I am nostalgic for the dusty roads of summer grass where the beggars were to be found. I am nostalgic for the child I was, walking down those roads.

(*Asahi News,* June 1, 1974)

III   Discovery of a Contemporary Author

Mishima Yukio: The Road to Defeat
of One Lacking in Political Sense

December 13, 1970. Sunday. Evening. The date has no significance. I don't have Mishima Yukio's interest in choosing dates. The end of a year that also seems, somehow, to be the end of the Showa era.[1] Nothing particular happened; a manuscript deadline merely grew closer. The only thing special about the evening was that it would be my last solitary one for a while because I was preparing for my next film, and I knew that once that began, I probably wouldn't have any evenings for myself. The night before, the rain had leaked furiously into the room in my usual hotel in the Yotsuya section of Tokyo, which seems to have been a dormitory of some sort during the war. Putting a bottle of whiskey on the desk, I begin to write this piece. I pass out, or the liquor runs out. In any case, the end of the liquor marks the end of the bond. For me, the evening somehow comes to take on the aspect of a wake.

Right now I don't feel like reading what others have written about Mishima's death. Nor do I feel like commenting on their views. I also don't feel like stringing together theoretical-sounding words predicting that the influence of the incident will be this or that. Right now I would merely like to tell a brief story about Mishima. I turned down all other requests for manuscripts except this one. There was only one reason I accepted this one: it had the latest deadline.

I hadn't met Mishima that often. One of the longest times we spent together was when he received from the president of the company, Nagata, a print of the Daiei film he had acted in, *A Man Blown by the Wind*, and I was invited to a preview of it at his house, which is said to be in the Rococo style or some such thing. The other time was around November 1967 when we participated in a dialogue for the 1968 New Year's issue of *Film Art*.

1.   The reign of Emperor Hirohito, 1925 to 1988. He is now known as the Showa Emperor.

The preview was a large gathering of people, so we didn't really have time to talk. Also, a social atmosphere like that isn't comfortable for a poor film director. I am the sort of person who, once he starts drinking, continues until he passes out, so I'm no good at sipping cocktails. I had seen the film before, but I was very happy to see the great Mishima Yukio in person. For a film director, watching people is entertainment. A person like myself can be said to live for the joy of being a peeping tom. I think about all kinds of things while I am watching people, but the most vulgar thought among them is to wonder whether that person can become an actor— whether they can act. And I can tell that at a glance. Mishima, however, appeared to me to be constitutionally unsuited to being an actor. Generally, there aren't many women who are absolutely unsuited to acting, but many men aren't suited to being actors. Within that group, Mishima's type is the absolute worst. When I talk about a person's temperament being most unsuited to acting, I refer to the person's psychological constitution. But among men constitutionally incapable of acting, there are those who want at any cost to become actors. I am occasionally descended upon by such utterly unmanageable would-be actors. They have their set convictions and won't listen to anyone else. Mishima appeared to me to be one of that type. I thought of Masumura Yasuzo, director of *A Man Blown by the Wind,* who had to use Mishima in a principal role, and I couldn't help feeling sympathetic. At the same time, I looked at Mishima with a kind of sympathy. He was someone who probably couldn't adapt to this world and who, moreover, was making a tremendous effort to do so.

Why did Mishima set his heart on body building? If he had a kind of complex about the body, then I have the same thing. During adolescence I was all bones. Then, just when I was feeling good about having gotten a bit of meat on my bones, I suddenly became a tub of nearly 100 kilos. With a bit of adjustment I have now lost a little weight, but mine is still not a shape that is pleasant to look at. I have already given up, however. Why was Mishima able to radically change his physique? Was it because he didn't want his literature to be seen as the product of a meager or abnormal body? Wouldn't literature that is the product of a healthy body or a normal body be subject to the same logic? Or did he want to say that even if his own body changes from meager to healthy or from abnormal to normal, his literature doesn't change? If so, wouldn't it have been more interesting if he had tried restoring his body to meagerness and abnormality once again? I wanted to see a doddering Mishima, an obese Mishima. Mishima, however, went to his death emphatically denying those possibilities. That is probably where the problem of Mishima's aesthetic sense lies.

Since I am not a literary critic, I shall not delve deeply into the problem of beauty in Mishima's writing, but I think I can say that Mishima's aesthetic sense differed decisively from my own. More than that, I think that the way I incorporated my aesthetic sense into my creative process differed decisively from the way Mishima did. During our joint interview for *Film Art,* Mishima said that he didn't understand my film *Japanese Summer: Double Suicide.* That's not unreasonable. There is absolutely no reason that it should be understandable in the context of Mishima's aesthetic sense. Then Mishima asked me why I don't use beautiful men and women in my films. This is the limitation of Mishima's aesthetic sense. In other words, Mishima's aesthetic sense was extremely conventional. If that were all, there would have been no problem, but because Mishima was such an intelligent person, he was, to some extent, aware that his own aesthetic sense was conventional. That is the origin of Mishima's worship of the spurious and the artificial. He attained death as a result of having fabricated himself as well.

This type of person exists in the law faculties of universities, particularly those of national universities. Their grades are good, but they aren't interesting as people; they lack artistic sensibility and they have no feeling for sport or amusement of any kind. In other words, they are lacking in human sensibility. Apparently Mishima graduated from the law school of Tokyo University with extremely good grades, but even if he had gone directly to work in government, he probably wouldn't have got very far. In particular, he probably couldn't have become a politician. People like Sato Eisaku, who don't have such good grades but who like to amuse themselves and have a liking for people, become prime minister. It may be terrible to claim that someone like Mishima is lacking in artistic sensibility. People carried on about the fact that his death manifestos and poems were awful, but I tend to think that they were a return to his original lack of artistic sensibility. Isn't it true that Mishima, insensitive to everything as a youth, put off the things that were difficult to conquer, like sports and amusement, and decided to concentrate all of his efforts on conquering what seemed to be the easiest to conquer—his lack of artistic sensibility? And after attaining a degree of literary distinction, didn't he shift the object of domination to the athletic, the physical, and the political?

Everyone probably felt as I did when looking at Mishima—that haunted feeling one feels when looking at an artificial plant. He even looked to me like someone from outer space. Even during our dialogue, something seemed to be missing: the quality of feeling you have when you are talking with another human being. Despite that, it definitely read like a dialogue when I saw it in print. It already contained phrases like "I don't want to live" and *seppuku.*[2] Others have used those words in

2.   Ritual suicide by disembowelment. *Seppuku* is written with the same two characters as the word *harakiri,* but in reverse order.

other places, however. Perhaps he was open with me because I am not a literary person. The words he used in talking about *Kyoko's House,* which I told him I liked, were desperate confessions of feeling. Now, as then, they are engraved in my memory:

> I am ashamed to say it, but I very much wanted everyone to understand *Kyoko's House.* When I am about to throw the baby into the river Imagawa, I stand on the bridge to see if anyone will stop me. But no one comes. In despair, I throw the baby in the river, and that is the end. Of me, too. It is done. I have not yet been arrested. So this time I'm doing all kinds of things in an effort to be arrested. But there was nothing as cold as the literary world at that time. In spite of the fact that I was throwing away a baby, no one looked back. This may sound like idle complaining, but those were my deepest feelings. After that I probably lost my mind.

You might call this selfish talk. Reading this dialogue, the woman who owns the inn in which I'm staying glossed over it, saying, "It sounds like you are the older one, Mr. Oshima." I do not, however, take this as a compliment.

Kyoko's House was published in 1959, and Mishima began to change gradually from about that time. Having conquered his physical deficiency, he moved on to conquer his political deficiency. Conquering his political deficiency, however, was not an easy thing—particularly for Mishima, given his lack of sensitivity to the left wing, either in terms of his constitution or his class. He discovered that in raising the issue of emperor he could transcend himself. This, however, was an immense contradiction, because conquering one's faults one after another is not a Japanese way of living. It is easier for a Japanese to live exposing his or her faults. It is terribly tragic, therefore, that at the very end of his life, Mishima, who had lived a life that was in no way typical for a Japanese—particularly not for a Japanese literary figure—had to stake his life on the most Japanese phenomenon of all: the emperor. This was doomed to failure.

First of all, Mishima's connections with other people were insubstantial. He had no opportunity for self-examination in the context of his relationships with others. For example, *Japanese Summer: Double Suicide,* which Mishima told me he didn't understand, is the story of a man who wanders about thinking that somewhere there is someone who will be so kind as to kill him. Mishima's heroes, however, were always people who die by themselves. Their deaths are inevitably self-terminations. No matter how Mishima tried to conquer his lack of political sense, there was no way he could succeed insofar as politics involves influencing others. Mishima knew nothing concrete about the type of people to whom he should assert his beliefs. Consequently, the group that ultimately formed, called the Shield Society, consisted only of pure, innocent youths. Their very purity and innocence, however, wouldn't influence others. Mishima influenced only himself. And because Mishima was paying for the Shield Society with his own money, this was not politics. Politics is something done with other people's money. People become political by spending money, and the basis of political action is getting other people to spend money. Spending your own money to get some youths together is not politics at all. For the most part, politics is asserting yourself to old women. Whenever the reform movement loses in a local election, my old mother, for example, says "Darn! Those incomprehensible old women voted for the Liberal Democratic Party," sighing and disregarding the fact that she herself is an old woman. The likes of Sato Eisaku and Tanaka Kakuei must understand the inner workings of that sort of thing. Ishihara Shintaro, who, like Mishima, is organizing youth, is also a layman politically, and he can't become prime minister. Thus, Mishima's urging the members of the Self-Defense Forces to rally was a heartbreaking act. Politics is influencing old women and setting them in motion. If you can't set old women in motion, how are you going to be able to move the members of the Self-Defense Forces? My immediate impression of the Self-Defense Forces is that they are probably a group of realists to be feared. They probably also have an instinctive dislike for politics. Unless they are ordered to fire or are fired upon directly, there is no reason for them to rise. This is because they are undoubtedly thinking day and night that they don't want to fight in a war, they don't want to die— even though that is their business.

Someone of Mishima's intelligence must have known this, even if unconsciously. However, Mishima's only possible political act was his appeal to the members of the Self-Defense Forces. To put it another way, Mishima may have selected the people to whom it was most difficult to appeal. Even if someone had cautioned Mishima to appeal to the nearest old woman, he probably would have refused. That was Mishima's political aesthetic sense. Terribly self-indulgent, terribly conventional. . . . However, Mishima must have foreseen that the members of the Self-Defense Forces wouldn't heed his appeal. We shouldn't ask now whether he thought they would listen to his speech more kindly and whether at the last instant he thought he had been betrayed in that respect.

And assuming that he reached the scene of his suicide just about on schedule, the last political object toward which Mishima directed his appeal must have been the emperor, through whom his immensely fickle object had to be the Japanese people as a whole. Why didn't Mishima appeal directly to the emperor and then die? Although he felt that the emperor was the sole object of his political appeal, he knew that the emperor would have no reason to receive it. Political acts consisting of an appeal to the emperor alone had been a pattern in Japan since ancient times. But that pattern had lost its *raison d'être* with the loss of the war. Although he was aware of the powerlessness that lay in the fact that his politics could only be realized in the context of that pattern, Mishima also knew that he did not have the power to create any other object for his appeal. Mishima's way of committing suicide in front of the Self-Defense Forces, which as a pattern was somehow unconvincing, exposes this contradiction.

By his own death, however, he communicated his appeal as a politician to many Japanese. Through his death, Mishima conquered his lack of political sense. He therefore conquered everything he had set out to conquer. Conversely, however, Mishima's death also exposed his lack of political sense, and even his lack of artistic sense. His *kendo* teacher said something to the effect that he had never seen anything so clumsy. But isn't that enough? He's already dead. All that remains for us to see is the road Mishima took as he tried to conquer everything. We may or may not learn from that. Everything he conquered, however, returned to its original state; perhaps the only thing that didn't betray Mishima was his body. That his second[3] failed in three attempts to stab him was not because the second was inexperienced or dizzy. Our cameraman, Narushima Toichiro, who is of the same generation as Mishima and who as a military aviator just before the end of the war was made to practice slitting the necks of prisoners every day, believes that Mishima—who had put all of his strength into committing *seppuku*—had muscles that he had trained over and over, which were extremely solid between his elbows and his neck. People will probably say that he hardened those muscles for his death that day; those muscles, however, opposed his death. This idea saddens me.

Saying that his muscles opposed his death raises the question of how the Japanese people will interpret Mishima's political signal, the assertion of which he exchanged for death. But I do not wish to pontificate about that as the critics are. Speaking for myself, I am amazed that something inside me could be so moved by this death, particularly a suicide. Is this reaction common to all Japanese? My political position is that I would like to try to make Mishima's death the last in a pattern of political deaths in Japan since the Meiji period. But if all Japanese are shocked by such a suicide, that will not be easy. Thinking about the fact that Japan's official left wing has been consistently apathetic about death, particularly regarding its political significance, I have the presentiment that the political signal launched by Mishima will

3.   The person who delivers the coup de grâce in the *seppuku* ceremony.

probably become a painful, heavy piece of baggage. It has become a painful, heavy piece of baggage for me, but through his death I have felt very close to Mishima. If I were with the Mishima I feel I know today, I think I could go drinking with him. I would have liked to make this person, who said he didn't know what a hangover was, drink like crazy and then show him how delicious beer can be when you are hung over.

"What are you saying, Oshima Nagisa? You're making another excuse for yourself to drink. Look at Mishima. That effort. That effort to conquer everything. That effort which caused him to drive his inept, insensitive self, which caused him to follow through on everything his own way to his death. Oshima Nagisa. You rely on a meager talent and don't try. You think that you are good just as you are. Bad, bad, bad!" Although I say that, I do want to drink. Goodbye, Mishima!

(*Film Criticism,* December 13, 1970)

IV   On Trial for Obscenity (1970–1978)

Between Custom and Crime: Sex As Mediator

"Between Custom and Crime: Sex As Mediator" is a title that was provided for me, but for the time being I will address it. Contemporary Japan is designed in such a way that news about manners and customs, crime, sex, etc., is given to us in tremendous quantities by weekly magazines and the like. We get information in its purest sense from newspapers and television, but because they impose on themselves the framework of public information agencies, they stop at mere descriptions of the superficial facts. By contrast, the weekly magazines devote all of their energy to descriptions of the inside or the other side. The highest aspiration of the weekly magazines is to report on manners and customs, crime, sex, etc., in a way that places the greatest emphasis on human interest. Consequently, we who read the weekly magazines seek human interest in them; you might even say we are trying to learn about the human condition from them. In the past, the study of the human condition meant reading literature, popular fiction, or drama; the fact that we have now been given the weekly magazine, a very speedy and easy medium, deserves more than a simplistic value judgment.

I know two extremely talented executive producers in a certain film company. The briefcase of one is always stuffed with weekly magazines. The other, who never reads them, provides an excellent contrast. The former continually produces large quantities of amusing popular work; the latter, although producing infrequently, occasionally creates work that is outstanding.

The question of how people living in Japan today assimilate the information they receive from weekly magazines is fairly important. I do not, of course, mean to imply that the information provided by the weekly magazines or their study of the human condition is accurate or unique, much less profound. I have started by discussing weekly magazines because the title provided with its theme of custom, crime, and sex, centers on subjects that the weekly magazines hold very dear. However, if you really read the articles on these topics, you'll find that there is nothing more ridiculous. Sometimes I laugh aloud at the stories of sex crimes presented in the style of true-life accounts. They invariably say, "I became a prisoner of X-ko's white skin,"[1] or "I can't forget O-ko's corpulent flesh," or "I was under the spell of his brawny muscles," next to which there is a photograph of X-ko or O-ko or the man, who aren't in the least white-fleshed, corpulent, or brawny. Don't the writers of this kind of articles notice the contradictions? And what must the readers be thinking? The key to the mystery of the connection between the information we are given about manners and customs, crime, and sex and our real lives lies here.

What are *mores*? The other day, during a conversation we had after appearing together on a certain television program, a Dietman from the Liberal Democratic Party said to me that *mores* have far more power to change society than politics. Of course, this may have been a mild way of flattery, because I am positioned more on the side of *mores* than of politics, or it may have been his own vanity as an intellectual Dietman. It is fundamentally impossible for manners and customs to have more power than politics, however. But after that, when he said, "Oshima, where on earth do manners and customs come from? I'd like to hear your thoughts on the subject," I sensed that he was at least somewhat serious. Of course, it is obvious that the part about hearing my thoughts on the subject was mostly flattery, since the opportunity for him to do so had not materialized before this, but the question of where manners and customs come from is important. How are *mores* changed, and by whom?

In a word, it is guerrillas who change manners and customs and make new ones. People don't pay attention to old ways of behaving People always pay attention primarily to new manners and customs, odd manners and customs. And those new ones and odd ones begin as expressions of dissatisfaction with the system that is trying to entrench the old manners and customs, to the status quo. That dissatisfaction, moreover, has shifted to manners and customs because it can't be expressed in the usual way. It is not, as that LDP Dietman said, that *mores* have more power to change society than politics; rather the forces unable to change society through politics shift to manners and customs. That is true even of political *mores*. The manners and customs of staves and helmets are an expression of the insufficient political strength of those who can fight only with them. Manners and customs are, more than anything, an expression of weakness. When people lacking in power try to express themselves, it takes the form of guerrilla tactics. It is guerrillas who change manners and customs and make new ones.

1.   *Ko* is a common ending of women's first names in Japan; "X-ko" indicates that the person being discussed is a woman, without giving her name.

Society's dropouts, such as the Beat Generation and hippies in the United States and the drifters in Japan, all began by expressing their weakness. Needless to say, they were guerrillas. I have always been supportive of their position, but my saying so makes conscientious people angry. I understand the anger of businessmen and PTA mothers who have conformed to the system, but it troubles me when young, serious-looking students and laborers show anger.

The other day at a small neighborhood gathering I got a reaction from a young man when I said that it was the dropouts who anticipate the destiny of those of us living in the world today. What is a pedestrian's heaven,[2] for example? It is the way the governor and the chief commissioner of the metropolitan police imitate the philosophy of hippies and drifters. Or, I should say, the way they steal it. More than ten years ago, hippies throughout the world asserted that the streets belonged to the people and began living there, as did Japan's drifters several years back. They have disappeared from the daylight streets, however, because the governor and the police commissioner built fences, chased them out, and, finally, locked them up. I have observed their weakness and gentleness in my work, from *Japanese Summer: Double Suicide* to *Diary of a Shinjuku Thief*. Those who, because of their weakness, can only become drifters are chased out by the governor and the police commissioner. And now the governor and the police commissioner brazenly say that the streets belong to the people and steal the hippies' and drifters' philosophy to make pedestrians' heavens, smiling complacently at the people as they walk by. The gentle drifters may not be angry, but my heart trembles with anger. My resentment probably won't even disappear with time. But I don't matter. Whatever anyone may say, the making of pedestrians' heavens clearly shows that the *mores* of society's dropouts anticipated the destiny of the people. And the first guerrillas, who created those *mores* were then chased out. Such is the fate of *mores*.

Crime, too, is an act of the weak member of society. People who are powerless in society, who are unfit, commit crimes. Those who have power in society, who are fit, can survive without committing crime. Even if they do commit a crime or something like it, they can cover it up and survive. Those who can't survive without committing a crime are always the weak ones. There is a saying that history repeats itself, the first time as tragedy and the second time a comedy; two-time hijacker Inagaki Sachio may actually have appeared comical to people. He said, "I had no desire to live; I was planning to kill myself. But I didn't have the courage to commit suicide,

2.   A reference to certain streets in Japan that are closed for traffic at fixed times, such as on weekend days, for the convenience of pedestrians.

so I planned to hijack a plane, make a stand, and be shot dead by the police or the Self-Defense Forces." The weekly magazines, among others, made light of these words, but I was unable to laugh. The hero of *Japanese Summer: Double Suicide,* which I made in 1967, is a man obsessed with the thought that somewhere there is someone who will do him the favor of killing him. He is swept up in a strange gang war and survives to the end, continuing his pointless rebellion, when he is shot to death by police. But Inagaki's case was pathetic because he wasn't even able to die as he wanted to. Inagaki's words, "I had no desire to live" and "I didn't have the courage to commit suicide," eloquently express his powerlessness and weakness. It is precisely this sort of powerless, weak person who commits a crime. Not only people like Inagaki, who look weak, but the so-called brutal criminals, too, commit crimes out of weakness and powerlessness.

Considered this way, the guerrillas, who change manners and customs and make new ones, and the criminals have something in common: weakness. But because the guerrillas are able to express their own weakness by changing the old and making new manners and customs, it doesn't take the form of crime. However, their new and their odd customs are like crime in that weakness is at their roots, so they draw strong reactions and oppression from the societal system and its representative, general opinion. But once the new manners and customs created by guerrillas have taken on a life of their own, don't weak people, by committing themselves to those manners and customs, become distanced from the danger of committing crimes? Aren't manners and customs therefore acting as a kind of safety valve for weak people against their committing crimes? Perhaps because new manners and customs and those in transition have the same basis for expression as crime, they are ultimately quite criminal in nature, and yet at the same time they also tend to act as a substitute for crime.

Once again I must return to the topic I was given. What on earth is meant by "sex as mediator"? At face value, the title seems to say that sex is a mediator between customs and crime. But I have always thought that no mediator was needed between customs and crime and that the two were in a relationship of mutual substitution. Accordingly, the concept of sex as mediator would have no meaning here. The only remaining interpretation for the words "sex as mediator" is that they mean sexual manners and customs, particularly changes in them, and their relationship to crime. As for the relationship between sex and crime, that is to say, sex crime theory, several essays in this collection discuss it: "Sex Crime and Penal Legislation," "Young Criminals and Sex," and others. Thus, instead of examining the direct relationship of sex to crime, I shall restrict myself to the relationship between sex and crime as it is manifested in manners and customs. [Oshima here refers to the supplementary issue of *The Jurist* in which this text was first published. Ed.]

Whether considered globally or in terms of Japan alone, sexual *mores* are unquestionably heading in the direction of freedom and liberation. When I say "freedom and liberation," I am referring to freedom and liberation from certain things that affect sex—that is, the regulation of sex by the values of the state, the society, the family, etc. When I was a child, I heard the story of a famous shogun who mounted his wife saying, "Endure it for the sake of your country." It was, however, told as a joke; people doubtless knew instinctively that sexual principles were different from national, societal, and familial principles. It is also true, however, that national, societal, and familial principles openly regulated sex and that those principles had to be observed. Today, too, many people believe that national, societal, and familial principles should regulate sex.

The other day I participated in a televised debate about the National Police Agency's issuance of a warning to the Motion Picture Code of Ethics Committee (Eirin) with a famous writer, a woman who was involved in the proletarian literature movement before the war. I was surprised when, slightly agitated midway through, she said, "At any rate, no matter how much you talk about freedom, things like sex and theft have to be firmly controlled by law." It appears that this writer sees sex and theft as the same sort of thing. In general, however, society has come to think that sex is not something to be regulated by other principles but that it must be regulated by its own principles. We should take our hats off to the women's magazines and popular weeklies that have written tirelessly about the issue of sex—although of course they do it as a marketing ploy—and I am not speaking ironically. It is laughable that the women's magazines and others pay lip service to public manners and customs by always preceding the word "sex" with the word "love," but the most fundamental aspect of the change in sexual manners and customs is the idea that sex be judged in a sexual context. On a deeper level, the tide of sexual *mores* will probably shift even further in the direction of a tendency to extract only the pleasurable element from sexual relationships. Approval of every sexual perversion—premarital sex, adultery, rough sex, spouse swapping, homosexuality—will be one of the fashions in that tide. So, what is the relationship between those changes in sexual *mores* and crime?

Is it acceptable to think of changes in sexual *mores* in the same way that I have come to think of changes in general—as being carved out by weak people? At first glance the changes seem to be part of a fad created by the women's magazines and the popular weeklies. But if you think about it further, you see that each one of them was also elicited by the demands of the weak. Premarital sex, for example, was a demand of powerless young people who, although desiring sex, cannot yet marry for economic or other reasons. Needless to say, the first people to engage in it were shunned by the public as criminals. Homosexuality is obviously the public expression of a demand by the sexually unfit, who feel sexual desire only for members of their own sex. When I say weak or unfit here, I mean only that these people are powerless or unfit in terms of the current societal structure.

Those who called them weak or unfit did so many other social reasons in addition to the merely sexual, but if you take away all of these reasons, weakness and unfitness will no longer enter into the matter and sexual principles will stand alone: we have premarital sex because we don't yet have the economic strength to marry, we are homosexual because we feel sexual desire only for our own sex.

Incorporating a variety of circumstances, then, changes in sexual manners and customs overall are heading toward the independence of sexual principles and the approval of every individual sexual configuration. One might say that the women's magazines and the popular weeklies have been a powerful force when it comes to bringing out new demands by revealing and publicizing those of the weak. Of course this is not to overlook the achievements of the many artists and scholars who have written about sex, but it is still the editors of the women's magazines and the popular weeklies who have made the most significant contribution. To put it jokingly, you might say that they have tried so hard to see sexual issues from the point of view of the powerless that you almost think that they themselves have become sexually powerless. If changes in sexual manners and customs are carved out by the powerless, then we can say of sexual mores that they relate to crime as *mores* generally relate to crime. In other words, to people like the writer mentioned, changes in sexual manners and customs may even appear criminal, or appear to be crimes themselves, but in actuality they substitute for crime. They prevent crime.

The so-called pink movies,[3] for example, are part of the new sexual manners and customs. People who see these films are able to satisfy their sexual desires by the mere act of seeing them. The prevalent opinion that people commit sex crimes because they have seen pink movies is definitely an error of judgment. Audiences of pink movies do not see them to prepare for actual sexual activity. Seeing them is itself a sexual activity for them. They are absolutely incapable of committing sex crimes. Anyone who doubts this should visit a pink-movie theater. You will be able to tell from looking at them that these are weak people who are satisfying themselves by

---

3.   Short, low-budget, maximally soft-core pornographic films.

seeing a pink movie. Rarely someone surfaces who says he committed a sex crime after seeing a pink movie, but such a confession is definitely a lie. That person would have committed a sex crime even if he had not seen a pink movie. The National Police Agency and the writer can relax. Pink movies are at least beneficial in that they prevent those able to thus satisfy their sex drive from committing sex crimes. If such films did not exist, some sex criminals would definitely emerge from this group—although their crimes would not be brutal sex crimes, but instead pathetic minor crimes or crimes of an entirely different sort.

Although sexual customs are heading toward freedom and liberation and the principles of sex are gradually becoming independent, *mores* are, after all, *mores.* The sex practiced by an individual will always belong to that individual. The sex drive of the individual cannot be completely satisfied in the context of custom. No matter how much one gives oneself up to certain sexual *mores,* the problem of satisfaction will rest with that individual. Thus giving oneself up to a certain sexual convention can also be called giving oneself up to an illusion. In that sense, the decay of convention is desirable for the true independence. It may be that the complete independence of sexual principles will not be possible until sexual conventions are in ruins. Even if that happens, it will probably be in the distant future. Or it may never happen. For the time being, we must say that conventions are good and that changing them is good. I believe in the present benefits of custom—particularly in the benefits of sexual *mores*—because I believe in the power of oppression and because I believe in the weakness of the individuals who must resist. Let's change conventions more, let's keep them in flux, let's differentiate them more. If you are at present unable to commit a crime individually or in a group—that is, participate in a revolution—then you have no choice but to devote yourself completely to convention for the time being. If that is connected to crime prevention or the genuine basic prevention of a revolution, for example, then that is the level of our weakness at present. By that I am not saying that we should become weaker. I am not waiting hopefully for *mores* subject to government oppression.

(Supplementary issue of *The Jurist,* December 1970)

We have all sorts of documentation of the student protests of 1968–69, but so far as I've seen, at least, there are none that mention male-female relationships behind the barricades.

That is most unfortunate. Documentation should definitely have been left concerning male-female relationships and sexual activities behind the barricades. Information to the effect that rough sex was taking place behind the barricades has been leaked by the enemies of the fighting students, but so long as those involved keep silent, it won't be possible to learn the truth. Looking around me, however, I see the vacant eyes of those who participated in the protests and who now lead the lives of average citizens. I also see the silhouettes of groups of students for whom no trace of the barricades remains, but who have instead been silently sucked back into campuses with new, higher, prisonlike fences. It is then that I want to think that something took place behind those barricades after all. And it would be good if it had been rough sex. In fact, I think it has to have been.

The other day a friend of mine appeared at a student gathering on the theme of freedom and made the young people uncomfortable by saying, "You have everything here, but you don't have unrest." Apparently he also actually thought, "You have everything here, but you don't have sexual freedom," and that night he slipped into the room of the high school girl next door, creating a fuss and ending up playing out a comedy in which he was forced to take a self-critical stance.

The other day I was a guest on a television program that gathered 150 young men and women together for critical discussion of the state of things. One young person suggested, "Instead of having this ridiculous debate, let's unzip our pants and ..." He put his hand in front of his pants and not a single person responded. He didn't have the courage to do it alone, so he ended up wilting there on the spot. Judging from these incidents, I think that there must have been not a hint of rough sex, even

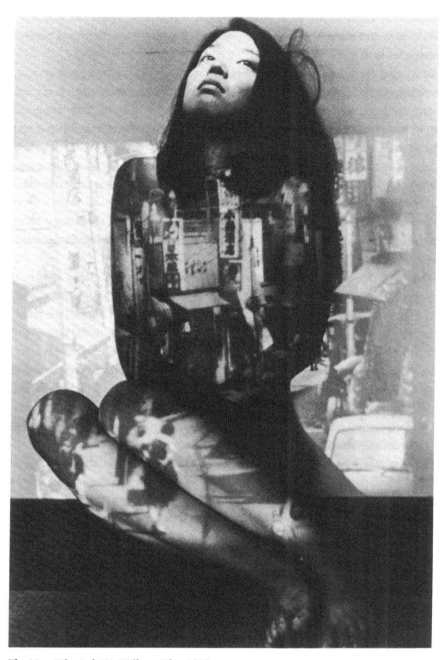

The Man Who Left His Will on Film. 1970.

in a situation as close to the ideal as behind the barricades. Rough sex probably chooses its time and place. That is precisely why whether there was rough sex behind the barricades is an important question.

I am using the words "rough sex" here because I want to risk being sensational; however, the words "group sex" could be substituted. The times when group sex can take place are good times, and the places where group sex can take place are good places. Wouldn't the time when there were barricades have been a good time and the place have been a good place?

I am now thinking about sexual abundance, because I usually think about sexual poverty. We are inundated with information about sex, and there are exhaustive descriptions of images of apparent sexual abundance, depicted in as much variety as possible. Of course, as I implied when I said "apparent" sexual abundance, most of those images are false. Perhaps we can call the main current of those false images "sexual GNPism" or "sexual careerism."

The issue of sex has been narrowed down exclusively to a matter of sexual organs and sexual pleasure. The majority of stories in the popular weeklies and middlebrow novel magazines and the supposed "sex education pages" that fill the women's magazines all concentrate on totally fragmented issues, such as the size of the sexual organs, the intensity of sexual feeling, and the frequency of sex. Praise is given to those who can accumulate the greatest number of sexual encounters, increase their sexual sensitivity, and have the largest sexual organs; efforts to achieve these goals are applauded. This is exactly the same phenomenon manifested by postwar Japan when it turned unquestioningly and single-mindedly toward economic prosperity, proceeding blindly toward a prosperity based exclusively on numbers.

This sexual GNPism or sexual careerism is the flip side of what should be called the sexual militarism of the prewar era. I immediately think of the sordid story I heard during my boyhood about General Nogi, in which he says, "Let me do it—for the sake of your country," and then rapes his wife. This story is too clever to be true, and I later learned that in his youth Nogi frequented the red-light district enthusiastically. However, the thought that he really did behave that way toward his wife has always remained fixed in my mind. That is how I got the idea that all people involved in sex are dirty and that it is only permissible when it is for the sake of the country— when it is carried out to further the goal of procreating subjects, particularly soldiers, to serve the country.

Before the Meiji period [1868–1912], this type of sexual militarism consisted of imposing the morals of the warrior class on the people at large. It is easy to see how it was used to implement the Meiji political strategy of "A Rich Nation and A Strong Army." We can conclude that this alone has come to dominate the way sex has been perceived in Japan ever since.

Does this mean that in pre-Meiji Japan people thought differently about sex and had a different sexual culture? During the Edo period [1600–1868] a free sexual culture centered on the pleasure and entertainment districts that were the world of the townspeople, and a culture of communal sex also existed in the folk customs of the farm villages. Not being a researcher, I can't produce definite evidence of either of these, but above all, I do know is that both sexual cultures were crushed in the process of modernization during the Meiji period and later.

Despite this a sexual culture like that the Edo townspeople had in their pleasure and entertainment districts has managed to survive in one corner of Japanese society as an institution bequeathed from the past, but its existence has served only to reinforce the facade of sexual militarism. Meanwhile, the communal sex culture of the farm villages was quite consciously emasculated as the farm villages became the strongest base of Japan's militarism.

With Japan's defeat in the war, the sexual militarism that had completely negated sex was thrown out effortlessly in a kind of inevitable upheaval. It was superseded by sexual GNPism, or sexual careerism, which affirmed sex completely. That this transformation of values took place without a single ideological struggle on the part of the Japanese determined the form of sexual GNPism or careerism of today. Even though they were told that sex is good and to enjoy it to the fullest, the Japanese, who had known how to think of sex only negatively, didn't know how to enjoy it. Those who asserted that in the past Japan's farm villages had a communal sexual culture and that free sex bloomed in the world of the Edo pleasure districts were being frank despite the atmosphere of sexual conservatism.

In the midst of the modernization of the Meiji era and afterward, however, those things either no longer existed or did so only in a different form and on a smaller scale. Society therefore turned instead to models that had no connection whatsoever to the past. People imitated Western, particularly American, sexual culture extremely superficially. A Japanese youth who became depressed and committed suicide after comparing the size of his sexual organ to those of the Western men cited in the Kinsey Report is a symbolic example. Because they were totally ignorant that sexual culture is a true culture, the Japanese imitated theories of sexual behavior with a crazed passion. The Japanese are probably the world's most fanatical students of sex today, too. Their perversion resembles that of the students who prepare for entrance examinations attended by their "education mamas."[1] The perversion of the mass media, which is the tool of education, is precisely that of the education mama. The novels beloved by the mass media are remarkable for their extreme crudeness. The aspect of Edo culture concerned with sex has an elegance and purity that provide a striking contrast to the crudeness and coarseness of today—although we may perceive it that way only because it has survived beyond its time. Today it can only be called sexual careerism.

Because I am from the country, I don't want to use the words "country people" in a derogatory way, but I imagine that the country people who would most certainly have been received coldly at Yoshiwara[2] are today's sex heroes. I use the words "country people" to mean those who lack consideration for others. That lack of consideration for others bears a close resemblance to Japan's national stance, which is that as long as it has its own GNP, the disaster suffered by the citizens of a neighboring country does not matter. This is why I call it sexual GNPism. This also resembles the education mama who cares only about her child's grades, no matter what else may happen. The ideological decay of postwar Japan, which unquestioningly accepts the ideas of "my car" and "my home," has reached this point. The depraved idea that ought to be called "my-sex-ism" is part of this.

I want to laugh mockingly at the poverty of this "my-sex-ism" that hides behind a mask of abundance, but I would be laughing mockingly at myself at the same time. The transformation from sexual militarism to sexual careerism took place inside me as well, with no personal crisis whatsoever. Trailing an ample residue of sexual militarism, I behaved on the surface like a champion of the new sexual age, as if I had no scars whatsoever. During the shift in values that accompanied Japan's defeat, I took a curious pride in belonging to a generation that was able to assimilate new things with freshness.

With that pride, I scorned the way the people of the previous generation who were then at my university approached sex. Nearly all of them were products of the old high school system. They seemed to think about women in an extremely mysterious way. Their quotations of abstruse passages from essays on women in foreign literary and philosophical works, for example, made me wince. Even while they were thinking about the sex question so abstractly, they would suddenly all get together to go out to the red-light district. Their reminiscences of the red-light district were

1.   Name given to Japanese mothers who involve themselves in their children's preparations for school entrance exams to the point of obsession.
2.   Location of the most famous of the government-regulated centers for prostitution in Japan from the early years of the Edo period (1600–1868) to the middle of the twentieth century.

told unashamedly as dirty stories. I scorned those older friends of mine from the depths of my soul. I wasn't alone: all my peers did so too. Needless to say, that was the flip side of a feeling of inferiority.

My older friends were clearly superior to us in that they had fully absorbed the sexual customs of the intellectual elite who had lived during the days of sexual militarism. As a result, we weren't included in their dirty stories. We told dirty stories among ourselves that we thought were more stylish. We did nothing comparable to visiting the red-light district in a group. Of course, individuals might have gone quietly on their own. For us, though, not being able to get a woman unless you went to the red-light district was a source of shame.

We each had our own regular partner. We didn't tell each other what level of sexual intimacy we had reached with those "regular partners." At the least we would all say something like, "We do it, of course," or assume an attitude along the lines of, "If I want to, I can do it anytime." The truth, however, must have been pitiful. While men were dragging behind them the old idea that sex was something to be ashamed of and kept hidden, women were deep in the grip of the ideas inherited by sexual careerism from sexual militarism: the prizing of virginity and the fear of pregnancy. Because the ideas of each side prescribed rules for and tied down the other, the self-proclaimed champions of the new sexuality of the supposedly free new age lived with an inner reality that was miserable when compared to the splendor of their outward appearance and spoken views.

I and others like me exposed the prewar notion that sex was something to be ashamed of and kept hidden to mystify sex. With the loss of the war, when the power of all mysterious things came crashing down to earth, sex was one of them. We were of course taught that sex ought to be glorified and enjoyed to perfection as the most beautiful act of mankind, but, for me at least, the feeling that something formerly mysterious had been exposed to the bright sunlight and revealed as a mere *thing* overpowered that lesson.

The people I saw during and after the war, the image of the streets as they appeared to me then in the form of literature and chronicles taught me that human beings are a *thing* and, accordingly, sex, which is one part of them, is also a *thing*. You might say that I scorned all human beings, including myself. I scorned sex, and so I scorned the sex of my women friends, the objects of my sexuality. Now I am able, sorrowfully, to understand this, but at the time I gave it no thought whatsoever. I was proud of myself for scorning sex, and that pride kept me going.

Precisely because of that pride I was able to survive among the ruins of Japan's defeat in the war. And wasn't that true of many Japanese? Self-scorn was the only way the prideful Japanese· could survive the shocking reality of defeat. Like starved animals, the Japanese had no choice but to live scorning themselves in order to fulfill that hunger. That was already the very road that headed straight to GNPism; in a sexual context, it had a direct link to sexual careerism.

However, Japanese society did not lack a movement that sought to drive a wedge into that trend. And I was also present in one corner of that movement. The human relationships in that context—the man-woman relationships, to be precise— were far removed from this type of scorn, because they had to be carved out on a basis of human respect and freedom. At least, that was superficially true of the culture held sacred by the movement. The reality was different, however.

The fetters of sexual militarism and sexual careerism bound the activists in the movement even more firmly than they did in everyday life. I saw women willing to throw themselves at those in power in the movement and men keeping women on the pretext that they were leaders of the movement. When I saw all of this being carried out under the pretext of "the protest" or "the revolution," I knew intuitively that there couldn't possibly be either a protest or a revolution as long as the evils of the present reality were dragged unchanged into the sexual realm.

I think I was a bit of an idealist and a bit of an introvert. I thought that we needed to establish a new logic—one that was separate from the rules of reality—regarding protests, revolution, and sex. The way I dealt with sex in that context was unspeakably poor. The poverty of that realization has remained unchanged through today in this age of the overflowing of images of sexual abundance. At the same time in the midst of this abundance, there is definitely the scent of falsehood.

The other day at a large meeting of hard-core members of the National Federation of Students' Self-Government Associations I heard that the women activists furiously accused the executive committee or all of the male activists of discrimination against women within the movement and denounced their lack of awareness of this. I am not at all closely connected to that organization, so I receive all of my information about it secondhand, but when I hear sharp words like "You fence in your own women. What is activist about that?" I feel a combination of despair—that just as it was twenty years ago when we were in the movement, even the center of the movement today is supported by the many evils of the reality that it is trying to overthrow—and a quiet hope that a voice was raised attacking it.

Even so, it is very interesting that the women's accusations about sex came at a time when the movement is ebbing, because I think that the movement at its height embodied even more images of sexual abundance.

"The greater your labor of love, the more overwhelming your desire for revolution. The more you revolt, the more overwhelming your desire to engage in a labor of love." This graffiti, written on a wall at the Sorbonne during France's May Revolution, is an extremely concrete expression of this. At such times, one person's sexuality becomes linked to all humanity. A sexual relationship with another brings about a connection with all humanity: by embracing one person, you are able to embrace all humanity. Even if I did not attain perfect joy, even if my sensation was slightly distorted, I experienced something close to that. I can't believe that sort of thing didn't take place behind the barricades in 1968 and 1969. I brazenly asked about that when I used the words "rough sex." Is sex really an individual issue? The concrete act of sexual intercourse definitely takes place between two individuals, but I believe through union with another individual one is attempting union with all of humanity and all of nature. When one falls prey to the delusion that the essence of sex exclusiveness—because at the moment of their union individuals are exclusionist—one becomes an eternal prisoner of the societal structure behind mistaken idea.

For nearly every moment of our daily lives, we are that sort of pathetic prisoner. Instinctively, however, people try to escape the fetters of such a delusion. Anticipating that, society creates purely technical escape routes, such as swapping partners and sex outside marriage. Insofar as these escape routes do not aspire to break through the myth of sexual exclusiveness and possessiveness, however, they have no essential power.

Looking back, I wonder if my group's nonstop telling of dirty stories, our sleeping together as a group, and our visits to the red-light district weren't a distorted expression of the desire for union through sex. The custom of group sex that almost certainly existed in Japan's farm villages prior to the Meiji period and the Okinawan custom of "playing in the fields" by young men and women must have been less distorted forms of safety valves, offering release from the frustrating fetters of the concept of sexual exclusiveness.

Today, too, many types of communities are instinctively created by young people who sense the falseness of the concept of sex socially imposed on them. What kinds of sexual relationships will be forged in these communities? When one distances one's self from sexual careerism and mutual possessiveness, things can begin anew.

Would it be possible, though, to build a sexual community where all of humanity were one? It is always easy to start something, but it is difficult to make a special moment last. Even if you extend the time by means of drugs, who can guarantee that the monopolization of woman by man or a man by woman will not occur? If so, have we any choice but to be perpetually renewing our sexual communities? The country we now live in isn't even a republic.

(*Perspectives,* October 1971)

Sex, Cinema, and *The Four-and-a-Half-Mat Room*

At hot times like this, even thinking about "it" is disagreeable. I don't know how much of their lifetimes people spend thinking, but I sometimes wonder how much of that time is spent thinking about "it."

Of course, when one is young there are even times when one spends the whole days thinking about "it." But if this condition were to persist for one's whole life, wouldn't that be a bit abnormal?

But there really are people like that in the world. Sex scholars and sex researchers think about "it" all the time without getting bored.

The late Professor Takahashi Tetsu appeared in some of my films, and I spoke with him on a number of occasions. One time, while drinking small glasses of sake, he talked at me passionately in waves that ebbed and flowed, practically pounding on the table. "Hey, Oshima. There are many unfortunate people in the world who go to their graves with complexes about sex," he said, with a poignant expression. I was suddenly at a loss for words, and although I didn't say it, I felt, "What? Is that all? Isn't it their own business if they die with a complex?"

Although surprised, I couldn't help feeling moved somehow by Professor Tetsu's excessive thoroughness. But the dislike and suspicion I always feel for the professors in this world who research and debate about sex is rooted in the question of whether they are really able to think seriously about "it" for an entire day or an entire lifetime. If they really can, isn't that abnormal?

Not that in itself the anomalous is bad. I have a friend who was ordered by his company to make a porno film as his first film. He made the film based on a crucial decision—that he had to shoot the anomalous. I think he was right. If you intend to pursue sex directly, you have no choice but to make some sort of anomaly your theme.

For example, the majority of Nikkatsu's so-called *roman poruno* [pornographic novel] films take sex as their subject matter but not as their theme. The themes of their most highly regarded films tend to be something like adolescent rebellion; sex is merely the seasoning. This old method has been used for a long time; it is precisely why these films are attractive to superficial critics and young film buffs.

Unfortunately, the film that my friend made with sex as its direct theme was unsuccessful. It contained some breathtaking fresh descriptions, but overall it was incomprehensible. The anomaly was not expressed in physical terms. For example, in the script he writes, "Then the three have sex using all of the body's orifices."

I understand the feeling he was trying to convey, but this is not something that can be captured on film. It is also questionable whether the actress who played the heroine would actually have been able to engage in abnormal sex practices.

My friend told me after he made the film that he knows a genuine masochist and that he probably could have made a far better film by shooting his friend's sexual activities with several cameras.

That probably would result in something powerful. But when you ask yourself what is being expressed in a film like that, you don't come up with anything substantial and you still feel that particular dislike and suspicion of sex researchers and sex theorists.

Pornography probably was invented as a way to avoid thinking about sex directly. If you think about "it" too intensely and become depressed, you certainly won't feel like doing "it," will you? Pornography restores sexual energy by eliciting them into a state of mind in which laughs foolishly about sex instead of thinking about it seriously.

In that respect, *The Paper Lining of the Sliding Doors of a Four-and-a-Half-Mat Room*[1] is a little too refined. It fails to realize the effect of pornography. Since the authorities would presumably be in a bind were people to lose the desire to do "it" and stop having children, they probably did not mean to ban pornography; rather they were concerned about its becoming too refined. That may be why this film was offered up as a sacrifice.

(Half-Kidding, October 1973)

1.   Reference to a Kumashiro Tatsumi film, *The Paper Lining of the Sliding Doors of the Four-and-a-Half-Mat Room*. Kumashiro joined the Shochiku Kyoto Studio in 1947 and transferred to the Nikkatsu Studio in Tokyo in 1949. His directorial debut film was *A Life of the Front Row of the Theater* (*Kaburitsuki Jinsei,* 1968), which dealt with the lives of strippers and their milieu. After Nikkatsu launched the *roman poruno (roman pornographique)* line, his career started to bloom with *The Wet Lips* (*Nureta Kuchibiru,* 1972) and *Ichijo Sayuri: Wet Desire* (*Ichijo Sayuri: Nureta Yokujo,* 1972), among others.

Theory of Experimental Pornographic Film

"I really want to see it."

"You can't see it unless you go to France?"

"When will we be able to see it in Japan?"

"I guess we won't be able to see the vital parts of it in Japan."

"Can some special arrangement be made so we can see it? Please let us see it."

I finished shooting *In the Realm of the Senses* at the end of last year, 1975, and at the very beginning of this year I went to Paris, where I finished making the film in mid-February and then returned home.

"Isn't this the first time people have wanted to see one of your films so badly? Think of it as an honor." My wife snickered. It was clearly a scornful laugh. What was she laughing at? At me, whose films people haven't wanted to see too much (she thinks)? At the people who want to see my film so badly (she thinks)? In any case, *In the Realm of the Senses* is now a film people want to see. Why do they want to see it? Because you can't see it in Japan.

Throughout the process of producing and screening *In the Realm of the Senses,* it became poignantly clear to me that the human being is an animal who wants to see something all the more when it is forbidden. This desire was intensified in so far as the film's timing overlapped with that of the Lockheed scandal, when people were eager to learn the identity of the high-ranking government officials involved.

Isn't pornography based on the showing of something that is hidden, something one longs to see?

Just now I said the "showing" of something that's hidden, but isn't it really just the pretence of doing so? If so, the essence of pornography may be that it makes people think that they will be shown something. It makes them think there is something there.

In the Realm of the Senses. 1976.

In the Realm of the Senses became the perfect pornographic film in Japan because it cannot be seen there. Its existence is pornographic—regardless of its content.

Once it is seen, *In the Realm of the Senses* may no longer be a pornographic film. That may happen in Europe and the United States, where it can be seen in its entirety.

In Japan, however, there is no hope now of its being shown in public in full. Thus, even if it can be seen, *In the Realm of the Senses* will continue to be a pornographic film.

That it couldn't be seen established it perfectly as a pornographic film, though that was not intentional on my part. I wasn't thinking that far ahead when I set out to make *In the Realm of the Senses*. The revelations always come after I make a film.

To begin with, when a film director sets out to make a film, he does not know what type of film he will want to make.

When I made my second film, *Cruel Story of Youth,* in 1960, I was already engaged to my wife. I hear that when her oldest brother saw the film, he said anxiously, "I wonder if Akiko will be treated like that too?" That was probably because of the scene where Kawazu Yusuke rapes Kuwano Miyuki at the big timber yard in Tokyo.

I am not compelled to say so at this point, but the fact is that I didn't take Koyama Akiko violently. However, the first sexual images to appear in my films were inextricably linked to violence.

It was publicized that Honoo Kayoko, the female star in my next film, *Tomb of the Sun,* said, "I love having sex," which seems to have given my films an even deeper sexual coloring.

Shortly before that, Honoo had been involved in a double suicide attempt with a youth of eighteen, one year younger than she. Deep down, we were afraid there might be an incident during the filming. Nothing happened, however.

But the night we shot the love scene in the grasslands with the woman on top of the man, against a background of a burning sunset, was the first night she didn't return to the hotel. I don't known what happened. But in the back of my mind I knew that she had clearly been sexually aroused during the shooting, and I wondered why it isn't permissible for real intercourse to take place at such times.

I hear that Honoo Kayoko is now happily married.

Matsui Yasuko appeared in *In the Realm of the Senses.* Long known as the "Pink Queen," she now has the dignity of being the "Pink Empress Dowager." At one time

Cruel Story of Youth. 1960.

she was the "Princess of Acting" at Shochiku's Kyoto Studios. During the shooting of *Tomb of the Sun,* the "princess" came to me for an interview. More than ten years later, she told me her impression of that day, so vividly that it was as if it had happened yesterday. We were at an inn called Shinjuku in the Tennoji section of Osaka. She came lightly up to the room at the top of the stairs into which the crew was crowded. I was in the middle of the room, half-naked, and Watanabe Fumio was next to me.

I wanted to give her the role of a student who goes mad after she and her lover are attacked during a rendezvous: he is killed and she is raped. She was perfect for the role. At that moment, the future "Pink Queen" had wept unrestrainedly, saying that playing that role upset her.

"I didn't even have to go naked. All I had to do was have my chemise ripped— that was all," said the "Pink Empress Dowager," laughing animatedly as she concluded her reminiscence. She didn't forget to add one thing: "Unlike now, though, in those days both you and I, Director, were really thin."

Tomb of the Sun, which featured at most a ripped chemise, was closely scrutinized by the Motion Picture Code of Ethics Committee. Sex in my films always invites warnings from the committee that are excessive because they go beyond what is shown on the screen. This was the first such instance.

I heard recently that the same thing had happened to *Tomb of the Sun* on the other side of the world, in Brazil.

In Brazil in those days, Japanese films were shown in their original language in the Japanese community. Young Brazilian film lovers would go to see these unsubtitled films. *Tomb of the Sun* caught their attention. They tried to get it shown at a regular Brazilian movie theater, but it was difficult to get it past the censors.

"But we did our best and pushed it through. That incident clearly marked the turning of a new page in sexual expression in the Brazilian film world," I was told by Glauber Rocha, who was then a young film lover and is now a representative of Brazil's *Cinema nuovo.* Rocha was staying at the same cheap hotel where I was staying in Paris's Latin Quarter. His story had a point.

"After that we waited for more than ten years, but no films directed by Oshima came to Brazil. We figured that Oshima must have been an old man who died after *Tomb of the Sun.*"

Censorship in Brazil is strict. Rather than merely banning the showing of a film, its director is thrown in jail. I am depressed to see that in recent years Rocha's work has been done chiefly in Europe.

I might have been mourned if I had died around the time of *Tomb of the Sun.* Some might have rejoiced. But I didn't die. I left Shochiku with *Night and Fog in*

Japan, after which I made *The Catch,* and then, at Toei, *Amakusa Shiro Tokisada*. After that there was a three-year period during which I wasn't able to make a film, but even so I didn't die.

In 1965, when I had read Yamada Futaro's novel, *Pleasure inside the Coffin,* I was given another opportunity to make a film. Shochiku insisted that it be an original work. The story is as follows. A man commits murder for the sake of the woman he desires. His crime is witnessed by an absconder of public funds, who coerces him into keeping his money for him until he leaves prison. When the woman marries, the man decides to use up all of the money and to die before the end of the embezzler's three-year prison term. He uses the money to buy one woman after another.

Taking a hint from posters and newspaper advertisements, I thought of these phrases: "Let's buy somebody. Let's buy a woman. Grab it: the joy of sex!" For the title, I decided on *Pleasure of the Flesh,* suggested by Daiei's Mr. Suzuki, always my best adviser. At the time of the shooting, this sexual expression was news, and the film was a big hit, but for me it was a film of many regrets.

On the one hand, during the writing of the script I was asked not to stray too far from the original work, while on the other I was compelled to omit important episodes. As always, I received excessive warnings from the Motion Picture Code of Ethics Committee before the fact, and they cut it to pieces. But more than that, I regret that my abilities were by no means equal to the task of coping with these problems.

By "my abilities," I mean things that are expressed in terms of vectors such as energy, sharpness, and courage.

My biggest regret about *Pleasure of the Flesh* related to the casting of the female roles. We should have used so-called pink actresses. I thought of that a number of times. But I hesitated each time.

Takechi Tetsuji[1] had already made *Daydream* and *Dream of the Red Chamber.* I don't remember whether it was before or after this that I met Wakamatsu Koji at

1.   Takechi Tetsuji came to public attention by a "radical" theory and staging of the Takechi Kabuki in Osaka. He turned suddenly to filmmaking with *The Night of Japan: Woman, Woman, Woman Story (Nihon no Yoru: Onna Onna Onna Monogatari,* 1962). In the following year he made *Daydream (Hakujitsumu,* 1963), which deals with a woman patient's fantasy of rape by a dentist while undergoing treatment, and *Dream of the Red Chamber (Koromu,* 1963). It was his fourth film, *Black Snow (Kuroi Yuki,* 1964), with its repetitive scenes of sexual intercourse and of a girl's nudity outside the U.S. Yokota Air Base and its appeals to anti-Americanism, that attracted widespread attention and generated debate. The result was indictment on a charge of obscenity. Nevertheless, he went on to make, in rapid succession, *The Tale of Genji(Genji Monogatari), Stories of the Postwar Cruelties (Sengo Zankoku Monogatari), Stories of Cruelty of the Ukiyo-e (Ukiyo-e Zankoku Monogatari),* and *The Lady of Scandal (Scandal Fujin).* His publications include *The Dawn*

the nostalgic, triangular-shaped "Unicorn" building in Shinjuku, but his name was already familiar to me. The new "pink" wave in film was already making ever-increasing inroads into Japanese film.

I shouldn't have hesitated. Using the so-called pink actresses would have forced a resolve on my part—a resolve to forge ahead in the direction of complete expression. The resolve itself would have brought direction.

At that time, however, I was ultimately unable to muster the resolve. In a word, I wasn't able to lower myself that far. I hadn't the courage to take the plunge. Another ten years would pass before I again faced that plunge and made the necessary decision.

After *Pleasure of the Flesh,* my films were usually sex films. I also made films about the "Daylight Demon," Ri Chin'u, and two major postwar sex criminals. I carefully avoided the kind of filmmaking that makes the sexual act its central concern, however. The wound from *Pleasure of the Flesh* was deep.

I had resolved not to make that kind of film if there were no possibility of complete sexual expression. Sexual expression carried to its logical conclusion would result in the direct filming of sexual intercourse.

I forget who said that films are desires visualized, but for me, at least, film is the visualization of the director's desire. But the director's desire doesn't appear in the film directly. It appears in all kinds of convoluted forms. My fear that my desire will appear in my films has always caused me to be extremely wary of making films, hasn't it? Haven't I made films to hide my desires instead? Trying to hide them made them appear even more vividly.

Other desires must also burn deep in the heart of any director. Film directors want to shoot the dying. And they also want to shoot men and women (or men and men, women and women, or people and animals) having sexual intercourse.

The other day I participated in a symposium with the director Shindo Kaneto. He said, in a voice full of emotion, that he envied what I had done in *In the Realm of the Senses.* His eyes were wide and shining, the way children's are when they discover something they want, and a strange energy radiated from his small body.

It was Sato Kei who said, "When I learn that I'm dying of cancer, I'll let you film my death, Oshima."

---

of the Kabuki (Kabuki no Reimei), *Tradition and Disruption* (Dento to Danzetsu), *Mishima Yukio: His Death and His View of the Kabuki* (Mishima Yukio: Shi to sono Kabukikan), and *Eros Accused* (Sabakareru Eros).

I should have had Sato Kei and Watanabe Fumio rape Yokoyama Rie in reality. If I had done so, something would definitely have come of it. This was at the time of *Diary of a Shinjuku Thief.*

At that time, it also would have been all right had Toura Rokko and Wakabayashi Mihiro done it. It was the kind of atmosphere in which it would have been totally all right. Rokko was the kind of man who could make love any time, and Mihiro was that kind of woman. I would have had to say only, "Do it for real." But I didn't say it, and though they actually did touch each other's genitals, they didn't do it, and Mihiro died, jumping from the roof of an ordinary building in Atami.

"Even so, I wonder why Anatole Dauman thought he wanted to have you shoot pornography?" I was startled when someone said that to me. I hadn't been asked that sort of question before. Nor had I thought about it myself.

Whether because of my own unworthiness or for some other reason, I don't get work from Japanese producers, but fortunately I get offers from Dauman and others in foreign countries. Thinking about it, though, the pornography suggestion is most unexpected. What made Dauman think of that?

I was disconcerted by Ogi Masahiro's excellent question.

"Hmmm. Perhaps it's because it isn't a discipline I excel in?"

"Why would that be?"

"Hmmm. Then it's his instinct as a producer."

I can't forget it. It was the end of the summer of 1972. I had stopped over in Paris on the way home from the Venice Film Festival, where I had taken *Dear Summer Sister.* Dauman suddenly came out with it in the anteroom of a small private showing room called the Club 70.

"Let's collaborate on a film, a co-production. A porno. I'll leave the content and the actual production all to you. I'll pay for it, that's all."

Working with him for the first time and hearing him talk about all kinds of things during the process, I gradually came to see that Dauman's greatness as a producer lies in the fact that after proposing a project he leaves everything to the artist.

That may make him sound like an articulate, administrative kind of person, but, to my dismay, Dauman, originally an artist himself, would make a suggestion of this magnitude while laughing as though it were a joke. When he finished talking, he snickered and stared at me with his big eyes. I was completely at a loss.

The only thing to do was to smile and agree. I answered that I'd definitely like to do it, but my words lacked conviction. To cover up for that, I smiled with all my might. However, that expression was far from what you'd call a smile; it was closer to a very untidy smirk. Our interpreters, Shibata Shun, president of a French film company, and Kawakita Kazuko, were probably even more at a loss than I.

In spite of that, soon after I returned to Japan I sent two sets of plans to Dauman. One was the story of Abe Sada.

Dauman replied immediately, saying, "I want to go with Sada." Over the next three years, however, I dissolved Sozosha and fooled around.

Three years is the same interval that passed between *Amakusa Shiro Tokisada* and *Pleasure of the Flesh*. That three years was long. I was always irritable. But the three months between the time that my first work, *A Town of Love and Hope*, earned me a demotion from the company's executive offices and the time that I made *Cruel Story of Youth* was even longer. I spent my days and nights worrying, thinking despondently that I would never be able to make another film.

If the three years between *Dear Summer Sister* and *In the Realm of the Senses* seemed short it was because of my age, unfortunately. When I was young and always irritable, the movement of time actually felt sluggish, but now that I am in middle age, at peace with myself and free of care, time flies by like an arrow.

If a director doesn't enjoy making a film, it cannot be interesting to its viewers. I had firmly resolved not to make any films that I could not enjoy making.

I wrote several scripts. I enjoy writing scripts, but when I am finished I feel that I needn't go any further. I don't have the bounce needed to leap to the next level and fix it on film.

Dauman continued to press me. During that time he must have been steadily accumulating successes, for the amount of money he offered increased little by little.

When Shibata and Kazuko left for the 1975 Cannes Film Festival, their parting words to me were, "But isn't this about the longest Dauman will wait?" They were headed for the third Cannes with no Oshima films to sell, even though they had sold Oshima films to the world ever since the 1968 Cannes Film Festival, interrupted by the May Revolution but at which they had sold *Death by Hanging* to Anatole Dauman. Instead, they left carrying *Akasen Tamanoï*[2]/*I Can Penetrate*, directed by Kumashiro Tatsumi. They wanted to take *The Paper Lining of the Sliding Doors of a Four-and-a-Half-Mat Room*, but they avoided it because it had too many black masks.[3]

On April 26 of that year, France launched a complete legalization of pornography. Cannes, naturally, was overflowing with it.

2.   A famous Japanese brothel district.
3.   Used to cover up sexual organs. This would have attracted the attention of the censors.

June 15: Shibata and Kazuko return. June 17: I hear about Cannes from them. I hear that all of the young directors are acting in their own scenes of sexual intercourse. They were scolding me for not shooting pornography immediately.

That evening I write in my notebook that I will make a "pornographic film"—not an average "film," a "pornographic film" all the way.

To me, a pornographic film was a film of sexual organs and sexual intercourse. A film that broke taboos was, to me, a pornographic film.

I would import the film stock from France, shoot it in Japan, and send it back to France for developing. That way, I could shoot everything I wanted to shoot. That is the basis on which the direction of the film was decided.

If the method of making films doesn't change, the films won't change. A new film will not emerge without a new production method.

This is how the pornographic film *In the Realm of the Senses* came about.

"If, hypothetically, we were to take a step back (No, go forward!) and think that our works and our actions are 'crimes' worthy of being called obscene, as in the indictment, I would probably shed tears of humiliation. They are just not worthy of that grand title, no matter what." So said the director Yamaguchi Seiichiro,[4] defendant in the Nikkatsu "*roman* pornography" case.

His intention and his feelings are clear. "If these films are repressed on the pretext of obscenity, the most effective way of fighting back would be to respond by working to make the concept of obscenity meaningless, that's by creating works that are even more obscene." His words communicated his bitter conviction that the work for which he had been arrested was not sufficiently "obscene."

Is that right? It probably is.

For the present, "obscene" is a legal term. To fight a legal term, one must travel the convoluted road of making it meaningless.

My question, though, is whether an artist can really attain "obscenity." Of course, it is easy to attain "obscenity" in a legal sense. If the point is "creating works that are even more obscene," as Yamaguchi says, *In the Realm of the Senses* is clearly "more obscene."

---

4.   Yamaguchi Seiichiro's first film, *Love Hunter* (*Koi no Kariudo: Love Hunter*, 1972), was suppressed during its first-run distribution. Prints were confiscated and the director was arrested. While the case was pending, he made *Love Hunter: Desire* (*Koi no Kariudo: Yokubo*, 1973) in which the heroine, a student stripper, is arrested by the Tokyo Municipal Police on the same charge of "obscenity in public" for which Yamaguchi himself was indicted. Nikkatsu has not employed him since then, but he directed *Kitamura Tokoku: My Winter Song* (*Kitamura tokoku: Waga Huyu no Uta*) in 1977.

But I don't feel at all as if I have attained "obscenity." I think this is no different from the Yamaguchi's feeling that on his arrest for *Love Hunter*. Which leads me to think that, generally speaking, nothing that is expressed is "obscene." Isn't "obscenity" contained in that which is not expressed, not seen, hidden? And in the part of the human heart that responds to these things?

I daresay that internalized taboos make for the experience of "obscenity." Children, on the other hand, don't feel that anything they see is "obscene."

The concept of "obscenity" is tested when one dares to look at something that he has an unbearable desire to see, but has forbidden himself to look at. When one feels that everything that one had wanted to see has been revealed, "obscenity" disappears, the taboo disappears as well, and there is a certain liberation.

When that which one had wanted to see isn't sufficiently revealed, the taboo remains, the feeling of "obscenity" remains, and an even greater "obscenity" comes into being.

Thus, pornographic films are a testing ground for "obscenity."

If that is the case, then the benefits of pornography are clear. Pornographic cinema should be authorized, immediately and completely.

Only thus can "obscenity" be rendered essentially meaningless.

As of now, fewer than two hundred people have seen *In the Realm of the Senses*, but nearly all the male viewers, who constitute the majority, comment that the moment they see O-Sada cut off Yoshizo's penis, they feel pain in their own sexual organ.

At the first invitational preview in Paris, a famous scholar (male, of course) paled instantly, grabbed the hand of his boyfriend, who was sitting next to him, and didn't let go of it until the end.

When the men are talking to each other about that painful sensation, Kawakita Kazuko, pointing out that she has screened countless scenes in which a woman has a light bulb or a pole stuck up inside her, said, "I bet you guys never felt pain then." And she is definitely not a feminist.

By the way, I never feel pain when I see *In the Realm of the Senses*. It may be that I am a little strange. But why not? I can't explain it.

And because it is galling to feel oneself strange, I have decided to think that I don't feel pain because I made the film.

Filmmaking is a very self-liberating occupation.

Previously, at the Venice Film Festival—I forget which year—I was interviewed by an extremely obnoxious German youth. "Why do you make films?" he had the nerve to ask. I realized that the only way to answer such an inane question was to say anything that popped into my head, but his attitude rubbed me the wrong way. It made me hunger for a battle of wits, so I answered extremely affectedly, "To find out what kind of person I am."

"Is that all? If that's all it is you might as well make them with 8-mm film rather than in wide screen and color."

I was irritated to find myself at a loss for an answer. Thinking about it now, though, there was no reason for me to feel stuck for an answer. Finding out the kind of person you are is something you do by finding out about your desires, and, insofar as those desires will naturally be related to beauty, then wide screen and color is the inevitable choice.

The desires and moods (chiefly playful ones) of myself and of art director Toda Shigemasa show through abundantly in *In the Realm of the Senses*. That's because we confronted the project feeling sufficiently free.

We felt like joining hands in a prayer of thanks for the two or three actors willing to do a scene involving real sexual intercourse. That was really a good feeling. Of course, we had no idea whether it would actually be possible, but we felt completely free when they said to us, "Let's do it."

Before we reached that point, we interviewed countless men and women. But it was not in vain.

At first it was exciting when the young women said, "I don't mind doing it," but we soon realized that this was natural. I was surprised when Koyama Akiko said, "I don't mind doing it if you can't find anyone else," and there was no point in her saying it, but later I realized that it was important both to the film and to us as a married couple.

The problem was the man. Nearly all the men flinched at the idea. They all said, "I'm afraid I won't get an erection when the time comes."

"You have a big one, don't you?" I asked audaciously over and over.

"I'm confident that it'll be big at the crucial moment, but I think that normally it may be a little smaller than most people's." Eight out of ten men gave that response.

Two out of ten said theirs was average. I considered them to be the confident ones.

I am one of those lacking in confidence, but I was delighted to find out that there are so many of us.

Let me take this opportunity to apologize sincerely to all of the timid fellows to whom I spoke about appearing in the film. I caused you unnecessary anxiety.

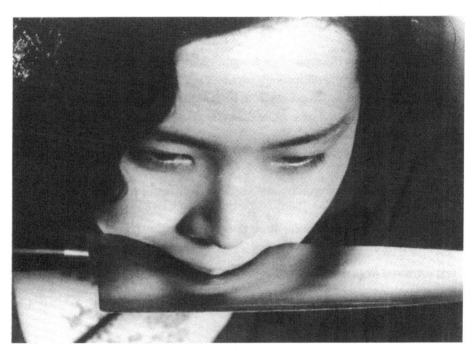

In the Realm of the Senses. 1976.

Please try to forgive me. I hope that all of us will find liberation from the grim reality of timidity.

It was unreasonable from the beginning to ask that the flow of acting be interrupted for sexual intercourse.

It happened, though. Furthermore, I think that the fact that it was done by a famous actor with a normal family must be considered not only significant in the history of film, but also as the beginning of a new chapter in the annals of the history of sexual love in Japan or perhaps the world—because the taboos surrounding sexual intercourse that derive from the sacralization of monogamy system were thereby broken.

No one spoke of the scene's great significance on the set, but the atmosphere was solemn, as if we were all naturally aware of it. It was not the gravity that comes from tension, but that which comes from liberation.

Everyone on the staff gave more than 100 percent. That came from the atmosphere of liberated solemnity.

I am grateful to fate, to the actors, and the crew for allowing me to live amidst of this solemnity.

"You are fortunate, aren't you?" said Komatsu Hosei when we had finished watching the film.

But I do want to make one more pornographic film, completely different in format from *In the Realm of the Senses*.

(text extracted from the book containing the script and stills from *In the Realm of the Senses,* June 15, 1976) by Defendant Oshima Nagisa

Here is my view of the indictment.

I would like to make two of my assumptions clear before I begin. One is my basic attitude toward this trial. I completely oppose the viewpoint so often evident in past trials involving Section 175 of the Criminal Code and the question, "Is it art or is it obscenity?" I have absolutely no intention of asserting, "Because this is art, it is not obscene."

To my mind, "obscenity" does not exist to begin with. If "obscenity" does in fact exist, it is only in the minds of the police and the public prosecutors who try to control it. It seems that the police, the public prosecutors, and some judges have concocted a sort of definition of "obscenity". Just how nonsensical this definition is will become sufficiently clear in the course of this trial, but for now I will clearly state that, even if that definition were acceptable, "obscenity" is not criminal.

To put it in terms of a catchphrase, my basic attitude toward this trial is "'Obscenity': What's wrong with it?"

A second point that I wish to make clear at this time is that the film, *In the Realm of the Senses,* on which the book indicted as "obscene" is based, is being shown freely all over the world.

It is common knowledge from reports in the press that the film *In the Realm of the Senses* contains depictions that are much more—to borrow the words of the indictment—"frank" than those in the book.

Since September 15, 1976, when the film was released in Paris, it has been shown freely in theaters in the European countries of France, Holland, Denmark, Norway, Sweden, Portugal, West Germany, Switzerland, and Austria; the North American countries of the United States and Canada; and, in the southern hemisphere, in towns throughout the various states of Australia. It has also been shown at film festivals in Italy, England, and Spain, where it will soon be released to the general public. Its showing has been banned only in Belgium, and in one or two countries it suffered minimal cutting, but the cuts were made because of violence, not "obscenity."

In today's world, then, the film *In the Realm of the Senses* is accepted in what are called the advanced nations—the free world. In spite of that, in Japan, where the film was made, it is being blocked by the censors on the basis of Section 21 of the Fixed Tariffs Law—notorious for its reputed unconstitutionality—and barely permitted to be shown even after we allowed one-third of the entire film to be edited. The book, moreover, has been called "obscene" and indicted. Where might you find an equally ludicrous situation? This really has to be a historic example of absurdity.

There is something even more ironic. The long run of *In the Realm of the Senses* continues even now, seventeen months after its release in Paris; over 350,000 people have seen it. How many of those people do you think are Japanese? According to Anatole Dauman, producer and distributor of the film, Japanese viewers of *In the Realm of the Senses* number seventy or eighty thousand. Three hundred thousand Japanese visit Paris every year. That means that one in four sees *In the Realm of the Senses*. And not only in Paris. Many Japanese are seeing this film in Frankfurt, Zurich, Los Angeles, New York, and Honolulu. Today, 1.3 million Japanese travel overseas each year. That means that hundreds of thousands of Japanese will ultimately see *In the Realm of the Senses*. Twelve or thirteen thousand copies of the book will be published at most.

Isn't it ludicrous that the same Japanese who are unable to see something in Japan are able to see it in a foreign country?

And I have a further question. Why is something that is not considered "obscene" in a foreign country considered "obscene" here? Isn't Japan one of the advanced countries? Isn't Japan part of the free world?

Lately I often hear the following: "The world is one family; we are all brothers and sisters." That's right. There were people on earth before there were nations. Laws are the result of an attempt to solve problems of human relationships through logic and evidence, rather than by violence. Nations and laws are justified only if the follow universal principles of humanity.

Today, the universal principles of humanity are progressing in the direction of freer sexual expression toward the goal of general freedom. The fact that the film *In the Realm of the Senses* is being accepted in countries throughout the world makes this obvious.

In the Realm of the Senses. 1976.

I recognize no necessity to prove that the book *In the Realm of the Senses* is not "obscene." The world and the fundamental principles of humanity have already accepted *In the Realm of the Senses.*

On the contrary, the prosecutors who have indicted me must convince me; they must use arguments and evidence to the fullest possible extent to convince me of the reasons for my guilt. They have to convince not only me, but the world.

Having explained those two assumptions, I will proceed to outline my position.

I will first discuss the photographs that are termed "obscene." According to the indictment, there are twelve. However, on July 28, 1976, the National Police Agency cited only eight of them as "obscene." That will be clear from a look at the newspapers of the time, for example.

I don't know which eight photographs they were and which four were added later; I would like to be informed of that during this trial because I would like to understand the standards used by the police and the public prosecutors to determine "obscenity."

Apparently the public prosecutors say that the determination of "obscenity" will be left up to the court. It can't be that they are leaving the judgment entirely up to the court while prosecuting and indicting everything and everyone. The police and the public prosecutors must be making their own judgment.

Based on what "judgment" was the number increased from eight to twelve? Does the fact that those four that were originally "judged" not to be "obscene" were later declared "obscene" mean that the first "judgment" was a mistake?

I would really like to have this explained by the police and public prosecutors in charge of my prosecution, interrogation and indictment. Their explanations may convince me of my guilt and at the same time teach me how to avoid being prosecuted and indicted in the future.

However, the mere fact that the number changed from eight to twelve clearly shows the ambiguity and haphazard nature of "obscenity" regulation.

As a citizen of a law-governed country and a defendant being judged according to a criminal code that is supposed to apply the principle of *nulla poena (nulla crimen) sine lege,*[1] I strongly request from the police and public prosecutors who prosecuted, interrogated, and indicted me the following explanations regarding the photographs that are said to be "obscene":

1.   The principle that a prohibitory norm must exist before an act can be prosecuted or punished.

1. The indictment reads "obscene color photographs depicting poses of male-female sexual intercourse and sex play." Of the twelve photographs, which show "sexual intercourse" and which show "sex play"?

2. Is it correct to interpret "sexual intercourse" in terms of the usual definition—as the insertion of the male sexual organ into that of the female?

3. Do "sexual intercourse" and "poses of sexual intercourse" mean different things?

4. Are "sexual intercourse" and "poses of sexual intercourse" "obscene" in themselves? Is it possible for there to be "sexual intercourse" or "poses of sexual intercourse" that are not "obscene"?

5. Are all photographs of "sexual intercourse" or "poses of sexual intercourse" "obscene"? Or is it possible for photographs of "sexual intercourse" or "poses of sexual intercourse" not to be "obscene"?

6. A lawyer has already pointed out that there is no definition of the word "sex play" in any Japanese dictionary. What on earth is it?

7. Is there a difference between "sex play" and "poses of sex play"?

8. Are all instances of "sex play" and all "poses of sex play" "obscene"? Is it possible for there to be "sex play" or "poses of sex play" that are not "obscene"?

9. Are all photographs of "sex play" or "poses of sex play" "obscene"? Or is it possible for there to be photographs of "sex play" or "poses of sex play" that are not "obscene"?

10. Can "obscenity" exist without there being "sexual intercourse/sex play" or "poses of sexual intercourse/sex play"? In what instances is this possible?

11. If those "instances" are photographed, would all of them be "obscene"? Or would it be possible for some of the "instances" to be photographed and not be "obscene"?

I wish to be informed of the principles underlying these eleven instances. I would like an explanation, based on those principles, of why those twelve photographs are "obscene." If there is no explanation, not only will I not be convinced of my guilt, I won't even be able to avoid committing another crime.

I have heard that the criminal code exists to punish crimes and also to prevent crime and educate criminals. If I do not receive a convincing explanation, the police and public prosecutors clearly will have neglected crime prevention and the education of the criminal.

Unlike text, photographs are a very concrete form of expression. As I said earlier, "obscenity" exists only in the minds of the police and public prosecutors who control it, so that there is no "thing" in the world that is inherently "obscene." But if the police and the public prosecutor adhere to the idea that a "thing" can be inherently "obscene," then photographs are a "thing" and a mode of expression that demonstrate an extremely clear standard for "obscenity." That is precisely why I am making a very strong appeal for the setting forth of a standard. If you can't set forth a standard for photographs, how can you be expected to establish one for more abstract, more complicated modes of expression?

I would like to make another important point about photographs. In photography there is the practice of cropping, which is the cutting off of one part of a photograph and using only the part that remains. Today cropping is a commonsense technique employed not only by professional photographers but also by amateurs. It would not be an exaggeration to say that nearly all photographs that are exhibited are cropped.

I would like to ask the police and the public prosecutors what sort of cropping I would have to do to make the twelve "obscene" photographs no longer "obscene." I will not accept, "They'd be obscene no matter how they are cropped." For example, there is the photograph that is referred to as "the reverse side of no. 2." A man and a woman are facing each other. I don't know if this is designated "sexual intercourse" or "sex play." The only thing I can say with certainty is that if you cut this photograph into a top half and a bottom half and exhibit just the top half, it would be almost impossible for it to be called "obscene." If that is the case, then what is "obscene" is the bottom half of the photograph. Let's say that the bottom half is cropped further. The candle and the brazier behind the man probably wouldn't be considered "obscene." You keep cutting away the parts that are not "obscene." Then the part that the police and public prosecutors consider "obscene" would necessarily be left.

Why don't we give that experiment a try?

Stop talking in ambiguities like "Male-female sexual intercourse/poses of sex play"! Say clearly that it is "obscene" because it shows this, that this part is forbidden!

It is only then that a discussion of why "this" or "this part" is "obscene," why it is forbidden, can finally begin. Insofar as the court is the proper place for an exhaustive discussion of this issue, I strongly request that the public prosecutor first specify the standards for "obscenity" in the photographs, a mode of expression in which "obscenity" should be very easy to identify. That will be the starting point for all of the discussions.

I will now proceed to the second part of my piece. This consists of my thoughts about the fact that when I was prosecuted by the police, I was told that only the photographs were "obscene," but the indictment also cites the text of the script as "obscene."

Before I go into my thoughts on the subject, I must confess that I made a big mistake when I was questioned by the police and the public prosecutors. I said just a little too much.

Of course, I answered no questions about my films, and I refused to give any explanation about the content of the photographs. I spurned the question, "What makes you think that this is not obscene?" by saying, "Unless you, who say that it is 'obscene,' first give me your reason, there is no need for me to say anything." And I refused to consider their modest request that I give them my thoughts on the subject of obscenity by saying, "That isn't something to be discussed in the interrogation room." In what respect did I say too much, then? I explained to them that they couldn't find me guilty merely by declaring my photographs to be "obscene." What do I mean by that?

The photographs in question are stills from *In The Realm of the Senses,* a film I directed. I call them "stills" here because in the Japanese film world, photographs made for purposes of publicity are conventionally termed "production stills" in contrast to "films," frames, or moving pictures. Naturally, these stills are taken on the set by a photographer. I am not the author of these stills.

It is obvious that in copyright law the "author" of photographs is the person who took them. But there is some doubt as to whether the author of film stills can, unconditionally, be considered the one who took them.

By this I mean that, even if the person who decides the composition of the still and presses the shutter were the photographer, there is a collaborative aspect to it in that the director stages the scene that is the subject of the photograph, the photography and lighting engineers control the lighting, and the art director oversees the design, makeup, and props.

On the other hand, according to the Section 16 of the Copyright Law, the author of a film is "the person responsible for the production, direction, acting, photography, and art and who does much to contribute creatively toward the entire form of the cinematic work."

The problem is whether this provision also applies to the author of the stills. If it does not apply, and stills are like other photographs, with the cameraman being the sole author, then I have absolutely no responsibility for the photographs in question. Only if it does apply am I included as one of the collaborating authors.

However, although Section 16 of the Copyright Law does make stipulations about films, Section 29 says, "the copyright of a film . . . reverts to the film producer."

In this case, the film producer means the company that produced the film. The authors of the film—for example, the producer, director, cameraman, and artist— have no copyright.

If Section 16 applies to stills, Section 29 must do so as well—in which case the copyright to the stills belongs neither to the director nor to the still cameraman, but only to the company that produced the film. That would mean that the copyright to the stills of *In the Realm of the Senses* belongs only to France's Argos Films, the pro- ducer of the film and actual possessor of the negatives of the stills.

Needless to say, only the copyright holder has the right to use a work freely. Although I may possibly be one of the authors of the stills of *In the Realm of the Senses,* I am definitely not the copyright holder. Accordingly, I would naturally have no responsibility for the photographs.

The police haven't the slightest knowledge of these sorts of copyright law issues, so they probably included me in the indictment on the basis of some crude reasoning along the lines of "It's Oshima's film, so Oshima must also be the author of the stills." But no matter what instinct may have been at work, at the time they did not prosecute me as a conspirator with Takemura Hajime,[2] but only as an abettor.

In fact, the only relationship I had to the photographs was to be asked by Tak- emura whether I could get them and to ask Shibata Shun—the president of France Films, the French film company coordinating the joint project—to contact Argos Films for me. I didn't look at the stills that were sent over, and I don't even know what was done in the way of cropping by Takemura or anyone else at San'ichi Shobo. I saw them for the first time when the book was published and Takemura brought me a copy. And anyone can see that on the back of the book jacket it says "photographs provided by Argos Films."

I explained the copyright law to the police and public prosecutors who inter- rogated me, asking how they could possibly find me guilty, even of abetting, when I had no rights to or responsibility for the photographs. In retrospect, I went too far.

There was, however, some historical background to this. For nearly ten years before the enactment of the new copyright law on April 28, 1970, as a director and managing director of the Japan Film Directors Association, I had worked with my elders in the field and my friends in an attempt to prevent the copyright law from being enacted in a form that would be disadvantageous to film directors. The result,

2.   Head of San'ichi Shobo, the company that published the book *In the Realm of the Senses*.

however, was defeat. We were unable to prevent the worst possible result, which was that the law made film copyrights revert automatically to the film company rather than to the director, the actual author of the film.

Bitterness over that defeat and pride in being one of those best informed about film copyrights led me to make that explanation of the copyright law. I learned from that experience that people make mistakes in those areas in which they are the most knowledgeable. I was also concerned about the effect of this unbearable accusation of a director based on the film stills on the members of the Directors' Association. At the time I thought that if explaining the copyright law meant that I wouldn't be indicted, that was what I wanted.

What really mortifies me now is that I thought the public prosecutors—if not the police—would understand the logic behind the copyright law. Being indicted led me to discover the true essence of the matter.

The police wanted to prosecute me in any event, as did the public prosecutors. With the indictment, the public prosecutors expanded the bases for their action beyond the photographs to include the citation of nine places in the script for "obscenity" as well. This was no doubt because they were uncertain about whether they could prove me guilty based on the photographs alone. They probably thought they couldn't even indict me on that basis.

I think that it was my explanation of the copyright law that caused this. If not for that, the public prosecutors might have indicted me on the basis of the photographs alone. In that sense, I made a mistake—a big mistake. But it was also a valuable mistake, because it clarified the intentions of the police and the public prosecutors, who wanted to indict me no matter what. That was all.

I will now present the third point of my argument.

I seek an explanation of what it is about the passages that have been designated "obscene" that makes them so. The indictment says that in nine places, "There are obscene passages in which male-female sexual intercourse or sex play is described frankly." It would be acceptable for it to read that way if, at the time I was prosecuted by the police, they had firmly believed that the passages were "obscene." But that wasn't the case. Instead, because they wanted to indict me no matter what, they must have selected passages in haste. The designation of these "obscene" passages is crude in every way, as well as nonsensical.

The clearest indication of this absurdity is that all of the "obscene" passages are designated in terms of pages. Everyone knows that sentences don't always begin and end cleanly in accordance with page breaks. There are places where a page begins in mid-sentence, and places where it ends in mid-sentence. This is the rule rather than the exception.

The indictment says, for example, that "from page 29 to page 31" constitutes an "obscene passage." But page 31 ends in the middle of a speech by a maid named Matsuko: "Because the mistress told me to take the sake bottle to," with "told" being the last word on that page and "because" being the first word on the following page.[3]

If you take the indictment seriously, then, all the text to the word "told" is "obscene," and "because" isn't. Could anything be more stupid than this? As long as something is called a sentence, it is one sentence with a beginning and an end. Could there be anything more frivolous than chopping it in the middle and coolly designating it "obscene"?

Moreover, between pages 29 and 31 there is a passage that says, "In the garden at night. The mistress, Toku, casually glances over to the annex." This is one independent sentence. In film or script terms, it is an independent scene, scene 17. According to the indictment, however, this too is an "obscene passage." The next scene, scene 18, is similar: "The annex. The sound of the *shamisen* and of Sada's singing voice can be heard." This is also an "obscene passage." Isn't there something wrong here?

This probably wouldn't have mattered to the public prosecutors. I have no doubt that they designated the "obscene" passages based on this kind of thinking: "We're going to indict him, regardless." "We're going to cast the widest net we can." "We're going to cast a lot of nets, and in doing so we should catch at least one small fish." That is why sentences are cut off in the middle and why there will be a sentence in the middle of a page cited for being "obscene" that can't possibly be considered "obscene."

To be indicted on such a haphazard basis is intolerable; it would be even more intolerable to be found guilty. The basis for a determination of "obscenity" in the text must also be clarified, and I strongly request that the public prosecutors who indicted me explain the following:

1. The smallest unit into which a sentence can be broken is a word. Is it possible for one word to be designated "obscene" by itself? If so, what are the words?

To add a brief note of explanation to this, based on my own experience, I believe that for young people it is possible for one word to be quite stimulating sexually.

3.   The word order is different in Japanese and English.

If so, I think that the words "sexual intercourse" and "sex play" used in the indictment fall into that category. What do you think?

2. Are there words spoken in the work that are "obscene"? If so, what are they?

3. Similarly, are any of the words expressing sounds uttered by the characters "obscene"? If so, what are they?

4. Are there sexual acts in the work that will invariably be considered "obscene" if described? If so, what acts are they?

5. Are there sexual moods in the work that will invariably be considered "obscene" if described? If so, what sexual moods are they?

6. The indictment says, "There are obscene passages in which male-female sexual intercourse or sex play is described frankly." What is meant by the word "frankly"? Semantically speaking, the opposite of "frankly" appears to be "euphemistically." A euphemistic expression is one that uses a different word to describe a thing or an act instead of a simple word, for example, saying "hair" or "thicket" or "mount of Venus" instead of pubic hair. Ikeda Masuo, who won last year's Akutagawa Prize for the novel *Offered to the Aegean Sea,* disliked all these words and says he hit upon the phrase "the underground sea" while he was thinking about it. If, for example, "pubic hair" is "frank" and "the underground sea" is not "frank," then I think there would be absolutely no problem if I said "metropolitan police headquarters" in place of "male sexual organs" and "public prosecutor's office" in place of "female sexual organs." Give me the basis on which the "frank" "pubic hair," "male sexual organs," and "female sexual organs" are considered more "obscene" than "the underground sea," "metropolitan police headquarters," and "public prosecutor's office." Why is "frankness" "obscene"?

7. There are intricate descriptions and simple descriptions in the text. In descriptions of "scenes of male-female sexual intercourse/sex play," which type of description has the stronger possibility of being designated "obscene"? Why?

8. Among the descriptions of "scenes of male-female sexual intercourse/sex play," there are four types of sentences: those with intricate, frank descriptions; those with intricate, euphemistic descriptions; those with simple, frank descriptions; and those with simple, euphemistic descriptions. Among these four types, is there any type that will always be considered "obscene"? If so, which is it? Which has the strongest possibility of being designated "obscene"? The weakest? Rank them.

9. Into which of the four categories above do the sentences designated as "obscene" in the indictment belong? Why?

Needless to say, what is designated "obscene" in the indictment is one part of the script of the film *In the Realm of the Senses*. This will be the first time that a film script is tried in Japanese court. In issuing the indictment, did the public prosecutors give sufficient consideration to the special characteristics of the prose used in the script genre?

Naturally, the public prosecutors, who high-handedly added the script to the reasons for the indictment in their haste to indict me, certainly could not have given this adequate consideration. If they had, they wouldn't have been able to indict me.

Or the public prosecutors would say that the fact that it is a script doesn't change the fact that it is prose. However, that is not true. Prose differs according to the purpose for which it is written and the form in which it is written. Novels, plays, scenarios: they all differ. Verse, such as poetry, *tanka*,[4] and haiku, and prose, such as essays, reportage, and travel writing: they all differ. It is extremely arrogant to accuse prose of a crime without knowing its special characteristics.

What are the special characteristics of the script form? The first is the purpose for which scripts are written: to make films. Consequently, they are not written for publication. Of the scripts that have been written since the invention of the film, 99 percent have not been published.

The script is written for an extremely small number of readers. It is written for the executive offices of the film company, the director, the crew, the actors, and a few others. In Japan, scripts written for film productions are usually printed and reproduced, but at the most one hundred copies are made. Seventy copies were made of *In the Realm of the Senses.*

If the script for *In the Realm of the Senses* is "obscene," it would have been appropriate for those seventy copies to have been seized and indicted when they were printed and distributed. However, the fact that they were not seized indicates that the police and the public prosecutors did not consider the distribution of only seventy copies to a small circle to constitute publication.

That is, in fact, true. The executive offices of the film production company, the director, the crew, and the actors are the kind of people who read the script, but they are not merely readers. They have the job of making a film based on that script. Would it be possible to write a script that "idly stimulates the sexual appetite" with

4. Form of Japanese poetry containing thirty-one syllables.

.those people in mind? First of all, if the crew and the actors were sexually excited by the script, the job wouldn't get done, would it? I'm not kidding.

Furthermore, in the case of *In the Realm of the Senses,* I myself am the director, the most important reader of the script and the only absolutely indispensable reader of it. The script is nothing more than my own notes. It is merely my showing of my notes to the producer, Anatole Dauman, and crew and actors. In which case, why would it be necessary for me to put material that stimulates me sexually into a script consisting merely of prose written only for me?

As I have said from the beginning, I don't think "obscenity" is a bad thing, and I don't think sexual stimulation is a sin. Even if—giving them the benefit of the doubt—the police or the public prosecutors were sexually stimulated by reading certain parts of this script, it is only too clear that, given the purpose for which it was written, that was not my intention.

Film scripts have another special characteristic that is a natural result of the purpose for which they are written. The usual length of a film is from about one and a half to two hours, and the length of the script is limited accordingly. It is usually about one hundred pages long in Japanese, on standard paper of 400 characters per page. At that length, one can't include detailed descriptions.

Writers can, of course, describe what happens within a given period of time either simply or in detail, and one characteristic of writing is this freedom in terms of length, but the script presents certain limitations.

Films, particularly dramatic films, employ a mode of expression that consists of describing things by means of human activity. In concrete terms, human activity is speech and movement. To give a certain speech takes a certain amount of time, and to complete a certain movement takes a certain amount of time. If a film is about two hours long, the total time allotted to the speeches and movements in the script can't exceed that. Those are the natural limitations on a script's length.

In spite of that, you might say, why couldn't you write as much as it takes to communicate a person's psychology and mood? That, however, would be a hindrance. If you included psychology and mood in the script, the imagination of the director, the crew, and the actors would be inhibited, and the film would lose its originality. Writing only the speeches and movements simply stimulates the imagination of the director, the crew, and the actors and brings forth positive results. A director, crew, and actors need fertile imaginations if they are to excel. A good film or a pleasant film can result from the same script, as can a bad or boring film. This is because of individual differences in the imaginative powers of the director, crew, and actors.

It is because of such individual differences that the positions that these people fill exist.

I would like the public prosecutors who labeled parts of the script of *In the Realm of the Senses* "obscene" to give a concrete explanation of the types of scenes they envisioned. If possible, I would like them to make these scenes into a film. That will be the best way to clarify what it is that the public prosecutors are considering "obscene." I would also like to submit as evidence the fact that, upon reading the parts of the script that have been labeled "obscene," one person has imagined one type of scene and another person has imagined another. If that is done, it will become clear to the public prosecutors that what is really "obscene" is not the "thing" called the script, but rather a certain "state" of consciousness of the person reading it. I would like to call that "state" of consciousness a "public prosecutorial state."

If the state of consciousness of the majority of Japanese is a public prosecutorial state, then I may be guilty. But I firmly believe that the number of Japanese who have a public prosecutorial state of consciousness is small. The public prosecutors will have to produce many witnesses to prove that they are in the majority.

Insofar as they do not prove it, I am determined not to acknowledge that the parts of the script that have been designated "obscene" are "obscene" or that I am guilty.

I will move on to the fourth and final point in my argument. I would like to touch on the problem of the book, *In the Realm of the Senses,* as a whole, and on words such as the following, which are used in the indictment: "plot," "sales," "possession."

According to the indictment, 12,524 copies of the book have been sold. I am the author of ten books; the number of published copies of each ranges from 10,000 to 15,000. One of them, *Night and Fog in Japan,* exceeds 30,000, but it is over fifteen years old, and that figure includes the various editions, so it is an exception. In other words, *In the Realm of the Senses* will not exceed the scope of my previous books, which means that the number of readers will be limited as a matter of course.

Books containing scripts don't sell well by their very nature. Because they are not written for publication, there is no reason that they would be of interest to the average person. They should be of interest only to film professionals. Accordingly, the people who buy scripts are film professionals, young people aspiring to be film professionals, or film buffs who buy the books as a memento of the films.

How can it be that this limited number of readers would buy the book *In the Realm of the Senses* and be injured by its "obscenity"? Who has been hurt because of this book's having been sold?

Moreover, it is not true, as the indictment says, that Takemura Hajime of San'ichi Shobo and I "conspired" to sell this book. The only one selling the book is San'ichi Shobo; I have nothing to do with the sales.

Or perhaps, as was determined in an earlier trial based on Section 175 of the Criminal Code, when a publisher requests a translation with the intention of selling it, and the translation is done because of that request, a conspiratorial aroma is not altogether absent.

In this case, it was San'ichi Shobo who thought of publishing this book and selling it and he did sell it; all I did was sell Takemura Hajime a script that had already been used to make a film. I'll say this half jokingly, but you asked Takemura's opinion at the first public hearing, didn't you? Do you think it would be possible to enter into a "conspiracy" with someone who has that strong a will?

Moreover, I speak as someone who does not make his films in "conspiracy" with anyone and who has made a number of films, based always on his own individual ideas, for which he is solely responsible. On Takemura's honor as a publisher, I am saying, as he did, that there is absolutely no "conspiracy." Even if I am said to have "sold" it, I have no knowledge of having done so, and as for being told that I "possessed it with the intention of selling it," I don't even know where the book was. For the person who "possessed" it to not know where it was "possessed" is utterly nonsensical.

Conclusion

The photographs and the passages called "obscene" in the indictment cannot possibly be "obscene"; therefore, the book containing them, *In the Realm of the Senses,* is not obscene.

As is clear from what I have already said, you have no right to accuse me of any crime regarding the content of the book or the way in which I handled it. In spite of that, why did the police insist on prosecuting me, and why did the public prosecutors insist on indicting me? This point will be the most problematic for the court.

I'll come out and say it: This prosecution and this indictment constitute repression of the film *In the Realm of the Senses.* The book has been its scapegoat.

As you know from the press reports, the film *In the Realm of the Senses* was made jointly by Japanese and French artists. The film was imported into Japan from France, shot in Japan, and sent back to France to be developed, edited, and completed. By so doing, it was possible to develop the sexually expressive scenes that couldn't be developed in Japan, and the resulting film couldn't be shown uncut in Japan.

I'd like to state clearly that in the process of making the film I have not violated the laws of Japan in any way. That the people who are trying to change the Japanese constitution for the worse would make the production of "obscenity" a crime is proof that it is not so under the present criminal code.

I wanted to show the uncut version of the film in Japan, even if it meant my being indicted. However, the wall erected by the unconstitutional Section 21 of the Fixed Tariffs Law is wide, and showing the uncut film wasn't possible. That impossibility also signified the impossibility of the use of the film by the police and public prosecutors as the basis for accusing me of a crime.

Consequently, the police and the public prosecutors used the book as a scapegoat. Their real purpose was always to repress the film *In the Realm of the Senses* in its entirety.

Until the end of the war, Japanese films were strictly regulated by the censors of the Home Ministry and the Film Law. Section 175 of the Criminal Code did not come into play. Kisses, for example, were not permitted to be shown in films, and the title *The Second Kiss,*[5] which had been permitted in the case of the novel, ultimately had to be changed for the film version. Repression isn't directed exclusively at sex, however.

The first film to suffer because of censorship in Japan was the French film *The French Revolution: The Final Days of Louis XVI,*[6] which was shown in 1908 at the Kinkikan Theater in the Kanda section of Tokyo. It was banned from screening by order of the National Police Agency. Needless to say, our own imperial family was the subject of certain taboos, as were the ruling families of foreign countries.

After World War II, the constitution banned censorship, but censorship was carried out by the U.S. occupation forces immediately after the war. In 1949, Eirin (the Motion Picture Code of Ethics Committee)[7] was established at the recommendation

5.   A short story by Kikuchi Kan, who embraced popular literary forms. In this he differed from contemporaries such as Akutagawa Ryunosuke and Kume Masao, who were committed to "pure" literature. A film of the same title, *The Second Kiss* (*Daini no Seppun*, dir. Shmizu Hiroshi, script Hasebe Keiji, 1953) was made after the war.

6.   Oddly enough, *The French Revolution: The Final Days of Louis XVI* was distributed after the title change as *The Story of the North American Monte Cristo*. Because it was a silent movie, the *benshi* (narrator/commentator) provided another story.

7.   Established in 1949 in accordance with the GHQ directive, the committee was composed of six representatives from each of the six major film production companies, five producers, four distribution/presentation division representatives, one independent theater owner, four film artists,

of the Supreme Commander of the Allied Powers[8] as a so-called self-regulating organ. After the occupation ended, Eirin was, as its name implies, the only organization that regulated film, but it gradually began to come under pressure from the government, the police, and the public prosecutors. Particularly noteworthy was the fact that in 1956, in connection with the problems of the "sun tribe" films, Eirin received a government-initiated drubbing by the public and was compelled to reorganize and enact a new code of ethics for motion pictures.

However, until that time the police and the public prosecutors had not been directly involved in repressing films. They first did so when they prosecuted *Black Snow* in 1965. *Black Snow* was indicted but found not guilty the first time, and this verdict was upheld the second time when it was said that "there are pictures that are 'obscene' according to the Criminal Code, but it has passed Eirin and the defendant had no criminal intent." The next instance of repression began in 1972 with the prosecution of four Nikkatsu films of the so-called *roman poruno* [pornographic novel] genre. This year the court is finally moving toward its first decision in the case. One notable feature of this case is that in addition to the people responsible for the film at the company and its director, Eirin's examiners are also on trial.

Considered in this light, the history of the repression of films by the police and the public prosecutors has two notable aspects. One is that sexual expression in film is always seized upon when it marks the beginning of something new. That was true in the case of the sun tribe film series; *Black Snow* was made at the height of the small-production film called the "pink film"; and the Nikkatsu *roman poruno* films were made at a time when Nikkatsu, one of the big film companies, suddenly put all of its energy into pornographic film production.

Also worthy of note is the fact that the police and the public prosecutors have been steadily gaining ground. Essentially, their position is that if *Black Snow* is not guilty because it passed Eirin, then, in the case of *roman poruno,* Eirin examiners will also be brought in as accomplices. It seems that the metropolitan police headquarters' goal of making Eirin their subcontracted censorship organ is gradually succeeding. As for the stills from the book *In the Realm of the Senses,* Eirin responded submissively to the questions of metropolitan police headquarters about whether each one would have been permissible.

---

and four third parties working in film. It underwent organizational and ideological changes in the late 1950s.

8.   Acronym of the Supreme Commander of the Allied Powers, Gen. Douglas MacArthur. The Office of SCAP was located at GHQ in Tokyo. Media-related matters were handled by the CIE (Civilian Information and Education) Section of the Civilian Division at GHQ during the occupation (1945–1952).

The repression of the film *In the Realm of the Senses* has something in common with the repression of films in the past.

First of all, the repression of *In the Realm of the Senses* was a prompt attack on the new method of using a collaboration with a foreign country to exceed the limits on sexual expression. In addition, the repression effort is attempting to extend its reach by assailing everything from the stills to the script. In particular, the fact that the police seized the script must be seen as a major development. The script of *In the Realm of the Senses* was published in book form after the film was made, but, considering that some scripts are published in film magazines before and during production, it would not be an exaggeration to say that the prosecution of the script paves the way for advance censorship of films in the future.

I am now approaching the last section of my conclusion. I have argued that the prosecution and indictment of the book *In the Realm of the Senses* is completely groundless and was merely a matter of the authorities wanting to prosecute and indict me. In its prosecution and indictment, the book has served as a scapegoat for the film. Considered in light of the history of film repression in Japan, the repression of the film *In the Realm of the Senses* was inevitable.

Furthermore, it was inevitable, historically speaking, that the police and public prosecutors would prosecute and indict me.

However, is it acceptable that these things be allowed to happen? I have heard that the most important principle to be upheld by those in the judiciary is to "hate the crime, not the person." In this instance, however, the police and the public prosecutors have turned these words around.

There is no crime here. The police and the public prosecutors fabricated a crime out of hatred for a person.

The police and the public prosecutors hated the person who made a film that went beyond the confines of sexual expression in Japan by means of an international collaboration. That person was also a witness for the defense in both the *Black Snow* and the Nikkatsu *roman poruno* trials, where he asserted the innocence of the defendants. Furthermore, that person boldly asserted in the book containing the script and film stills at issue here that Section 175 of the Criminal Code was a meaningless, bad law. Out of hatred, the police and the public prosecutors fabricated a crime.

This indictment resembles a false accusation. A false accusation—not to mention crime that doesn't exist—occurs when the true criminal in a real crime is not found and one who is not guilty of the crime is accused instead.

In the past, when trials were carried out in the name of the emperor, the Japanese police and public prosecutors charged many people falsely. Our hearts ache when we hear the stories of the pain-filled lives of people like Yoshida Ishimatsu and old Kato Shin'ichi. There have even been false accusations in postwar Japan: the Matsukawa incident, the Yakai incident, and the incident of the murder of the Hirosaki University professor's wife, in which innocence was recently confirmed. Many other such incidents are now before the courts.

Why do false accusations occur? They arise from the police's anxiety about their reputation when a crime has taken place and the perpetrator has not been prosecuted. Even when they learn that a suspect is not guilty, they can't make that information public because to do so would have an adverse effect on their reputation. In nearly all cases, the public prosecutors tend to work on aspects of the case that preclude any adverse effect on police reputation. And so the web of lies grows thicker and thicker. At times the courts, too, have as their chief aim the preservation of the reputation of the police and the public prosecutors. This is how false accusations are set up.

The case of *In the Realm of the Senses* is also one of false accusation. That is the point that I most want to stress. At least in the case of the film *In the Realm of the Senses,* even the police were not able to establish any crime. Nevertheless, the police still wanted a criminal. Because for a film like *In the Realm of the Senses* to be made and there to be no criminal would have damaged the reputation of the police.

Therefore the police fabricated the "crime" of "obscenity" regarding the photographs in the book.

In the case of a false accusation, when a crime exists and no criminal can be found a criminal is fabricated. In the case of *In the Realm of the Senses,* the criminal existed but there was no crime, so the "crime" was fabricated. In that sense, this false accusation is worse than most. But what the two have in common is that the "crime" or the "criminal" is fabricated because the police's reputation is threatened. That is why I call my current predicament a false accusation.

Should we allow the perversion which fabricates a criminal in the absence of a crime?

In reality, however, the police and the public prosecutors often engage in such perversion. In essence, you can replace the words "police and public prosecutors" with the word "authority." I won't say that they constitute all authority at all times. However, even when there is no necessity for its display, decaying authority wants to demonstrate its own power. The display of authority becomes its only reason for being. This is perversion. The easiest way to display authority when there is no crime is to fabricate a criminal and attack him.

Japan's postwar constitution prohibits censorship and authority has lost a way to display its own power over expression. All that remains is Section 175 of the Criminal Code, which was left by mistake. It is not unreasonable for authority to cling to Section 175, because it has no other way to display its strength with respect to popular expression.

In that sense, Section 175 is no longer a regulation controlling "obscenity." It is meaningless to control "obscenity" when there is no defendant. All "obscenity" cases are cases of false accusation. All "obscenity" defendants are falsely accused. Under Section 175—which exists only so that authority can display its power and say, "Hey, people, we're not going to let you get away with doing just as you please"— the defendants are not actually "obscenity" defendants but are instead judged as rebels against authority.

I now stand before this court as such a defendant. Thus I wonder if my being here was inevitable.

I think now of two of my teachers who had the strength to make me choose this kind of life. They are Professors Masaki Hiroshi and Suekawa Hiroshi.

When I entered the law school of Kyoto University in 1950, the *Compendium of Laws* that I carried was Iwanami's *Student Compendium of Laws,* edited by Professor Suekawa. Today, as I have set forth my opinion, I have kept one hand on that student edition. I was poor when I was in college, so I wasn't able to buy a larger *Compendium* to replace it, and after graduation I left the law, so I had no occasion to buy a new one. The preface Professor Suekawa wrote for the student compendium has provided moral support for many years, however. In the preface, Professor Suekawa quotes from the beginning of Jhering's *Fights for Rights*:

> The goal of law is peace, and the way to accomplish this is through conflict. As long as the law has to be on guard for violations by the unlawful— and that will probably continue for as long as the world exists—the law will not be able to avoid conflict. Conflict is the livelihood of law: the conflict of all kinds of nations, national powers, classes, and individuals.

Professor Suekawa wrote that every individual's interpretation of these words would be different. When I read these words, I decided that I would be a fighting man with respect to the law. I decided to become someone who would always be involved in law-related conflicts for the freedom and liberation of mankind.

In the course of my student council activities at that time, I met Uchida Takehiro, who is my chief counsel in this trial. For us, student council activities truly were a struggle for the freedom and liberation of mankind.

Nearly thirty years have passed since then. I have observed him only from a distance, but it appears to me that Uchida has followed through on his youthful aspirations and devoted much of his energy to fighting for human freedom and human rights in Japanese judiciary circles. Having my defense handled by Uchida and his trusted colleagues is a very high honor.

Looking at myself, though, I am plagued by shameful thoughts about whether I am worthy of that honor. I don't believe I have deviated from the path of fighting for the sake of human freedom and liberation, but I think that I have accumulated many mistakes along the way.

My biggest mistake was probably my tendency to think that freedom and liberation are imposed from above. I tried to accomplish mankind's freedom and liberation on the basis of the ideas and logic I learned at the university known before the war as the Imperial University.

In recent years, I have become somewhat free of that mistake. Now I don't want to get my ideas from anywhere except the pain experienced by the women who live in the lowest depths of society.

I made *In the Realm of the Senses* with that in mind. The heroine of *In the Realm of the Senses,* Abe Sada, kills her lover because of love, cuts off his sexual organ, and goes around wearing it next to her body. The heroine of my new work, called *The Ghost of Love* (the French title of which is *L'Empire de la passion*), also kills her husband for love. She and her lover are haunted by her husband's ghost. The heroine, Sakata Seki, a poor farm woman of the Meiji period [1868–1912], is ultimately arrested and given the death penalty. The "passion" in *L'Empire de la passion* can be translated either as "passion" or as "love and hate," but it also means "suffering." Now I think only from the viewpoint of "suffering" women like O-Sada and O-Seki.

Accordingly, I am now standing trial because I believe in freedom of expression, and I am certain that my trial is meaningless unless freedom of expression is considered and argued about in conjunction with the freedom of people to listen to and read that which is expressed. Formerly I prided myself on being an expressive person, but now I am rather ashamed of it. I find the lives of the anonymous people who go to their deaths without expressing themselves at all and without making any pronouncements are far nobler than my own.

Those who express themselves and their work shine in the light of the lives led by silent people like O-Sada and O-Seki, unable to articulate their difficulties. We must not be confused about the relative importance of freedom of expression.

In that sense, I am struggling in this trial to expand freedom of sexual expression, however minimally. But more than that, I am fighting for the freedom of people to see, read, and listen to expressions of sexuality.

Earlier, I said that I am on trial as a rebel against authority. Certainly that is how it must look from an authoritarian point of view. But that is not really the case. Now, at the very end, let me speak the truth.

I am here for love—out of love for suffering women like O-Sada and O-Seki. I firmly believe that it is precisely for the sake of women like them that freedom of sexual expression must be expanded and, eventually, totally secured.

I am standing in this court right now with my left arm around O-Sada and my right around O-Seki.

Honorable Presiding Judge and Judges:

History's last judgement will be a court of love that embraces not only the human species but all living things. I believe that when this final judgement comes— as it one day will—it will seat us on clouds of light, crown us with flowers, and lead to the heights of heaven.

However, the happiness of Japanese now living in Japan is important. I would like to end my opening statement by expressing my earnest hope for a trial in which the public prosecutor and I and the lawyers can sincerely offer arguments and evidence regarding the rights of Japanese citizens as free individuals to see what they want to see, hear what they want to hear, and read what they want to read—never for myself alone, but for the sake of all Japanese.

(February 27, 1978)

Regarding the Proper Attitude when Seeing a Film

Speaking at a preview of *Japanese Summer: Double Suicide,* I said that in the future films may come to be shown accompanied by an interpretation. I also asked that people who felt that a film was hard to understand after seeing it once see it two or three times. I was criticized for these comments in several weekly magazines and newspapers.

Naturally, I didn't say these things in complete seriousness. I have become thoroughly accustomed to being criticized for the incomprehensibility of my films, and I have no intention of raising my eyebrows and getting into a debate about that. I meant only to express my feelings in a slightly ironic way. However, as long as there are people who will criticize me for this again, I have to speak directly.

First of all, it is only natural that the day will come when films are shown with an accompanying interpretation. Not that all films will be that way, although even now interpretations appear with the classic films shown by all types of film clubs. The future of the film lies in the groups of young people who read these interpretations with great interest and stare intently at the screen. People who feel that interpretations are unnecessary should go to these places.

And just as some novels are accompanied by interpretations and some are not, there are novels that you read once and don't want to read again and those that you read two or three times. The same holds true for films. Who ever said that films were a one-time thing? This holds especially true for the critics. In what other discipline are there critics who write reviews after coming into contact with their subject only once? Why are film critics allowed to be called critics when their viewing practices are no different from those of the general viewers? I don't understand this.

I realize that even now some film critics see the same film twice or more. Their writings definitely stand out. It is natural for the filmmaker to ask that the viewer see a film two or three times. However, I'd like to make this a clear demand of the critics. See films two, three, five, or ten times, then review them—whether you understand them or not.

(*The Nikkan Sports Journal,* September 14, 1967)

Filmography

1962. *Youth in Ice.* (*Kori no Naka no Seishun*).
    Producer: Toshizo Yuki, NTV ("Theatre without Fiction" Series). b/w. 16mm. 25 min.
    Script: Nagisa Oshima. Cinematography: Yoshitsugu Tonegawa. Music: Riichiro Manabe.
    Narrator: Nagisa Oshima.
    Documentary on the young fishermen of a village on the Hachiro Lagoon along the Sea of
    Japan in Akita Prefecture.

1963. *A Forgotten Army.* (*Wasurerareta Kogun*).
    Producer: Junichi Ushimyama, NTV ("Theatre without Fiction" Series). b/w. 16mm. 25 min.
    Script: Nagisa Oshima. Cinematography: Sadanori Shibata, Masaaki Susawa. Sound: Takao
    Morimoto. Editor: Kurahei Tamario. Narrator: Hosei Komatsu.
    Documentary on the Korean veterans of the former Imperial Japanese Army.

1964. *A National Railway Worker (Before and After the Called-Off Strike of April 17th).* (*Aru
    Kokutetsu-Jomuin (4.17 Suto Chushi Zengo)*).
    Producer: Junichi Ushiyama, NTV ("Theatre without Fiction" Series). b/w. 16mm. 25 min.
    Script and supervision of direction: Nagisa Oshima. Directors: Susumu Hani, Hideo Seki-
    gawa, Noriaki Tsuchimoto, Yoshihiko Okamoto, Takeshi Tamura, Tetsuro Onuma, Shinki-
    chi Noda. Cinematography: Yoshitsugu Tonegawa, Akira Kimura. Editor: Nagisa Oshima.
    Narrator: Matsuhiro Toura.
    Documentary on a railway strike.

1964. *A Rebel's Fortress.* (*Document of the Bee-hive Castle*). (*Hachinosu-jo no Kiroku*).
    Producer: Junichi Ushiyama, NTV ("Theatre without Fiction" Series). b/w. 16mm. 25 min.
    Script: Nagisa Oshima. Cinematography: Hiroshi Ichimura, Akira Kimura. Sound: Kiyoshi
    Iwami. Editor: Yusuke Miyamoto. Narrator: Musei Tokugawa.
    Documentary on a man who, in protest, built a castle on his own property, a part of the
    site set aside by the government for construction of a dam.

1964. *Crossing the Pacific on the "Chita Niseigo."* (*"Chita Niseigo" Taiyeiyo Odan*).
    Producer: NTV ("Theatre without Fiction" Series). b/w. 16mm. 2 × 25 min. Script: Nagisa
    Oshima, based on an original idea of Kazuya Tamura. Cinematography: Kozo Itaya. Sound:
    Kiyoshi Iwami. Editor: Yoshio Matsuno. Narrator: Asao Sano.

1964. *The Tomb of Youth.* (*Seishun no Ishibumi*).
    Producer: Junichi Ushiyama, NTV ("Theatre without Fiction" Series). b/w. 16mm. 40 min.

Script: Nagisa Oshima. Cinematography: Yoshikazu Komuro. Sound: Kiyoshi Iwami. Editor: Yusuke Miyamoto. Music: Toru Takemitsu. Narrators: Hiroshi Akutagawa, Tomoko Naraoka.
Documentary film shot in South Korea: a young girl who had lost her right arm during the student movement of 1960 is forced to survive by prostitution.

1965. *The Trawler Incident: The Forgotten Typhoon Catastrophe. (Gyosen Sonansu: Wasurerareta Taifu Saigai)*.
Producer: Junichi Ushiyama, NTV. b/w. 16mm. 25 min. Script: Nagisa Oshima. Collaborator: Yasushi Toyotomi. Director of Cinematography: Akira Kimura.

1968. *The Pacific War. (Daitoasenso)*.
Producer: Junichi Ushiyama, NTV (The "Hour of the Twentieth Century" Series). b/w. 16mm. 98 min. Script: Nagisa Oshima. Sound: Takao Morimoto. Editor: Takashi Ueno. Narrators: Hosei Komatsu, Mutsuhiro Toura, Ichiro Shimizu.
A montage of Japanese newsreel footage and newly released American documentary footage from the Ministry of Defense.

1969. *Mao Tse-Tung and the Cultural Revolution. (Moutakuto to Bunka Daikakumei)*.
Producer: Junichi Ushiyama, NTV (The "Hour of the Twentieth Century" Series). b/w and color. 16mm. 50 min. Script: Nagisa Oshima. Sound: Takao Morimoto. Editor: Yusuke Miyamoto. Music: Naozumi Yamamoto. Narrators: Mutsuhiro Toura, Hideo Kanze.
This film compilation, made of archival footage, traces the history of the People's Republic of China. Oshima's commentary is composed of questions addressed to the Chinese leader: the images are intended as replies.

1972. *The Giants. (Kyojin-Gun)*.
Producer: Junichi Ushiyama, Tatsuhiko Goto, Nippon Audio Visual (NAV). b/w and color. 16mm. 42 min. Script: Nagisa Oshima. Cinematography: Seizo Sengen. Sound: Takao Morimoto, Tetsujin Kimura. Editor: Yoshindo Hasegawa. Assistant Director: Shizuo Sato. Narrator: Mutsuhiro Toura. Interviewer: Nagisa Oshima.
Interviews with baseball champions.

1972. *Joi! Bangla*.
Producer: Junichi Ushiyama, NAV. Color. 16mm. 25 min. Script: Nagisa Oshima. Cinematography: Seizo Sengen. Sound: Takao Morimoto, Kiyoshi Ogasawara, Tetsujin Kimura. Editor: Ryoichi Tomizuka. Narrator: Akira Kume.
A celebratory documentary of the newborn nation of Bangladesh.

1972. *The Journey of the Blind Musicians. (Goze: Moumoku no Onna-Tabigeinin)*.
Producer: Junichi Ushiyama, NAV. Color. 16 mm. 25 min. Script: Nagisa Oshima. Co-Director: Kiyoshi Ogasawara. Cinematography: Yasuhiro Yoshioka. Sound: Kiyoshi Ogasawara. Editor: Ryuzo Ikeda, Kazuhiko Hiraga. Narrator: Mutsuhiro Toura. Interviewer: Nagisa Oshima.

1975. *The Battle of Tsushima*.
Producer: Junichi Ushiyama, NAV. b/w and color. 16mm. 50 min. Script: Nagisa Oshima. Cinematography: Yoshitsugu Tonegawa, Yoshimune Watanabe, Hisaichi Inaba. Sound: Hiroshi Hiraga. Editor: Kazuhiko Hiraga. Narrator: Mizuho Suzuki. Interviewer: Nagisa Oshima.
Documentary on Japanese war survivors.

1976. *The Golden Land of Bengal. (Ougon no Daichi Bengal)*.
Producer: Junichi Ushiyama, NAV. Color. 16mm. 50 min. Script: Nagisa Oshima. Co-Director: Yuji Yamazaki. Cinematography: Yuji Yamazaki. Sound: Hiroshi Ikebe. Editor: Ryuzo Ikeda. Narrator: Mizuho Suzuki.

1976. *The Life of Mao.* (*Denki Moutakuto*).
Producer: Junichi Ushiyama, NAV. b/w and color. 16mm. 65 min. Script: Nagisa Oshima. Sound: Hiroshi Ikebe, Tetsujin Kimura. Editor: Ryoichi Tomizuka. Narrators: Nagisa Oshima, Mizuho Suzuki.

1976. *The Sunken Tomb.* (*Ikiteiru Umi no Bohyo*).
Producer: Junichi Ushiyama, NAV. b/w and color. 16 mm. 25 min. Script: Nagisa Oshima. Cinematography: Hajime Masuda, Yoshitsugu Tonegawa. Sound: Hiroshi Ikebe, Hiroshi Kawai. Editor: Ryoichi Tomizuka. Narrator: Mizuho Suzuki. Interviewer: Nagisa Oshima.

1976. *The Isle of the Final Battle.* (*Ikiteiru Gyokusai no Shima (Saipan no Kaitei o Yuko)*).
Producer: Junichi Ushiyama, NAV. b/w and color. 16mm. 25 min. Script: Nagisa Oshima. Cinematography: Koshiro Otsu, Enjiro Manabe. Editor: Ryoichi Tomizuka. Narrator: Mizuho Suzuki. Interviewer: Nagisa Oshima.

1977. *Yokoi and His Twenty-Eight Years of Secret Life on Guam.* (*Yokoi Shoichi: Guam-To 28 Nen no Nazo o Ou*).
Producer: Junichi Ushiyama, NAV. b/w and color. 16mm. 50 min. Script: Nagisa Oshima. Cinematography: Koshiro Otsu, Enjiro Manabe. Editor: Ryuzo Ikeda. Assistant Director: Shizo Sato. Narrator: Mizuho Suzuki. Interviewer: Nagisa Oshima.

Feature Length Films

1959. *A Town of Love and Hope.* (*Ai to Kibo no Machi*).
Producer: Shochiku Co. Cinemascope, b/w. 35mm. 62 min. Distributor: Shochiku Co. Script: Nagisa Oshima. Cinematography: Hiroshi Kusuda. Editor: Yoshi Sugihara. Music: Riichiro Manabe.

1960. *Cruel Story of Youth.* (*Seishun Zankoku Monogatari*).
Producer: Shochiku Co. Cinemascope, color. 35mm. 96 min. Distributor: Shokiku Co. Script: Nagisa Oshima. Cinematography: Takashi Kawamata. Editor: Keiichi Uraoka. Music: Riichiro Manabe.

1960. *Tomb of the Sun (The Sun's Burial).* (*Taiyo no Hakaba*).
Producer: Shochiku Co. Cinemascope, color. 35 mm. 87 min. Distributor: Shochiku Co. Script: Nagisa Oshima, Toshiro Ishido. Cinematography: Takashi Kawamata. Editor: Keiichi Uraoka. Music: Riichiro Manabe.

1960. *Night and Fog in Japan.* (*Nihon no Yoru to Kiri*).
Producer: Shochiku Co. Cinemascope, color. 35mm. 107 min. Distributor: Shochiku Co. Script: Nagisa Oshima, Toshiro Ishido. Cinematography: Takashi Kawamata. Editor: Keiichi Uraoka. Music: Riichiro Manabe.

1961. *The Catch.* (*Shiiku*).
Producer: Palace Film. Cinemascope, b/w. 35mm. 100 min. Distributor: Toei Co. Script: Takeshi Tamura, with Nagisa Oshima, Toshiro Ishido, Toshio Matsumoto, Shoumei Takamatsu. Cinematography: Yoshiji Tanegawa. Editor: Shintaro Miyamoto. Music: Riichiro Manabe.

1965. *Pleasure of the Flesh.* (*Etsuraku*).
Producer: Sozosha. Cinemascope, color. 35mm. 90 min. Distributor: Shochiku Co. Script: Nagisa Oshima. Cinematography: Akira Takada. Editor: Keiichi Uraoka. Music: Joji Yuasa.

1965. *The Diary of Yunbogi.* (*Yunbogi no Nikki*).
Producer: Sozosha. Standard, b/w. 16mm. 25 min. Distributor: Sozosha. Script: Nagisa

Oshima. Cinematography: Takashi Kawamata. Editor: Keiichi Uraoka. Music: Takatoshi Naito.

1966. *Violence at Noon (The Daylight Demon). (Hakuchu no Torima).*
Producer: Sozosha. Cinemascope, b/w. 35mm. 99 min. Distributor: Shochiku Co. Script: Takeshi Tamura. Cinematography: Akira Takada. Editor: Keiichi Uraoka. Music: Hikaru Hayashi.

1967. *Manual of Ninja Martial Arts. (Ninja Bugeicho).*
Producer: Sozosha. Standard, b/w. 35mm. 131 min. Distributor: Nippon Art Theatre Guild. Script: Mamoru Sasaki, Nagisa Oshima. Cinematography: Akira Takada. Editor: Keiichi Uraoka. Music: Hikaru Hayashi.

1967. *A Study of Japanese Bawdy Songs. (Nihon Shunka-Ko).*
Producer: Sozosha. Cinemascope, color. 35mm. 103 min. Distributor: Shochiku Co. Script: Takeshi Tamura, Mamoru Sasaki, Nagisa Oshima, Toshio Tajima. Cinematography: Akira Takada. Editor: Keiichi Uraoka. Music: Hikaru Hayashi.

1967. *Japanese Summer: Double Suicide. (Muri-Shinju: Nihon no Natsu).*
Producer: Sozosha. Cinemascope, b/w. 35mm. 98 min. Distributor: Shochiku Co. Script: Takeshi Tamura, Mamoru Sasaki, Nagisa Oshima. Cinematography: Yasuhiro Yoshioka. Editor: Keiichi Uraoka. Music: Hikaru Hayashi.

1968. *Death by Hanging. (Koshikei).*
Producer: Sozosha-ATG. Vistavision, b/w. 35mm. 117 min. Distributor: ATG. Script: Takeshi Tamura, Mamoru Sasaki, Michinori Fukao, Nagisa Oshima. Cinematography: Yasuhiro Yoshioka. Editor: Keiichi Uraoka. Music: Hikaru Hayashi.

1968. *Three Resurrected Drunkards. (Kaettekita Yopparai).*
Producer: Sozosha. Cinemascope, color. 35mm. 80 min. Distributor: Shochiku Co. Script: Takeshi Tamura, Mamoru Sasaki, Masao Adachi, Nagisa Oshima. Cinematography: Yasuhiro Yoshioka. Editor: Keiichi Uraoka. Music: Hikaru Hayashi.

1968. *Diary of a Shinjuku Thief (Diary of a Shinjuku Burglar). (Shinjuku Dorobo Nikki).*
Producer: Sozosha. Standard, b/w and color. 35mm. 94 min. Distributor: A.T.G. Script: Takeshi Tamura, Mamoru Sasaki, Masao Adachi, Nagisa Oshima. Cinematography: Yasuhiro Yoshioka. Editor: Nagisa Oshima.

1969. *Boy. (Shonen).*
Producer: Sozosha-ATG. Cinemascope, color. 35mm. 97 min. Distributor: A.T.G. Script: Takeshi Tamura. Cinematography: Yasuhiro Yoshioka, Seigo Sengen. Editor: Keiichi Uraoka. Music: Hikaru Hayashi.

1970. *A Secret Post-Tokyo War Story,* or *The Man Who Left His Will On Film. (Tokyo-Senso Sengo Hiwa).*
Producer: Sozosha-ATG. Standard, color. 35mm. 94 min. Distributor: A.T.G. Script: Masataka Hara, Mamoru Sasaki. Cinematography: Toichiro Narushima. Editor: Keiichi Uraoka. Music: Toru Takemitsu.

1971. *The Ceremony. (Gishiki).*
Producer: Sozosha-ATG. Cinemascope, color. 35mm. 123 min. Distributor: A.T.G. Script: Takeshi Tamura, Mamoru Sasaki, Nagisa Oshima. Cinematography: Toichiro Narushima. Editor: Nagisa Oshima. Music: Toru Takemitsu.

1972. *Dear Summer Sister (Summer Sister). (Natsu no Imoto).*
Producer: Sozosha-ATG. Standard, color. 35mm. 96 min. Distributor: A.T.G. Script: Takeshi Tamura, Mamoru Sasaki, Nagisa Oshima. Cinematography: Yasuhiro Yoshioka. Editor: Keiichi Uraoka. Music: Toru Takemitsu.

1976. *In the Realm of the Senses. (Ai no Corrida)*.
   Producer: Argos Films, Oshima Productions. Vistavision, color. 35mm. 104 min. Distributor: Argos Films. Script: Nagisa Oshima. Cinematography: Hideo Ito. Editing: Keiichi Uraoka. Music: Minoru Miki.

1978. *Empire of Passion (The Ghost of Love). (Ai no Borei)*.
   Producer: Argos Films, Oshima Productions. Vistavision, color. 35mm. 108 min. Distributor: Argos Films. Script: Nagisa Oshima. Cinematography: Yoshio Miyajima. Editor: Keiichi Uraoka. Music: Toru Takemitsu.

1982. *Merry Christmas, Mr. Lawrence*.
   Producer: Cineventure Films (London), Recorded Picture Co. (Wellington), Oshima Productions (Tokyo), Asahi National Broadcasting Co. (Tokyo), Broadbank Investments Ltd. Vistavision, color. 35mm. 122 min. Distributor: Shochiku/Fuji/Herald (Tokyo), Soprofilms (Paris). Script: Nagisa Oshima, Paul Mayersberg. Cinematography: Toichiro Narushima. Editor: Tomoyo Oshima. Music: Ryuichi Sakamoto.

1986. *Max Mon Amour, Max My Love*.
   Producer: Greenwich Film Productions (Paris), Greenwich Films USA, Inc. (New York), Films A2 (Paris). Standard, color. 35mm. 94 min. Distributor: AAA. Script: Nagisa Oshima, Jean-Claude Carriere. Cinematography: Raoul Coutard. Editor: Helen Plemiannikov. Music: Michel Portal.

Index

Printed in Great Britain
by Amazon